DESPERATE DEVIL

"Sheer Evil"

JOHN J.D. LAGBENEKU

outskirts press

Desperate Devil
"Sheer Evil"

v3.0

This is a work of poeticized fiction. The opinions expressed in this manuscript are solely the opinions of the author and do not represent the opinions or thoughts of the publisher. The author has represented and warranted full ownership and/or legal right to publish all the materials in this book.

Outskirts Press, Inc.
http://www.outskirtspress.com

ISBN: 978-1-9772-6791-7

PRINTED IN THE UNITED STATES OF AMERICA

DEDICATION

GOES

TO

My Classmate, Professor Richard Kofi Asiedu.
My Children, Oscar Daniel Pöhlmann &
Aseye Michelle Lagbeneku

APPRECIATION

GOES

TO

Marie Pöhlmann

*For Her Continuous **&** Unwavering Support*

Our hypocrisy and duplicity have caught up with us that has taught us lesson. Our nation was like a ship stranded on high seas, rudderless and with broken navigational aids. Our years with were full of hypocrisy, duplicity, fabricated integrity, false piety, empty morality, fraud and Pharisaism have caught up with us. Ghana was on the crossroad, and its future hangs precariously in a balance but as the Nation Builder, John Dramani Mahama has now become the president of Ghana, he is going to change the lives of Ghanaians from nobody to somebody and from nowhere to somewhere.

CONTENTS

EMPTY INTEGRITY

INTEREST & HABIT OF KILLING INNOCENT FOLKS

REVOLUTIONARY WAR NOW AND HYPOCRISY

EMPTY MORALITY AS THEIR WEAPON

CHRONIC ILLNESS IN THEIR BLOOD

NATIVE AS AN ALIEN IN HIS OWN LAND

KICK THE EVIL NPP OUT

EMPTY INTEGRITY

Disgrace Wears You

The black suns are working.
Effectively & efficiently.
Colours are under the watch

Of telescope. The travelling
Of the former is dense to the
Satisfaction of every well.

Looking into the moisture,
We saw countless empty
Integrities in the life of NPP

& John Agyekum Kufour.
They deceive to scare away
The attractive suns at work.

They are being baptised with
Insincerity & confirmed with
Other social vices. They are

The disgrace of the sky. The
Smell that kills the living smiles
Of glory. Lies have become

Their national anthem, the words
They live on to shine in the dark.
They are the stars of hell.

After Obligation

See this old liar, whose name can never be
Deleted from the book of deceivers. The mis-

Spell of the truth, fear to say the truth to beauty.
John Agyekum Kufour had fooled nature million times.

He had deceived the globe billion times. He had wounded
The culture & traditions of honour. The blue sky will

Never stop exposing the evil calmness in the waves. The
Cliffs continues to protect the images of the light-blue sea.

Watch the greetings from the trees in the morning. The
Whisper of the little babies will tell you that he had misled

The holy land into a satanic paradise. He could misinform
Like a mentally ill person who does the difference between

A shrine & church. Study the moves of serpents & calculate
How many times he could falsify the importance of water.

Your Office

The grime powdered all over NPP.
The stream from health has now
Landed on the land of disappointment.

Counting the rest of the energy, there
Is no purity standing at the entrance of
Reserved forest. The office of the NPP

Is as dirty as their tongues. Going to
The east forest of the pains, no light
Could be identified in the blue suns.

Lies upon lies are winning the dirty games.
Flags of black soil have occupied the
NPP's office. NPP was founded on lies.

The Three-Time Cough

The games of the day,
The players selected
To play the match,

The coach of the strategy,
The technics needed now.
All are on the desk to change

The moves of the dwellers.
The presence of the moons,
The confusion sailing on the

Minds of intelligent people.
Read the days spent before
Development. Count the

Shocks making you blind. Let
The surprise speaks for herself.
Drink whether you can drink.

There is nothing stars can be
Proud of. Find out whether
Singapore exists in the land.

Slow Motion

It is too much for light.
False words are heard
Every second on the skin of
The whiteness & pure water.

There is no channel to sail on
To feel the presence of deserted
Nutrients.

Look at the moves of their lips,
Measure the length of their
Wrongs alongside the breath of
The atlas in which we are living on.

Through the microscope, the title
Of the debates dancing on our
Brains questions their ages. They
Are younger than their mouths.

A Liar Is a Liar

Now, we've witnessed what ears
Are tired of hearing about the same
Songs on his birthday. To play the
Music well, Kenliar cannot stop
Telling lies & devouring fresh meat.
Hiding behind the wicked clouds,

Assorted suns have no right
To attend to their duties. Before
We could hear the whisper
Of the white birds he has lied
A trillion times before the
Shrine of the incorrect gods.

Look around the living oceans
& calculate the worries
Jubilating their anniversaries.
Nothing has been offered
At the sight of the blind. We
Could only feel the tolling

Drum of his words. There he
Goes again, again & again.

National Patriotic Party Still at Work

He is always at work
24/7 misinforming the
Charming rhythm in the

Science faculty.
The beat of the day is the
Continuous deceptions

From him. He cannot rest
Without lying to attractive
Leaves in our gardens.

Whatever he writes is full
Of untruth eating the most
Richest food.

What He Lives With

He drinks lies.
He eats lies.
He sleeps with lies.
He dreams lies.
He relaxes with lies.
He rests with lies.
He clothes lies.
He dresses with lies.
He thinks lies.
He plans lies.
Lies are all that he has.

Dying Look

We have not waited for
The so-called uncomforted
Paradise. The second of seconds

Knocking at the wrong doors
In the church. We cannot hold
The doors behind us.

The eyes of hour of hours
Ready to deliver the jobs awaiting
The jobs pile on the mountains

In the forest. The time isn't for liars
Him who has created a new world,

Full of mates. Count the mess,
Scan the items he has produced,
Bring out the results, so we cannot

Patronise the other side of the
Activities. A liar like him deserves
No place among the righteous.

NANAliar's Stories

Every word comes from
Him is full of sickness.

His words are misspelt
On the board. His letters

Are combating for comfortable
Positions. We've remembered

What we learnt. & our memories
Cannot disappoint knowledge.

It is the true that what he has
Learnt is not acceptable.

We have noticed what is taboo
At the sight of vision & mission.

No way for these letters, no more
Foreign words on the typing board.

Call Him a Liar

Whenever he is there,
Read the lips of the serpent,

We don't want to read
What we will not understand

After heavy rainfalls in the winter.
The face of the words matches

With the ugliness of the moonlight.
Let's go there now before the wrath

Of the winds, with feathers & uncertainty.
Let us hear the talk of his footsteps, the

Record is there for the truth in the fridge.
Let us see the banks of the rivers at his post.

We can say more about the Jubilee House &
His messages on the front page of the floating rivers.

Dark Uncertainty

A huge liar in the
Clothes of an elephant.
It enlarges the environs
Of his colleagues

Whose body is
Unclean as evil.
We always shut
Our noses & mouths

Whenever we are
Swimming around
The vicinity. No
Response to wipe

Off the sweats.
The fear of the dark
Uncertainty is poisonous.
Shock in the blood

If the danger is always
Wearing his crown, let
See how lies have been
Nominated as the king
Of the devils.

Double Worlds

We walk around them in the daytime.
We drive our eyes in the clouds of debates.
We stroll our noses in the air during summer.
We feel the weather hunting our feelings.

We study the result of the publish on air.
Yes, we are experiencing another weather
At the wrong time of the season. We look up
To productions smiling at us, not what all the

Seasons are informing us. They have double
Lives & uncountable stories hidden in their
Visions. They are friends of winter & close
Classmate of stains. They are liars of double

Games, & double worlds are their homes. It
Is extremely expensive to purchase their notions
At the cheapest market. Double lives, double
Worlds are their life partners. Liars of demons.

Is It a Film?

We can't stop watching the new films
Which the market does not want to promote.
We can't entertain forbidden food in the
World of living when the rejected lives

Are still hunting for healthy lives.
They sell lies on Amazon & sacrifice
Poisonous articles to the healthy
Villages of good smiles.

Look into their eyes with telescope &
The laboratory tests will not disappoint
Your handwork & hard work. They hate
Sincerity & marry insincerity on their

Birthdays. They can misinform & create
Their own worlds that disorganise the
Smoothness of plans. Their plan B always
Helps them to sneak in & out of lanes.

Wide Road

Loot at these liars of this century.
Look at the way their mouths invent
The phrases of another cottage.

They promise heavens of tomorrow
Which seers don't have any ideas
To foretell. Lies of lies have soaked

Them & they have their productions
That have sickened thousands of trillions
In their visions. They salute deception

& kill out moral integrity of the season.
They are deceptive and sick of telling
Truth in their lives. Huge liars.

Are We Having Nightmares?

All of sudden we woke up on a floating river.
Floating into the arms of unaware invitation.

We saw a rapid move of backwardness whilst
The heels of the forwardness joined him. The

Tongues of NPP had turned the world upside down.
New paths had been constructed at the cheapest

Price. The flourishing forests lost beauty on
The calm sea. Rivers changed into lakes whilst

Lakes converted into pools for unpleasure.
No more fire in the tongue of the living word.

The narrow path had eroded away from the land
Of the breath to the land of camera. The saints

Had vanished into the bush because they didn't
Want to stain their spotlessness. The dishonesty

Now is growing dense wings & its shoes are car-
Peting ups & downs of rich land. Lies are sitting

In the palanquin, dancing before serpents, waving
Handkerchiefs at darkness that she won the game.

We saw the empty integrity's appointees of NPP
Deceiving themselves like there is no tomorrow
To take care of the awaited songs in the wind.

Scanned Machines

Now, you have seen Kenliar
Deceiving the nature at her comfort

Zone. He is like Satan in his world
Because he is part of the family.

He is an international liar & have lied
Many times, which the world has

Sickened the plants & crops on the
Plantation farms.

We tried to comprehend the music
He has been composing on his

Social media platforms. He is
A disease in every food. Because his

Lies, sea cannot breathe well to
His satisfaction, lakes cannot the water

She wants to drink, rivers cannot
Entertain swimmers at their holidays,

Lagoons cannot boast of their beauty
In festivals. His dangerous lies have

Polluted the handsomeness of the
Goodwill of good moves.

Million Lives

The selection of his words
The movement of his face
The picture of mouth

Read his invention at the Trade
Fair. He has wounded the fantasy
Of creativity. He has destroyed

The well-planned the timetable
Organised for the incoming
Visionary leaders

Sick Driver

Nowhere is safe under Kenliar watch.
His air farts deadly illness.
Our noses are restless because of

His unkempt talks making plenty
Of folks uncomfortable. We are tired
Of hearing sick words displacing our

Wishes. Whenever we scan his life
In the public, we cannot afford the
Evil lessons he has lectured to the

Innocent. His speeches have landed
The living words in the hospitals. We
Don't have any medical assistance

To the patients. We have a driver who
Is morally sick. He is a sick driver
Adulterating the precious lives.

Enormous Insincerity

As he came into an existence,
Lucrative programmes have
Ceased to become known, to life.
We could not see what our
Destinies have promised our souls.
Yes, everywhere we go, we hear
The same songs championing
On air. The enormous insincerity
Is recruiting the saints into his
Kingdom & the Christendom fails
To shine during both day & night.
He is a cobra of devil. He lies
So that he survives his goals.

His Ambition

Before he was born, he knew how to deceive
All the nine planets around him. His first smiles

Were dirty lies which tricked his parents & brought
Them to sleepless mood.

His cry landed his innocent parent into an indescribable
Confusion for long period of time. The could not

Describe it because they haven't experienced them
Before. They could not illustrate the art.

The sound of his voice, the primary statements dis-
Appointed the parents & they asked the person

He was named after. Their religious belief could
Challenge the other religions. Born with different

Characters from crocodile. He is a fake rainbow
Capturing the minds of saints. He is not part of us.

Memorable Days

his name is deception in our book.
His birthday is a deceptive number.
His place of birth is unknown to the ears.

His hometown is not found on the atlas.
His country is outside the globe. No name.

Napo started his game of multi characters
From the Palace where light had no place.
From the rising of the sun to its setting,

He has contaminated the foodstuff on the
Farmland. Ears could not effectively labour.
Understanding could not go & come.

Hear him again, again, he continues to lie
& paint ill images of the dark. The complexion
His tongue is a deadly cancer.

Read his lips, calculate the movement of the
Mouth, estimate the activities now.
He is a shameless liar at work.

Mouth Washer

The odour in the oxygen,
The velocity of the air,
The movement of the ailment,
We cannot stop ceiling our noses.
He has planted everywhere spoiled seeds.
He has grown deceptions on the large land.
He has reaped uncalculated kilograms & tonnes.
His language is now streaming from head to toe.
His body temperature depicts many times he has
Turned the earth down. We need therapy to survive.

Plenty Of Lips

Hear his songs of the season,
Listen to the rhythm in the music.
Nobody's movement will buy the style.

His lips cannot pronounce the right
Words at the time. From the beginning
Of his logopaedic therapy, he refused

To articulate the healthy words that
Opens the gate of morning & closes
The mighty door of night.

Fatal News

Let's read his manuscripts of this novel.
The dedication of it at the book Fair is healing.

The appreciation of the person who motivated him
The content of his creativity underscores the expectation.

Editing the manuscripts, we saw forbidden statements.
Finding their ways into friendly atmosphere is brown. Cooked

Narrations came to stay. Pages and paragraphs
Struggled to buy the ideas behind the scenes. He can

Image situation which has never existed. Because he
Must change the lifestyle of rivers & lakes around him.

Everywhere he goes flies are celebrating their festivals.
His jobless tongues must utter clause of catastrophe.

Yes, he is known for his deceitfulness that gives him
Strength & happiness. The earth knows him as a liar.

Sick Mask

NPPliar wears a sick mask hiding
From Mr. Nature, from Mr. Globe.
Gruesome, filth from the real village.
Pandemic arises.

I am seeing what I have vowed not
To witness on the altar.
I feel the falling of
Mt. Kilimanjaro on my fruits.

Innumerable chains; wasted sadly,
Shabby appearance at sight.
A useless, sick mask threatens
The ecstasy of joy, happiness planted.

A thousand tongues overflow
The IMF Account. Good but caution,
Smell of the highest duplicity,
Bend of heads in disgrace.

A deadly, heavy blow in the face,
A sick mask because of triple-character
Living with the saints. True enemies
Of progress, the agent of destroyers.

The pride of creation is shamed.
The attraction of another lifestyle sings praises.
I sing the song of lamentation because
the earth is ready to lose its dignity & prestige

To recklessness. I learned many about hills, rocks.
The business of sightseeing. I am worried.
Concerned about cooked words. Ring
On the minds of fanatics. Fear threatens

Growth of vision & mission.
Gorillas promise to us. Bitter than death
We witness it on the Black Friday.
Questions chase questions. Answers are

Hard to find in sacred talks.
Artificial seat in the blood. I am very proud
That I do not have their rips.
Because their goods on the markets

Have killed the appetite of customers.
They need the first negotiation to wash
Away the expired products from the stores.

Bleaching The Clouds

The rumours are floating to the banks.
Lakes cannot harbour the broken promises.
I hear thunderstorms in the rumours. They
Are towering into the sky but a pyramid
Tease them. The winds from the north
Pole have planned to mount its exercises.

I look around me in the flash. I stare at the faces.
The presidential debate questions emerge
On my mind quickly. The brown leaves of
Crops feed me the answers. The look
Of today can run without seeing his tail.
The whispers carry out the evidence.

He promised to construct new harbours at
Jamestown in Accra, Keta in the air.
Up till now nothing has come out from
From the kidney of the lamb of the devil.
Fishermen & fisherwomen are wrestling to
Converse their sweats & transact

The plenty of fishes at the shore.
They're still staring at the cross.
Articles are being scattered on the skins,
Digested by the scorching suns
By the readers, by the hungry,
By disappointment.

The investigation of folks
At the grassroots cannot stop
Pouring out the pains dragging them
Into unforgettable experiences.

Nakedness Of Time

Now we have seen the end of the sea.
Side of the castle computes the source
Of a river. See lies running faster than
Truth in the race.

NPPliar sits at the peak of the mountain
As hills were looking at him closely. We see
Him fell at once.
Because his sentences are weaving, oblique.

Even in the night, the searchlights keep
A watch on him. Not a particle of an atom is
Suited on the ground upon
My meaty fingers in his mouth; more sizable

Than his ocean.
Slowly, the babies are growing sharp teeth,
More than crocodile teeth or more poisonous
Than serpent liver. Lips to say the truth only

To the blueprint,
Nothing else. The work on the ground is
Impatiently waiting for them to bite, to chew
Like vultures munching on human meat.

We are interested to know the time
In the moonlight, whether their performance
Will score the marks the goddesses predicted.
Pictures on the screen tell the story

Of the people who have multiple mouths,
Assorted drawings & have represented them
On their platform. Upon the aimless
Noise, they cannot create a dog out of

A leopard on the fifth day.
Their fall is about a trillion metres above Neptune.
The famished optic is fed with famished meals.
Likenesses are sadly portrayed in the museum

Letting my soul down. I can only see fishy things
Which river Jordan & pools do not want to work with.
Highlife music Begins to pity lives. The touch of
Ticker is roaming for a new life. The white birds

Have slumped into their seats. They are waiting for
Summer so that they can have their long trips
Without him.

Live Report

We are not comfortable in the boat
We are travelling with the navigator
Even though, the waves are gentle.
A liar like NPPliar is telling a conflicting story.
The reflection on the sweats
Reveals the mysteries which interrogate

The goals of the land. The sea mother
Holds everything on.
The stars weave through among the moons,
The clouds stop by the suns. Live report.
The awaited time has come to be liberated
From captivity. The fishes have come out

To help the less unfortunate to exercise
Their franchise. Unexpected-heart failure
Has eroded the glory of the land.
A broken-hearted news, every living will
Dodge to accept as a gift, is posted.
We remember the cry of the ten at the

Election 2020 who lost their lives because
The cannibal still wants to be a president.
The pool of tears of the pregnant woman
Overflowed the statues in St. Peter Basilica.
He is being smeared by a severe hit of
Misbehaviours. He is being surrendered

By angry ghosts. The bell tolls Continuously.
Altars are shrouded with violet. The sorrow
Of the soil. Statues outside there always
Remember the loss.

We Signed an Agreement

Nearer. Today, we have much
More work to do, tomorrow,
Much more to deliver.
Many more are floating in.

Live secret in the briefcase.
We will not sleep on our energy,
Ahead, blurred because of him,
Because the houses were built

With broken machines,
with patients with less vision.
Lies had been their neighbours
From generation to generation

To the clouded images to come.
A journey undertaken by
Family & friends in one boat,
For themselves, all for them.

A period that has lost his way
With gold & diamond in hands
Reaches its destination of
Questions on the altar. We cannot

Sacrifice what we don't have
Neither does he have something
To offer during an offertory.
As we were in our mothers' wombs,

We signed an agreement
To say the truth but nothing else.
Murky portrayal, hues of the birds
Of prey on the tree showcase

Their temperament.
What will be the next life?
Nobody suspects that he wears
The cloth of charlatan in the day

& speaks the tones of
Mephistopheles in the kingdom.
Before we could chant in many
Proverbs, let's not provoke the
Climate in Norway.

How serious is the talk today?
How dangerous is the effect
Of the culture of silence?

We've come out from our holes
To the pavement with fresh wounds,
To stand at the main junction of
A twin city to study the argument

Between transparency & obscure.
It is a mendacity as a lifestyle.
Choice at the age; for these grey hairs,
Worst with grey hairs,

Best without grey hairs.
It is a compulsive violation of the ninth
Commandment. So, muscles embrace
Veins, intestines arms
Shoulders, weights on the heads,
Hearts are to accept to
Accelerate & dribble & dabble through.
Question us.

His spirits collide with honesty.
Unprepared situation sneaks into
Heavens on the sabbath day.

Today's temperature is a question
For all of us to answer on the
Examination's day. No legacy for fishing.

Duplicity

We tried to remember the parables that
Have been journeying to the Indian Ocean

But the interrogations surrounding them need
Debates. They echo several times stealing

The worthy ideas in the temple. On the left side,
Questions hold the attention of all the women,

Gorgeously slipping in difficulties; out on pyramid.
We express the down-hearted jeopardy. We see

Minus & division in their lives like flowers
Struggling for help, like sick plants in

Remembrance of the wounded.
They grow bigger & taller in insincerity.

Everything falls deeper than thousand
Feet in worries, more than gold mines in Akyem,

More than the practice of geoscience in the
West region. The fake kenliar holder sets

175 questions but he doesn't have the materials
To build his life better. As the puff of pollution

Enlarged its territory, days fought for a week.
Months run away from its problems.

Then years start to breed offspring to many issues.
We have the men, but the men vanish magically.

It wasn't the same when I left. The beauty
Totally fades, nowhere to be found. I refuse

To pick a call in my dream. Honey & meat
Was too bloody. The option on the desk.

The fire burning in our eyeballs, stands boldly.
I tailed the wonders which were signalling to me.

Full of messages, rough in practice,
Hard with thorns & joints. We walked through

The merciless winds, whispering & whistling
The songs of deceiver. Questions &

Answers still are strangling problems.
Refuse to provide the necessary feed

Weed Of Backwards

Huge words give troubles to a false
Disappointment at the end of the mouth
Like the tongue of camel unfolding from
From its wrestling Eden, like the tongue

Of cow which is ever ready to lie a million
Times per day. Before the suns close
Its eyes. A grand preparation
Has already been organised at the palace.

Babies like synonyms also give birth to
Siblings likewise antonyms give birth to
Enemies. I wished we could read
The mind of the River Tano.

The types of words they employ in their
Everyday languages are dead but with
The help of Kaleidoscope
Their asses open widely.

Their faculty is impregnated with
Words & undefined action.
They convey unclear messages.
We try to comprehend the actions,

Which know the number of stars,
The activities under the sea.
We know them & are ready to
Discharge their duties.

We always know what they are
Studying. We know their words &
The type of life from above. They dig
Immeasurable feet into the ground.

Uproot the problem that have been lynching
Mercilessly but no situation runs for life.
We remember the words of their leader.
Sweeter than honey. More than Gucci perfume.

Their phrases are sharper than new knives.
Their clauses are stronger than metal.
We feel we are being flattered & blackmailed.
Things aren't on the right pathway

But a snake has sneaked into our vicinity.
Their introduction of added information &
Formation & their poison smartly withers us.

The Injured Rhythm

For sometime now
There is a new style of rhythm
That stabs into our bodies &
Tries to disarm the existing beauties
Which has kept us alive.

We play & pray it again.
We listen to it carefully.
We define it in detail.
We sieve it well without
A drop on the white soils.

We scan it.
We hand it over to experts for scrutiny.
Our tiny ears at work.
Our tongues fall ailments.
Our hearts box the chests.

Our arms tightly fold.
Our lungs thunder.
Our feet screw into the ground.
Our feelings visit an unknown
Planet for an answer.

Genetic Devil

The land in the hands of indescribable tones.
Its drama disses
At every corner of the village.

We decide & shoot our heads in debates.
We cannot always caper to an old
Choreography, however, the feelings advise

The peels of the watermelon & pawpaw will
Not guarantee us. How sweet will be the taste
Of the stick that needs huge attention.

Has it signalled to the right pathway?
Are we dancing to the painful decision?
Are we safe with the little we have?

Will it yield more fruits?
We are dancing in a dilemma.
The season is still in her maternity period.

Was/Is

A roaming, disowned odour sneaks
Into a forsaken village.
Homeless ashes inhale & give birth
To what we are expecting now.

The good lamps have uncovered
The hidden atom Which we think is
The fruit that can chant rocks
To say hi to unproductive visitors.

The hope of the earth is still counting
The trips of sand. We see something
Mingling among humans.
We are not expecting
A visitor at this novena.

The nightmare knows the game
He is playing with Mars.
We don't see the stars in the clouds
Or in mathematics lessons.

The climate knows the stars
& his siblings will pull
Out from nowhere &
float on his transit planet of ours.
Spare us the acidic dialogue, look at

Your height before your lies,
Before judgement.
His clothes, their clothes (extraordinary).
The words are immaculately ill.

Kenliar, as doubled-faced as
A wicked goat in the human woods.
His deception as ugly as his copy.
Side of the music confesses

The reality in the sanctuary.
Spread yourselves.
The suns are the feelings.
He is rather an imposter in nature.

Decayed Weather

We're still witnessing the dirties tongue of *NPPliar*
Longer than his brain in the rubbish. Decayed & cursed,
Can dodge medicine & slaughter truth at birth.

He eats his delicious lies three times a day
& drinks different thicker sweats of the drought.
He can't survive without a chameleon.

Lies are his saviour & sustainer. They are like
Clumsy trees living in a possessed ambush.
Their presence signals pictures in the moon,

Hidden under the armpits reserved for saints,
Pure wine. Soft to touch & kiss many times.
(la verdad) The Volta River foresees the clouds

Which are to blind the Eden.
The throne is heartily. Now as hollow as Satan.
There was a smile but now the smell has a

Home to lay her head. On the ground with the
Help of the sky. Knife stabs through the mess.
The voice in the air signals.

The rustling of the dry leaves continues to ring

Its bell. The explanation is too difficult to com-
Prehend the tongue of a camel. After the sunset,
The waves are gaming with the empty throne.

New Beat

We cannot dance to the music
The fake NPPliar plays nowadays.
Atmosphere has frowned his face.

Smiles have faded out.
In the wind, a strong discussion
Table for a while.

The pictures stand there,
Open the doors to dive deeper
Into the sea, whether there are

More dead answers.
The stand sends narrations to
Those whose ears

Could hear the real air.
We clap three times
To wake the silence from its job.

The bite of snake
In the hallucination prepares a
Channel for a particular action.

The microphone has not taken
Its position as an announcer at
6 am & 6 pm news respectively

But the seers doubt the new
Best plants in it.
A transit in a small domain is a

Boot for boot game. Its depiction
In circulation clothes. A stained dress,
The alien odour inside has made

The citizens are speechless.
The dance of the shamelessness
Embrace a new beat. Warm arms

Are slowly needed.

Black Smoke in The Air

We gaze closely into the worries.
They are bigger than the final products.
We see black snow covers our lives
More than two third of our heights

Widening its horizons aggressively,
Greedily encouraging the territories
Of its interests, the already-existent.
Properties are being threatened.

We gaze closely into calculation.
Nowhere is clean like spotlessness
Or shines like Dubai. Village in towns
& cities fight against hell on the tongues.

A blatant liar like him,
Yes, he's a leopard in a sheep's skin,
A chameleon with diabolic tricks.
A million colours are still stealing places.

We cannot trade moonshine for a liar
To create decayed lessons.
We wheel in doubt for affliction &
Carefulness paves for a wakeup.

Malicious Mercury covers the key lives.
Only a new globe is invented in
The centre of regret.
Noses & astronauts wrestle for the truth.

His throne has been overthrown
Unceremoniously. The unwanted paint
Has come to draw the homeless image.
Because of that we're now struggling

With poisonous lessons.

Catching Up the Trash

We are inhaling a forgotten object.
What is it about?
Show its face. Even at all.
That is a deceitful sign of forwardness.

We look closely into the bottles.
We read the difficult veins.
Past questions in the corner of Mars.
We take every word into account

& the master Google is to bail us from
The hell of shame which is about to give us
The conflicting identities.
We search closely into the affairs.

We think about our present humans like animals
Who could help the black smoke in the air,
Widely spread in stretch, carpet under grass.
We eye attentively into the matter. So many

Answers are displayed in the cabinet meeting.
They vow to solve the catastrophe hanging
Around our necks like necklaces
Drop from Akyem Palace to feed us about

Nothing emerges.

New Compose as A Toilet Paper

The sound in the blood,
The sound of disappointment.
We are continuously hearing
Hundreds of thousands of
Sounds echo in the realm of
Those artificial bodies around us.
They combat against the
Smile of the question.
For dreams & greener pastures.

Their voices roar like famished
Tigers that have not seen water
Before but tasted types of soup.
For a couple of decades in shame.
After the beneath groundwork,
Karaoke machine cries loudly.
It mourns nonstop.
The wounded reject lives.
Allergic to taste & choice of patients.

They inject fear into the footsteps,
Arms into another weave to
Keep them mute. We thought.
They think their voices are like
Immaculate angels that could bring
Heaven down & sit inside a tabernacle.
He loves lies more than truth. He fancies

Darkness & hates sunlight around.

Chopping Words in Falling Words

As I dived through the newspapers
Gossips of Kenliar champion the headlines.
Favourite columns are swollen with different

& intriguing articles that will keep the day
Restless & debating. He vomits the heavy
Words but full of hoes & crawl for a hide-out.

Lies more than fishes in the Indian Ocean,
More extremely sick than cancer patients.
Yes, get your healing now. A shameless liar.

Unlocked boxes have finally arrived at
The right time. Shock, heartlessness on fire.
The sentences open their doors for analysis.

The Latin lessons I had in school did not
Fail me. Conjugation of verb & declination
Of noun, adjective pave way for easy jobs.
I read the length. The breath

Of the heads. The tails are bitter. I do not believe
The existence of the rivers on the mountains, as
For the land of the plateau,

I dance in the conflicting answers.

Lucifer At Work

The sound on the street.
We pay an attentive attention to shrill
Whispers. Their ill whisper drums
Are like foreign drums that smell dead.
The words in it are sickened.
We read them & we salute our maturity,
Days of energy. We are the
Ladies & the gentlemen of the day,
Apart from him.

Natural resources are in large heads.
We can't measure the worries chasing
Us out of the world of Greenland.
Protruding eyes want to smuggle
Oil & gold out of the lane.
They rail off & trail off tracks.

The sound of the wicked,
The sound under the feet.
His voice, their voices sound like
The songs of hungry dogs whose
Messages are unclear
& have brought a thousand heads together.

The praise of cheers conveniently convinces
Gullible who swim in dilemma, whose minds
Continue to chase the answers which the elders
Refuse to provide the necessary feed.

One Name

He has a name which
Everybody knows,
Which meanings sound
Well & clean but
Now this is the time to
Call the real names.

He wanted to be called
On the new ceremonious day.
If we could buy these names
At the prices of salt
& sugar, sea will not allow
Fishes to celebrate their

Festivals. His lies have named
Him multiple times that,
Clean water fears of having
Contact with him. One
Name, a ridiculously huge problem,
To write about image,

Many names will fill the
Pages of his biography. His
Dreams are to be named
After the images he
Continues to produce.

Don't Leave Anyone Behind

If I knew where the smoke
Would be coming from, I would
Not ask the rainfall to call off his
Duty. Many have happened in
The days of nightmares. I can
Still hear the unhappy songs
Of the moon on her birthday.
I was living with them until I asked
Permission from the hands of
Erosion. It is too much for a single
Broom to sweep the entire horizon.

Faulty Sheep Is There

There is always night
In the days' dreams.
Why at this time of the
Season when there is

The start of double tongues
With different features?
Cooked words find their way
Into the wrong places.

Look around the cold corner,
Nowhere to experience
The snow which is whiter
Than their tongues.

Their eyes have started
Making huge confessions
Because new cameras are
Sincerely discharging their

Duties without delaying &
Consideration. Ears have
To attend to doctors. Apart
From this news, there is no other

Life in their sayings. Naadadeceiver
Always lies & he continues
To paint the skies with his
Favourite colours. Lies upon lies

Are reigning in his kingdom,
Cloth with stains & useless
Appearance. A high class
Liar at the sight of sunlight.

Unwashed Stains Stain Us

I need to stay away from them.
Something has become nothing.
Watch out the display on the platform
On the face of the green grass. I could

Only see the red-light stopping heavens
To exist on a small planet but hells have
Taken the broader spaces. The taste of
Hells & stains in his life. Uneroded records
Are in our memories warning our minds.

The burning fire is cooking me alive.
I have become the most delicious meal.
I am for the narrow path, the tasteless meal
Not the lamp to be enjoyed with another

Methods, for the other side of the toss are
Full of stains & clouds assisting him to create
The Sahara in the sea. I see possibilities
Wearing the shoes of impossibilities on the cross.

Cobweb

For years I have been training hard to know
How to weave through many lanes under

The watch of the owls which has brought me far.
I can tell the stories of building a skip from

The childhood. Now I can say a word of suns
In the moon but the sky still looks questionable.

If inconsistency is the true definition of deceiver,
Then he wrote the root of his dictionary.

Crazy lies & dirty serpents have come from
The bush to live with saints.

Hear the untold stories from Mars.

The Wall Has This to Say

Call him the names he deserves,
That swallow his poison, that entertains
The dry land. Upon the noise in the

Music, the clumsy trees on the lake,
The business under the sea, the waves
In the winds, shout from the ground,

Fake statements on the papers,
The excuses in the answers,
His words are tinted with plenty of faces.

I have counted the troubles on the wall.
I have described the evil air in the bodies.
I have weighed the deaths in my hearts.

Read the music he composed. It is written
In The Guardian. The Daily Newspapers have
Much more to say about their anniversaries.
Sing with me now.

Natural Disaster

I gave Kenliar a name,
Sweeter than honey
But as he grows up he
Goes for new programmes

That have changed them,
& he has baptised
Himself with another name
Because nature is tempted.

I could read his mind a thousand

Times & feel disaster on the fire.
So, you can now call him a
Natural disaster. He's a
Good friend of dishonesty.

His Nakedness in The Public

Soon & very soon, we are going to
Hear the confession from the horse
Mouth. I can write good speeches.

You can write better testimony than
The experts but a perjurer like him
Can write his biography better than
Professors. Born of a serpent. If a

Newscaster will not feed the air with
Gallons of humid then hear the cry of
The hungry farmland. Hands cannot

Shake hands with suns on the rise. I
Wished the continuous dishonesty of
Him will further expose the snake.

Lack Of Assets

What does he have to show to the village?
What can he boast of after a heavy downpour?
What can he smile at during the days & the nights?

The pictures around him preach the homily.
From east to west the same songs are played
On the platform, but we can dance from the north

To the south. We are testing the bitter truth of the
Century. The disfigure of destructions, the flood
Of incorrect testimonies, when truth has lost her

Title to lies. He can narrate his story & there is
No need to ask winds to explain the current
Situation. Ask him why there is heat in winter.

Unlimited Breakdown

As we could testify the work hanging
Around the neck of our strength,
We could not read the brightness of the

New-born day in the hands of Neptune.
We breathed & we could inhale
The worries of the hours that wanted to say

Hi to us. Until we define the meaning
Of the promises to the suns of the hearts
We will continue to chase the rain from

The womb of the clouds. We could drive
Ourselves from the flashlight to her. Settling
There was a big no, there isn't a hut shielding

His lies, rather championing in his life.
Gullible who swim in dilemma, whose minds
Continue to chase the answers which the elders

Refuse to provide the necessary feed.

The Knock

The knock sounds three times.
Not the call to serve but to be served.

We live with this knock like
Living with our greatest enemies.

We ask for heaven & earth kisses our feet.
But discomfort & conflict knocks at our doors.

Fear no question & prepare for battle.
Intimidation responds several times.

No! No! We have not thought about it.
The knock is too much to bear now. The

Invitation of the archangels could rescue us.
For that matter we do need angels.

We cannot entertain ourselves to our satisfaction.
The blow has completely taken our joy away.

The restless feelings run to snap the beauty
That has been purging our worries & sorrows away.

The wind blows & we could not build a new world.
Our favourite songs are under threat.

We do not understand the invasion of
Rivers in the cities. We must keep

Watch on the spoiled fish. Camera doesn't lie.
Because they are severely hungry
For uncompleted jobs.
Because they are scorchingly thirsty

For the real materials.
Because they are lazily jobless.

Their dream for opportunities.
Because they are dirty & homeless.

They have nothing to offer wholeheartedly.
They cannot sacrifice themselves.

The Bank of a River

I have already drunk gallons of water.
Upon the scorching suns at work telling tales,

The bank of a river seems uncomfortable
With the interpretation of the crocodile,

Parading At the sight of the moonlight.
I could not buy the presence of many

Words from him.

Yes, I got what history told me in the siesta.
Take every word into account & never let the

Waves of lives prepare another world for you.
No, I do not believe myself, because autumn

Prepares the way for winter to come & enjoy.
But the corridor of confusion made me always

Dream about him.

Look at him on the terrace of the anxiety.
Look at them on the levee of the catastrophe.

Hiding From the White Snow

How far can he go?
How long can he hide?
How often can he say the same thing?

Playing the same melodies indoors will
Make the walls of the skies fall sick
At the wrong period. We

Always hear what hands & legs cannot
Produce during examination; bigger than
The heart of the authenticity.

Whose words are not to be written.
Whose plots are being a warning to
Viewers. Whose faces are rejected
On the first day of creation.

We heard what stars didn't expect.

True Nightmares

You told us that before you went to bed
You didn't eat any foreign meal at your usual place.
You've calculated the steps ahead of the journey.
You've weighed the energy needed to climb high.

When we could have true nightmares.
When we could not count them.
When we could not recognise them.
When we could not feel the heat.

The knock at the main gate of deceit,
We have heard it before. The tone softened
The healthy hearts. We always walked here
& there for already cooked
Paradise but the referees blew the ill whistle.

The Rainbows of This Hour

Do you know the type of weeds
Displaying around the gardens &

Growing wings on the false part of
The tongue instead of allowing teeth

To chew the edible meat on the weekend?

Can you count many roots
That are pulled out of the holes?

If I could count them as easily as
Possible I wouldn't have asked you.

Whatever I am seeing now is not
On the lists of a blue sheet.

Whatever I've heard never existed in
The tabernacle. He conjured them

& they never appeared in the glass.
I could not feel the presence of life

In the green life. There is nothing
To build life with.

Spelling The Names

We do not want to call him names but
He prefers his characteristics to his names.
Their names are found in every register.

His name is jogging at the peak of mt. Everest.
Plenty of names are dancing on the minds.
Terrible heat from them; questions about them.

Until we ask night to open her eyes, we cannot
Comb every corner of his when his cup is
Full of illness & poverty of the triplet designs.

We can pronounce them even if we close our eyes.
We can do well without phonology at work.
Because we have been competent since our childhood.

We don't need to mark the logopaedic on his anniversary.

We can better spell them without visiting
The ancestors in the forest. No debate on the edges
Of the rain. We can write all the names without
Saying dear to Mr Google.

Revelation

Siren is everywhere
Because untold stories are
Being fished out from the net,
Celebrating their feasts.
Disappointment wears
Her white dresses

Celebrating over immeasurable
Lies. Shock to confidence.
That's struggling in the typhoon.
The degree of becoming
Breathless on our eighteenth
Anniversary. Now the door of failure

Has undressed the sanctuary.
Insincerity, dirt is dancing on
The altar & prayers have no
Capacity to climb the edifice in
Endeavours. Lies are leading
Their games. Lies are championing

The debates in all activities. He's
The mastermind of infernos & deteriorations.

Typing The Wrong Letters

Deception has introduced letters
That do not match with the suns,
With the moons, with the stars, with the

Skies: currently, real letters,
Extremely different from the
Roman letters; inexplicable
Nature, a paralysed wisdom.

We read them several times
But could not comprehend the
Methods & structures in shape,

Neither could we buy the existence
Of the nine planets with their tincture.
He hates their lifestyles & he doesn't

Love a broad day at all in his life.
He does not want to see the
Good work of other siblings
Exposing him here in Jerusalem.

The persistent change of the
Universe; the blow of dust
On the cassock of the saints,
Creating a non-existent world.

Bad Boy on The Street

Who baptised him with dishonesty?
Where did he learn this from?
How long will he continue?
Does he know the consequences?

A bad boy on the street,
Only bad words are rolling
From one end to the other.
Heads can't enjoy the siesta,

Conversations are full of illness,
Headlines are struggling to
Survive on the street because of
The bad boy on the street. Still

Operating in the skin of elephants,
If he could sow beans in the Sahara
& harvest them in the sea, then he's
A wicked & an immaculate liar.

Unforgettable Phrases

Whenever he opens his unkempt mouth,
Flows his unpolished assurance
From the land of living to
The land of the dead.
He has introduced
New courses in our habits.
We tried to study their
Bodies in our walks
Mars, Earth, Venus & Uranus

Could not understand
The biblical quotations involved.
We've tested our enemies
At the fourth banquet of uncountable
Deceptions in the black shoes
Much more to read for the yellow grasses,
Which are fighting to survive.
Bitter than premature death now.

The sign of poverty at hand.
Heavier than our poverty in the sacks now.
Necks cry for help.
Huger than the earth we are living on.
Endless wars.
We can forget everything but not this.

Wretched Old Liar

He started lying as he was
In his mother's womb.
Before he could feel the
Presence of the world.
In his life he had lied
Uncountable times, a shock to energy
Of Jupiter. We could no
Longer accept this concert anymore

Before his traditional naming
Ceremony with the drop of
Water & alcohol on his tongue.
He is continuously
Fooling & playing in the gutter
& polluted key notes on
The pianos. Before his teen
Period he had painted the

Youth with anticlockwise moves.
The youths copied fake,
Faulty lives, which were poisonous
& acidic. Days & nights
Are now tired of hearing the same
Message; Weeks, months
Are ill & admitted in the hospital
Because of continuous,

Cooked stories. He always
Has something to deceive
Nature & laughs at injuries.
It isn't a new animation to
Test rather it is a genetic,
Chronic illness. Lies are his
Foods to attain his goals,
To break the record of
Lucifer. Nobody can challenge or
Compute him in terms of fake narrations,
The wretched, old liar.

Wicked Character

Describe him with any adjectives under his watch.
He won't respond to the call in the air,

But if you call him a liar he will spring
Wholeheartedly & sincerely & embrace

It in the winds. He can say a statement
Which can't hold water & sand in the

Sea. His sentences find no meaning in
The dictionary or brings death back to life.

His lies have beheaded the entire country
& replaced peace with injustice & misunderstanding.

Should he stop telling lies & fight vultures
Over carcasses? Bad names & stolen wealth

Wear the same shoes he does.

INTEREST & HABIT OF KILLING INNOCENT FOLKS

National Patriotic Party Is a Human Slaughter

UN, listen to the citation of NPP in the tummy.
The earthquake in the blood of the pregnant woman

The deadly cancer hovering the strongest forest.
The knock at the gate the blessed safety.

Let the human blood pour on the holy land.
Let their bodies cut into pieces for sacrifices.

Let their skeletons hang in the shrine of the wicked.
This is their song on air for the primitive goddesses.

Yes, grey weather is losing her attraction in the daytime
& we cannot purchase inedible winds in the rains. He

Vowed to sweep the existence of healthy flowers on our
Eyes because he hates good morning, born of the stars

With pure hands. The fresh laughter of the newborn
Babies on the third day.

Good afternoon, the first face of the handwork. The
Decision of the moves in the race. The break of water

In the throat. We can now count our stars under the sun

Good evening, the equality in sizes of the shapes. The
Square of the brains of NPP. The anticlockwise climate

Is still killing the investment of the seasonal jokes. No
More the tone of good evening on the leaves of air.

Good night could not tummy the activities of NPP.
The sorrow of the voice, looking for a peaceful rest.

He's still reducing the handwork of music, the killing
Of holiness in person. He is the most senior slaughter.

Killing As a Hobby

National Patriotic Party has done so many evils to joy.
Darkness is persistently
Eroding the joy on the mountain.

The fishes speaking in our
Dreams, has become the
Acidic in the birthday's cake.

People are missing wherever
These slaughters are found.
Sorrow has come to dwell with

The greenness of pastures. &
Memory could not work without
The assistance of history.

Yes, they cannot see the fresh
Nature & smile at her. They love
To terminate the growth of

Production & kill little babies on
Their naming ceremonies. They
Are slaughters as the world knows.

Heartless Mother

We cannot stop crying over
The missing creatures on the temple.

White suns could not purchase

The behaviour of Hawa Koomson.
The manner she slaughters breathe

Under the watch of mercy. The suns

Can no longer circulate around the sea
Looking into telescopes. Physically

Disabled at the sight of snow in summer.

Whenever she lacks human meats
In realm plus zeal to end lives of angels

She must change the music at the

Background. She has killed the goodness
Of the universe & reduced the population

"I kill ...& I'll kill." She always said.

Worse Teacher

In the year 2020, Hawa Koomson
Composed, which the land completely

Disowned her invention. Even darkness
Could not effectively discharge her duties.

Pool of blood sprang from her handwork.
The earthquake could not tummy her

New product causing draught in rainy season.
Even though heavy downpour, which

Buried storey buildings on the peak of
Mountains could not soak the ground for new

Babies to be planted. She is known as a
Human slaughter. Her smile needs the pouring

Of blood from every lifestyle so that she can
Sell unproductive stuff on the market.

Angry Blood

Have you ever heard the speeches of Hawa Koomson?
Have you ever read the novels she has written?
Have you profited her experience of her?
Do you know the other side of her?

Trust, you have already heard the
Recitation of vulture in the wilderness,
The wrath of acid attacking the growth
Of sanity on the surface of smooth river.

We cannot swim from the lips of safety
Neither can we say hi to the conducive air.
Before seconds or minutes close their eyes
She has gunned down millions of persons.

He has shortened the life of virgins. The young
Stars could not grow to surprise the stems they
Are living on. As the stems supported to grow
Their teeth, they are supposed to replace the

Deteriorated teeth with hope on the fertile land.
But her behaviour has uprooted the strong
Foundation of rainfalls, which waters pure smiles
Purging away the worries & problems of the dying.

Human Eater

The butcher of Ghana who fed her wrath
With human beings, whose joy is to see
Immaculate flowers losing heaven & skills.

Hawa Koomson has removed the liver of the heart.
She has poisoned the kidney of the moon.
She has polluted the lungs of the rains.
She has disconnected the circulation of blood

Always, the same news on air.
War drams are toning above
Unborn babies are missing.
Children never return after school.
The skies cannot penetrate the moons.

The echo of gunshot around the ears.
The sound of the clash of waves & cliffs.
The thunderstorm in the throat.
The reborn ghost on the throne.

Sadness has come to live with us.
Broken heart is still enlarging his territories.
Hospital is full of numberless patients.
Cemetery does not give invitation anymore.

The leaves on the branches are calling for help.
The air in the atmosphere is hotter than oven with
The temperature of trillions of Celsius to the degree
That air could not sleep with conducive weather.

Found Breathlessness

NPP is a killer, a slaughter, a shooter.
They kill pregnant women, beheads

Children of the future. The missing
Laughter of the saints; the voices of

Days cannot stroll on the farmland

& come back to see the reflection in
The moist to say their problems.

Hear the songs of NPP on air again, that
Challenge the wrath of epidemic.

He is wicked to the extent that
Mediterranean Sea does not want to set

Eyes on their tail. Go to him & you will
Never come back to laugh with the valley.

Cry Of the Vacancy

After controlling the register
The beginning of the month,

The news of challenge on the ears
Streaming here from the depth of

The stop of the trip, full of pool of
Blood has become carpet surrounding

Life & death. Many stars have gotten
Vanished. The cry of the vacancy

Hunting the happiness in the heart.
We are losing the oxygen in preservation.

The Soul in Pains

What happened on the 1st of May 2001?
Which of the cities did it happen?
Where at all did it happen?
Who was the master-minded behind?
What was the result on that day?

This is the day we cannot pooh-pooh
In the history of the land.
Calculation could not meet heads & tails.
Hear the evil story of performance of NPP.
Our days are numbered in their hearts.

We could not devour the situation with plane glasses
Neither could we major in any word we knew before.
Look at him, he engineered the killing of over 116
People because he had to pacify the god that
Made him who he was. He isn't a stateman rather

A stateman murder who had terminated the lives
Of thousands of smirks in the wings. Laughter ran
Away for his image, the blueprint salutes the heroes
Who are dining with the ancestors.

Unbearable Scent

Nobody has conquered the record of NPP
For bombing happiness that swims on

The surface of the River Jordan.
When it comes to the matter of death,

NPP does not wage war against.
It is becoming the peak on the pathway.

Bodyguards faced the wall of their time
That turned the other side of doors. The

Rhythm in the slow talk sparks sad songs that
Play in our ears. The voice of the black birds

Of NPP has swept the entire family. We scan
Their hands in the holy water & the tears of

The goddesses in the land cry loudly for the
Vanished folks on the road of the life

Because Of The Missing Year

Time & time again,
Sadness has come to settle with us,

Because around the table is still empty &
We could not see the pictures of the

Century. There was, still, green folks & pink
Colours speaking about the worries

In the winds. The lessons in Good Friday
Have another meaning of the rock on the mountain.

Since the foundation of NPP, many souls have not
Felt the presence of blue suns with no reason. The

Missing year still knocking at the door of the wicked.
We cannot stop asking for justice for the innocent.

His Lookalike

As the killing was streaming from
Nowhere to somewhere, NPP increased
The execution of Eden & Earth.

Loved ones could not hold their breath
To the heat in the chilly water.
Neither the news of yesterday was

Different from the news of today. Indeed
Naada's cargos weren't different
From present cargos. Still, one plus one

Is one said NPP. The same calculation
He learnt from the family, is being copied
By his mates. To poison the oxygen of laughter.

The Same Wings

Open your eyes now & then
Before your nightmare floods
With pools of blood at your sight.

Hear the ears in the storms
Before the Tornadoes shock you
At your own grave. On the right

Side comes the noise we could
Feel the wind blowing from the
NPP's camp. The same wind in

Appearance. The same colour in
Rainbows, being shadows on
Narrow way. The same size in

Inexplicable form, we cannot
Explain why the earth smiles at
Them. Devilish minds of clouds.

Calamities Slap

The music they play nowadays in the wind,
Sounds a note of warning even to those
Who could not hear the footsteps of the real winds
But still the seers doubt the substances planted in them.
A transit in a small domain. Ring the bell many times.
Its depiction in circulation clothes
A stained dress & the evil odour inside
Has made the citizens speechless.
The dance of shamelessness is seen all over.
The sorrowful agony of the pregnant woman.
Plus the disappearance of the *PINKS.*
Throats lake up gallons of waste juice.
Voices become totally & severely injured,
Multiple times. Hearts soak of cuts.
We are chasing what is missing in us.
The whisper of the ambulance.
If we can rest, it & hide it from the look
& the touch of the people then
Who wants to harbour all the booties
Paraded left & right? Then the lake
Of blood streaming from head to toe,
Over its boundaries
Cannot satisfy him with human blood.
Like dripping 1000 litres of blood in a patient's veins.
He is heartless plus stoney = a chief murder.
He is like a vulture that eats human flesh
& anything served at his banquet.
Homeless souls are in a sorrowful prison.

Hundreds are visiting unknown places
& care less about songs.
Heaven is around me but
He thinks of assorted planets.
We can't go there & receive our portions.
We have been denied all
The benefits that keep us alive.
Nightmares have now become
Heavyweight title holders.
We can talk about Jerusalem
But we can't feel Babylon.
The streets have become
Empty like a deserted hope.
Extremely sorrowful like a funeral ground,
Extremely lifeless,
Like a harmless dead body which does
Not belong to heaven & hell
Or to chase the person who likes him.
Children chase their vision.
Poem is ready to soup-feed them.
Poem can engineer the mission
Without rain & shrine.
Was it our mistake to accept
A Mafia in our midst?

The Homeless Ghost

If we look at the features around
Us in our dream, many questions
Pump out from their castles.

Everything has been reduced
Totally & completely including
Persons who are strong & healthy

For tomorrow. Nowhere to see
The real images signalling at us.
NPP has physically eliminated

People. Buried alive on their
Birthday. We cannot forget them
On the Independence Day.

Friendless Blood

From the beginning of the day
To the end of the night, there have

Been a reduction of comfortability.
We are still hearing strength cries.

The campers in the forests could not
Buy the loud cries streaming on air.

The tragedy that has soaked face of the
Earth. The complains in the throat of

Dying, have contributed to the plenty,
Empty apartments in our lives. Around us

Is empty like desert around rivers & lakes
The living laughter has been wearing

Black clothes even on their birthday
Parties. Because nobody is there to celebrate

The fresh hours with.

Boiling Images

NPP have terminated Ghanaians.
They have slaughtered them live & coloured.
She has chopped them into pieces.

The cry of the weather in their season
The scream of the living beings
The sadness of the land, every time.

Blood is seen everywhere.
The flow of blood has flooded to
Everywhere & anywhere.

They have injured billion of people
& killed trillion of people under of
The elephants. They are killers, keep watch.

Untimely Knock-Out

Naada is fun of gunning
Down the sun & the heaven.
NPPkiller's hobby is to

Sacrifice breath in paradise
Ken celebrates whenever
Blood drops on his mouth.

NPP as a political party
Organises party when dead
Bodies are scattered every

Walk of life.
If we hear the reportage of
The dead bodies, even more

Than the count of sand on the
Shore. We could perceive the
Wrath of ghosts. We could hear

The lamentation of the land.
We film the broad daylight
Killing of the saints.

There were killings
They are still killing friends of joy
They are plotting to empty the land.

The Blood Flows

Why are you assassinating
The creatures of tomorrow?
Why are you plotting to murder
The happy souls in the gardens?

Why are you hunting their days
Ahead of them when they have
A lot to discharge on the day?

The pain in the blood, heated like
The smiles of Sahara Desert. It
Could be hot air in the winter when

The living could not communicate
With nature. A few have we become
Because they have made their minds

Clear the healthy happiness on earth.
Their song is let the blood flow, let's
Swim in the blood of future generation.

The Missing Future

We are still looking for the late former
President, Jerry John Rawlings.
We are missing the fertile contributions

Of the late J. B Danquah in the parliament.
We are hungry of the handwork of
Ahmed Suale that feeds the billions

Of people. Many others were strangled
Because they danced to the righteous rhythms
That bring down rain in the fruitful time.

They are human executors in the form of
Saints. Their best meat is human flesh.
More delicious than

We cannot go & return in white.
We cannot sleep peacefully in our dreams.
We cannot enjoy the healing atmosphere.

The agitation of the promised land.
The suffering of visions unattended.
The ailment of standstill in life.

Death Pronounced

Every day, children are being
Kidnapped into unknown cottages.
Youths' lives could not actualise

The visions piled before them
Parents could not enjoy the presence
Of their children & grandchildren.

Because NPP kills them for sacrifice.
The world knew them that they are.
We know them as professional killers.

Their song of the day is to butcher the
Honest folks, to remove them from this
World to another world where darkness

& hell contributed to the effectiveness.
They are what we are experiencing that
Sheer evil activities have covered the land.

Disappointment In an Ajar Room

Journey on an unknown lane,
The overtaking of vehicles reminds us.
The full box has become an empty head.
Answers have large wings so that they can
Fly through the closed windows in the
Middle of the clouds.
The ajar box lives on the billows.
As I started walking in the virgin forest

All the trees were wearing shrouded clothes
& the elements of the life were nowhere
To be found in the race.
The bell of the church continued
To toll. The rustling of the dry leaves drew
The last strength in us, then we saw inside
Of the ajar pot & we held a big funeral.

Still Reading with Glasses

Ready for Sunday move to go out.
The dearest coat & its pair of trousers.
The Italian black shoes,

The stained pink shirt,
One-in-all flying tie; hmmm!
His good look would catch eyes, he thought.

They thought of something else.
The images in the sanctuaries at
The peak of the mercy of cobwebs.

The winds in the sky were uncontented.
What has the earth contributed for her children?
In the air I found only fishy tongues licking up.

I wished the reading glasses would not dodge
The important assignments on the ground,
Because the present planet belongs to a family

& friends whose motives are to kill, destroy, steal
But their buckets are already full, floating over.

Immaculate Hell

Born into this world
With the leading nine stars,
With the wings of the angels

Fanning me, welcoming me
With their unique reverence
That cannot be found in the doubled world.

The loads on the back of a camel
Counting thousands of miles ahead.
He has commenced to somersault.

The breadth & the length of the speed of
The symptoms of the immaculate hell
Slowly walk into our brown tummies.

A new architecture at work of
The rapid speed of a horse in the race,
Its boss has dreams in a nightmare.

I also have feelings like you.
The movement of tigers on the errand.
It's inexplicable. I know the category

I belong to now.
As seconds are older than minute,
So, an hour is older than creation.

Week is also older than words, read my mind.
Then the year is younger than itself, calculate it.
This pain is beyond human measurement.

Even more painful than what Jesus
Enjoys on the Good Friday; was for a purpose.
Suns outside, the type of air inside lungs

Isn't what I ordered. Tongues are itching
To air out grievances. The atmosphere is
Not cool to store the ingredients.

Deeply Asleep

Like residing on a foreign skin
Like a Christian practising his faith in Mecca

Like others are suffering because of their colours
Like a stepson living with his wicked, half blood

I have a sharp tongue, but I can't talk
I have a healthy nose, but I can't inhale

I have sharp teeth, but I can't chew
I have iron arms to wear a stormy jacket

Aber ich kann nicht nach hochbringen
I have fitted legs to walk miles in my mind

Aber ich kann nicht laufen
I believe I am a prisoner in my own abode

Interview At the Scene

There is an uncontrollable noise
Disorganising our daily initiatives & ambitions.

Feelings have listened to many sermons,
They're cooked & crock as *International*

Central Gospel Church mafia, the scammers.
Its arguments have reached the height

Of the pyramid. Facts from pastor Mensah Otabil
Has reached the throat of the discussion.

This church has scammed & made us as laugh-
Ing stocks, as a church mouse. We count ceilings

& lose our efforts in the journey without arms & legs.
Our labour is what the sunlight is depicting.

The time has come to testify to the real outputs.
Pictures are ever ready to confess to Judas. There's

Nothing to showcase. Worse than slaughtering human
beings.
Because death pities conditions of empty cooking pots.

Lost In the Combat

The speedy reverse upon the congestion,
He wages a mighty conflict against
The living spirit of forwardness, & never
Praised the possessed spirit of backwardness ever.

He breaks the assurance he made to greens.
We look at the machine closely &
The equipment surrounding it.
Heart interrogates soul several times,

Neither are we seeing Malaysia in Kumasi,
Nor South Korea in Akyem.
We are about to feel a method of challenge.
Evening isn't found

In the wild animal kingdom.

We could only sink our heads in the mud.
We could only struggle through thorns & torn.
We could hold on to the little we have.
We could only say there is a time for the master.

Untold Time

Deep in the icy winter, we read
Million books that are published
Under the scorching heat of hell.
The makeup of the front covers

Illustrate types of stories dancing on the
Nose. To new readers who are eager
To bite & taste every meat in the books.
The meat is heavier than the books,
It doesn't weigh us down.

They frown broadly at the beginning.

Finally, something unusual has shown its head,
They whisper. Flowers die off untimely.
They grow leaves at the time they are off.
Research on the desk. New research

Should be conducted, we thought smartly.
Nothing in the moons. Sunlight cuts into
Chapters & pages. We read the skins of
The lions & crocodiles.

We take every single bone into account.
Naadalooter, where is the money we saved
For many years?
koathief, where are the bars of gold

We deposited in your bank?
Gaodarmedrobber, where are our sweats we toiled days
& nights in the wilderness?

But the moonlight has numerous times carpeted
Some stuffs, which could explode in the library.
The thunder strike undresses the weak points
& underlines the dangerous contents

& the light from nowhere claps his hands joyfully.
The exposure of the other side of the past & present.
We wanted to waive up while reading Mercury.
The signal shown in the quarter wine gave us an

Extra energy. I am tired of the way good visions
Cannot walk in circles.
The talk in the air is trying to explain
The differences in the passages. We understand

The song, composed of an untold story.

Smell In Smells

We are getting sick now & then
Because it is too much for the motor
To move the motion in the front of us.
Without titles we can neither describe
Physics or Chemistry in us.
Clauses & phrases are quoted from
Nadaa's authors. He does not bath well,
Says River Volta. His name could not be
Forgotten, says he-goat. He has looted
Everything in us, says the camera. I wished he
Could listen to *River Tano* & tap her Solomon.

Not To the East

For five calendars now,
I've been on many roads
Trying to reap my goals.
As I woke up from one
Side of the weather
I've gotten to know
My shortcomings.
Not everyone is qualified
To sit behind a steer.
Starting a machine
Needs to be learnt.
Heating the machine
Requires unfailing wisdom.
Now I am travelling on the
Path of hopelessness,
No yield has been put
On the dining table.
Regret is painted all
Over our bodies.
I can't say to our enemies
That we love them because
The combat isn't ended but
The words of inspiration
Calculated in us is the assurance
& the amazing love
Keeping our smiles not
Withered in the winter.

At The Tail of The Lake

We're still greeting our shadows
In the morning, weighing our intelligence.
The brightness of the day is
Nowhere to be found.

The tail has already started
Complaining about the deterioration
Of the morning. Strength begs to live
Longer to accomplish his
Assignments. & the bell of trust rings

Unfriendly. The sound gazes
At the bell scornfully.
It must deliver the parcel in
The transport as soon as possible.

The sound is in a new cloth.
All the spirits of the land cry.
The talk of the high heels
Sends a dangerous warning to

The stanzas of the sentences to
Move alone on a single lane.
When it comes to the brilliant planet
We are physically dead, far away

From reflection of plateau
That dwells in a tiny village-world.
We can now witness the true game
Of livers & kidneys dancing on statements

That wear the right clothes.
The cement blocks can no longer hold mortar.
We can see joints all over them,
Problems & troubles are unrest. Inside

Them are wretchedly unkempt & they
Push citizens away from enjoyment.
Every structure is hanging on the eyes like
A hanging valley of dishonesty.

There is no system
Is alive now at the tail of the lake.

Worn-Out Destiny

A lifeless handshake.
Naada, Bawuliar, Gaod, Koa, Ab
Are destined
To become shepherds of Satan.
They fear the words
Check & balance in white clothes.
That's why the River Oasis

Doesn't speak to them.
Rather he advises the
Sea in times of confusion.
They always come out
Of the water & listen to the nice weather.
NPPliar is allergic to songs
Of correctness.
They stretch himself
To the conflicting layers.
They are still driving at their
Destinies at all costs.
We know that suns
Will not disappoint us.

They dwell with his malice
With describable colours.
Night has finally run away
So we've seen their asses.
Even though they have

Stolen billions of dollars,
The land of resources will
One day bail the saints
From Starvation.

REVOLUTIONARY WAR NOW AND HYPOCRISY

No More Nonsense

The pulpit has been starved
Of the rich messages.
Still, he is hungry for nutritional
Supplements. Only
Useless sermons have been
Cooked to poison minds.

The audience always sleeps
Off when the messages are
Ringing across. The right
ingredients gaze into the
Searchlight so that they
Will be acknowledged.

Good literature books that
will talk to hearts & display
Their talents on the platform
Are left under the malicious
Darkness & carpet.

The microphone has been
Resting without a job, he
Cries. Half a million people
Are always ready to attend
Scamming classes. Instead
Of them being with living

Water to kill their dry throats,
They chase homeless spirits.
Satan laughs at them.
The pulpit is pregnant with
Numerous duties. Around
It is as naked as a desert.

It is a dead candidate. As
Quiet as the oldest cemetery
In Kumasi. So dirty to see.
When we see the pulpit, we
Touch it & we feel something unusual.
Worn with layers

Of dust, thicker than excavator's
Tires, heavier than sin.
The stench infects the
Congregation with Covid 19.
The pulpit of incorrectness.
Its stains have enlarged its

Territories. Idioms are being
Tormented by evil spirits,
Powerless tongues & weak products.

Pastor Mensah Otabil needs
to confess now because
He has killed many Christians.
He bends iron rods to
Hate souls, minds & hearts
That need to polish the

Shrouded world which has
Been denied her legitimate
Weapons. The dying fire
Needs to be resurrected
Immediately from his tomb.

A fake man of God like
Vitor Kusi Boateng, Power
Chapel Worldwide. Says *this*
& does different things.
He lives with deception,
scamming & extortion. Mafia.

A sanctimonious man like
Rev. Prof. Martey is
Persistently deceiving the
Village. We hear his
Language, which the local
& the international

Markets reject. By their
Fruits we shall know
Them outside the wide door
Around their scamming
Temples.

Comprehension

Mrs. Poem, Mr. Poem,
Miss Poem,
Your seats are totally
& completely vacant.
Wherever you're,
Your home is in the hands
Of a Dracul.

We sincerely & wholeheartedly
Miss you, poem.
Your presence is our
Delicious meal.
We don't need to search for
A green pasture elsewhere
To breathe.

We're living on a mighty land
Blessed with richest minerals
But cursed with diabolical leaders
Like Nadaa, Gaod, Ab.
They loot.
They are criminals!
They are armed robbers,

Jogging on the Ebiri mountain
To strengthen their ideas.
We cannot purchase
Their dangerous games.
The spring of the living water
Has let the locked bounties out.
We gaze into the body, bodies.

Planets laugh at rainbows.
The horizon is not well cooked.
But we believe in poems.
Mr. Poem will bring Singapore
Back to the rejected land.
Mrs Poem's beauty will never
Miss its loyal & royal throne.

We miss you Poem, come &
reign as the *queen of queens.*
We always select your words.
Because your inspirational
Words renew the faded
Ideas of the aged.
They settle conflict & establish

An everlasting food.
We wish leaders like you
Will repair souls, renew
Hearts & build new engines.
There are exorbitant perfumes
In the virgin forest
But your aroma tells how

Powerful & dearly the pains
& shamefulness is.
The poems disinfect
The wretched behaviour.
You, poems of fresh air,
Cool the temper of the sick water up.
What an affordable assignment!

Your commandments are
Enshrined in the life of
"Do the right thing,
At the right place,
At the right time."
You friends of healthy tools,
Seal a deep,

Huge hole but you've
Already fallen into it
Yourselves for the sake
Of your neighbours.
Everything about you is
Incredibly special & one in the
Blueprint we need to get a copy now.

Crawling Class Work

As we heard the introduction of new
Syllabus fishes ran for a new post.
Because. The new tools do not have the
Necessary B12 to breed rich
Materials. The students always complain
The bitter meal in the lecturing hall. They cannot
Do the class work. The devilish ideas & explanations
Have despaired the progress & developments.
Now, continuous heavy showers have finally visited us.
Still, the earth is harder than stone or metal.
Light has sneaked into shields—smartly
Because of the threat from her siblings.
The land, too big for them.
Temperature is 1000 degree Celsius @
Workplaces —-inanis—-mortiferum
Tools are there // plenty // wrong ones // fresh //
They have men to handle the position // manage lives //
To rescue the situation upright.
Sie sind lugner und sie haben verschiedene Gesichter.
Upon their constant noise, no output has been given
Birth to productive babies.
Colours on the leaves are in mortuary.

Sorry With Theories

After glancing through
An agreement, disagreement
Dances against the new agreement.
The new products have

Neither gold nor crude oil
To offer. Transaction cannot
Invite rainfall in the dry season.
This transaction can only trade

Blames & insults. When it comes
To it, our golden food will be
Taken away from our mouths.
No season but there is harvest.

SM has stolen our
Two million Us Dollars.

His backdoor contract on the rise,
Taller than *Shanghai Tower*
Turning down fortunes & hindering
The walk to the home of homes.

Golden envelopes no longer come
From the mouths of the fishes.
Warnings are ignored & accumulated.
Debts give birth to dry rivers. The body

Of the transaction is infected with deadly
Diseases. The mood of the flowers
Tells the visitors their present situation.
Heads collide with their enemies
On the battlefield. Visions hoot at
Gaod for stealing the state.
Destinies curse him & his generation.
Mission becomes angry at him & says

This Is an Evil Transaction Ever existed.

Subject Matter with A Serious Headache

Reading this century,
We see the birds flying
Down with casualties.
Two-third duty, ugly.

Morally questionable.
Parade before their master // zero //
They float here & there,
They fly up there for anything.

Inside the briefcases,
Headlines on the newspapers,
Clauses in the documents
Signal red lights.

Phrases in the documents
Cripple the affected people.
Words cook new figures,
Paint the pink sheets yellow.

The minds of the people
Have been captured by fake goods.
Predictions appear with white wings
On the screen of a plank double lives.

Primitivity With Long Wings

Definition of today is found at the dustbin
In the eastern zone & *Bawuliar* is still cultivating
One-man seedlings. He has withered edible

Ideas in the tabernacle. He has killed the light of
Brilliant babies. A complete portion has visited
The land of no return. Birds of the same feathers

Fly from a point & land on the altar to make
The last sacrifice. Not only there, in the chambers
(many, bold items) are discovered on his brown

& wine faces but his sight asks for rejected phases.
No planet wants to entertain him when it comes
To the workplace. Arms know their fruits without

Labour. The speeches of chameleons spell out.
The household is full of sad memories. Weight
In the pockets challenges the prices of goods.

The greedy politicians can explain the problem
At the back. The nakedness of their family has
Exposed them at the workplace. The symbols

Are extremely ill of primitivity. Up till now his
Statements do not cross, heal the sick. Upon the
Plenty of new songs he has composed

He is still dancing in the acrobatic theatre.
His different heads scan boxes in the bellies.
Files are on the table. More headaches

In the winds. The fishy results. Years of no products.

The oldest crucifixion of the holy place welcomes
All who have chronic pains, diabolic ailments
For treatment. Hope is a good friend of a good driver.

Announcement In Announcements

Thief, thief oooo!
Long hands, wrong hands harvesting
Golden opportunities in summer,
Hollow features have diverted its channels.
So many minuses in our sweats,
Writing the reports on the fresh branches
Deserting the fruits at the light,
We toil tediously here & there.
There's no there to see in the computer.
Nothing can find something in the fishing net.
Naada has stolen happiness in Lebanon.
Numerous lives in his pocket,
Because his hands cannot sleep quietly.
The announcements in the interrogations,
The hymn from the hideout; the throat
In the freezer, not anything there to boast off.

Desperado

Persistent alarm at his presence.
He has changed the complexion
In the tummy. We haven't taken
Any purgative in the morning. The
Rise of the sun, thickness of the
Mist, the shock in the bank account
Of family & friends; with the criminal
Records towering the firmament.
We could remember the agitation
Of the tireless soils. We weigh the
Gravity on the fire. He has thieved
Our souls. The unproductive time
Has come to stay with us.

Immeasurable Hands

If a rainbow doesn't know how many colours
That make up a new colour then those dogs
Who were barking yesterday, were under the

Influence of marijuana. All vanished in the
Whisper of vultures, all inclusive. I know how
Many days can predict the sound of the old

Engine car. The immeasurable hands of Naada
Have made the third planet loser before Jupiter.
Always. The same way in the ghetto. I could feel

The wretched, oblique line leading into the
Mouth of the erosion. He has pilfered the
Treasure of the souls, sang the song

Of the stone-hearted father.
He is homunculus like his head.

Wires In Wiring

At this hour, let's see what we have heard.
We are counting what we are supposed to

Have in the pocket. As it has begun to narrate
Tornado stories, we can still question the lifestyle

Of the weather. Everything is gone, leaving
The dry land to narrate the outcome. He is always

Happy to be called mafia in the goat's uniform.
He smells like a he-goat in the ghetto. Endless.

Rough Road on The Wilderness

Late news at the hour of heartbeat.
I have prepared the table for new
Gardens. Nothing in the life of assurance.

Again, the old faces have shown up
Studying the information like plies of clay,
Like cooking pots; the taste of caution.

Noise in the talk overshadows the honour,
I protected the walls which was about to break into
Pieces. Directions in the algae, sail on

The rough channel. I work labouriously
Above the tower of gains, but I haven't
Stopped counting trenches in destines &

Out on the papers.

Account Of the Ingredients

Voices are roaming on the edges of strength.
They need attentions of the footsteps
In the snow. Coldness & heat on the same ground,
Left & right reflect on the assignment hangs

On the dead conception. Not even half of the
Hope could be counted for. Macho drops
Into deep, sharp ditches, chasing the account of
The ingredients, two plus two = -4. This is what

Naada has turned the promised land to. Look
& search the plantation, full of illness & interrogations,
Early in the morning, the crawling of hours in growth,
Around the necks, goddesses complain bitterly.

Interrogation After the Exams

I ask the night to tell his stories
He has been telling his colleagues

When the clouds are present at work
But I don't perceive Canada in this land.

Too much of swimming in the night when
Day has been asked to leave his post

For thieves like Naada, Koa. Their hands are
Richer than their brains. Worthless folks of the century.

Journey Of the Devil

Good morning
The newest page is created.
Moisture & indescribable chapter.
Nothing is good about morning.

Bawuevil dresses up but we
Do not patronise the night. The designs
Do not catch sight. They do not stop
The bleeding hearts we've dressed up for.

According to the talk of the newly-
Bought speedometer, usual clothes
Snap the attention. We could only feel
The journey of the devil on the boat

Cruising the multitude to where
Their neighbours went & they never
Came back. He bakes our sweats
Into ashes. Wrong themes show

Their heads & wings. Fabricated
Statements travel with swollen, brown
Envelopes. Another responsibility
Overtake old work. His purpose runs

Faster than wings. Well-attended & flourishing.
Shout for bailout in spring. Our souls ring
In the ears. Clap of tiny hands breaks
Down in tears. The tone of the sad bell

Speaks to the planet. Smile on my face
Tells my siblings the suffering my sweet mum
Sailed through in labour (the wrath of the sea).
We have decided to channel through
A new path. Light should create a new path.

No Computer Answer

This search on the floating earth,
This light in the reflecting globe,
Under the water digging out the facts
On the ground, has intensively laboured.

What do we see around us today?
What do we hear on air around us today?
What do we smell around us today?
What do we touch around us today?

What do we eat around today?
What do we drink around today?
What do we sleep on around today?
What do we wear around today?

Heads never stop wiggling in investigation.
All the struggle falls away. 25th on the calendar
Wakes us up & questions hostile manuscripts
Which will retire at night at once.

We comb all the triangles of the *Whitehouse*
In the heart of the globe & no intelligent faculty
Has had an answer to the war between Russia
& Ukraine. Astronaut asks Southern Ocean if she

Could find psychological walk but medicine men
Burst into laughter. The overall *Google* rejects
The questions & says *Venus* is the question &
That *Venus needs to shoot some of her branches*

Down. The problem is uselessly foolish, say night.
A desperate, evil doer says Saturn. We promised
The temperature is fresh.
The family graves that we won't do *DNA until*

Saliva tells us the secrets of his action.

River Tano In Distress

We love to be with River Tano because
Her love endures forever but her children

Come from another planet which does not
Have human names. Their ways always

Conflict against different moons. When we
look at the movement of the River Tano is not

The language she speaks at home. She
Cries loudly for her children. We fish in

The home of the River Volta but her kids
Will come & smuggle them out of our lives.

We can no longer dive in the River Dnipro
Because there is *No Justice & Peace.*

Nothing hopeful can change black into white
Because an umbrella cannot cloud an elephant.

An elephant has become a thorn in the flesh,
The wall clock hops its steps immediately.

Hours speeds up without waiting for us
Because the rain has just started its duty.

It's time to cultivate our rich plans. A final combat
Has come to uproot the happiness of The Niger River

Kids. We're completely prisoners because of our trust.
Kingdom against her blood. We've lost the meaning of

The naming ceremony. In the name of the water we
Feel the true testimony of the culture. The citation plus

The pillars could measure the ingredients that will
Outsmart the vitamins & the proteins on our skins.

Unfolding Calls

We entered the Vatican City with
One leg & the other one debated hard.
A war to fight. There were many ancient
Lives not forgetting reading
& understanding in Padua. The words
Could teach the blueprint. Son in the sack.
We stood on the peak of a mountain
Looking over worries & spices. The branches
Tell us the stories. Sadness of the living.
We saw Jerusalem in Afghanistan
& Kremlin in Ghana ringing strange bells.
No smile. No enjoyment. No life.
Call for alarm,
Call for a positive change,
Call to wake up the sleeping rivers,
Calls from human beings & nature,
Call now, because we desperately need resurrection,
We asked ourselves whether we could not
Stand the seasons without answers. Why?
We could jog a stretch of afflictions without
Envying the stars in the sky.
Like being chased for its evil deeds. We can no
Longer boast of strength & sound bodies.
(We have no titles to challenge the behaviour
Of hot weather in winter) because of him, because
Of them.

Listening To Reality

On the hill, I now see near, I saw yesterday far away.
Christian organising a mighty crusade.

The wounds on the faces, injuries in visions.
Intervals between the poor & the rich.

The distances between the skies & the missed treasures.
The intervals between lagoon & sincerity.

Criminal like OM, looters like Bawulooter, KOAcriminal,
GAODthief & NAADAsmuggler,

Like those whose tongues receive the *Body Of Christ*
& preach the gospel of Judas.

Like those who hate to archangels & angels & accept
Destructive witchcraft & their apparatus at their workplaces.

They're far away from each other. I follow the Google map.
No positive change. Nothing new has been pulled up.

Foolishness On the Platform

We find it difficult to cooperate with Neptune.
We are tired of seeing what kill our appetite
When the night is struggling with the day for an immeasurable
Space to darken hell & death on the screen.
No respect for the book of life & taking the only oxygen
Left in the mercury. They don't listen to the injury of plants
Which are there to depict their generosity. Sight wished
He was not born at all because his siblings have disappointed
Him. He can no longer boast of being one of the children
of blue.
A final ploughing has come with his sharp teeth
To peel the rest of the layers on our bodies.
Sparkling bodies that catch the eyes of the land,
That have touched the hearts of many, have been
depreciated.
Even our neighbours can no longer identify minerals.
Our sweet voices have lost their titles on the stage
Because of poverty & hardship by the current devil.

Confession At the Spot

In summer, the temperature reads=Celsius.
Volcanoes have come to erupt our daily activities.
The pens have not locked up articles & novels.

It's time to wait for the season.
A list of items is jogging on the brains of many
Who could be new or old.

They could be bad because they are animals
Ready to get them out as soon as possible.
We have the patience to wait for the harvest.

We sail through wilderness & the message is
= no wasting of time.
Final erosion has come to bring out

What is under the soup.
We toil hard to guide & to
Enjoy the harmonious song.

To plan with the experts in the walk
With the richest knowledge on the earth
That has enriched thousands,

The eggs have fallen into the life of return.
Our fingers never get tired when the fishing nets
Have not told us the good news they have.

We sleep when the goddesses
Want to loan us their ideas.
Because of our goals.

But what are we seeing now?
But what are we feeling now?

We shall not give up at all.
We rather be the men who
Can change things around.

It's In Their Blood

The eyeballs of a cat have never lied to the morning smile.
I walk early in the morning among the lions & tigers.
Their greetings never allowed the temperature to
Visit the true poems of the period.

It's in their blood always. I spoke to nature about it.
They carry the world to the edge of discussion. I
Asked afternoon & I never felt any good thing
About afternoon until my skin reminds me.

The unforgettable history. Seasons came & narrated
Their stories. I was half fed but the knock at the brain
Opened many chapters to the globe. There have been
No difference between yesterday & nowadays.

It's in their blood.

Handover Ceremony

Now they pretend they like to fight.
They always gambol the issue consuming
The sea in the river. The lake can stream
To the north pole & rest at her tail.
From memorial to this generation
There hasn't been any beauty at sight of praise.
Acidic bombs cannot say they are more friendly
Than an earthquake on the happiest day.

It's Not New Environs

Their body speaks language
The rest of the souls complain about it.
The upper parts of the upper room.

Listen to their stories.
I can't speak the language of the stranger.
I understand a little meal on the dining table.

I want to travel to the city I've dreamt about
When I was in my mother's womb. Goals are ever
Ready to be attended but the wicked

Stands on the way. I can't respire the air.
Nature has provided to me freely because
Of them. They're inhumanly heartless.

Old Song

We read novels as if we are learning
How to paint the life to come.
We speak the language we
Weren't taught on our birthday.
The rhythm of their song is as hell as their output.

We are reading their biographies.
We read out the hell they are pushing
Us into. Heaven & earth don't see their glory.
The feet that step into
The sanctuary, is the same feet that walk &
Shut down the sunshine in our lives.

They always wanted to endanger the
Sweetness of paradise. The pride of
Nature has been deteriorating.
Nature can no longer hear the cry of the poor,
Nor respect the climate in our daily lives.
The same blood, the old song.

Repetition

Shame unto you *Naada, Bawuliar, Koa,*
You liars of the century.
You criminals of the generation.
You, murders of all time.

We sail from continent to continent.
Only Russia can boast that she is
The largest country in the world but
Freedom of speech & a pure democracy

Is dead & buried before creation of the
World. Ghana has copied their dirtiest
Practice that there is no Jerusalem in Venezuela.
We can only toll the bell of Afghanistan

In Burundi. A strength travels far miles
& come back home with an immaculate
Disappointment. Regret investigates the
Sky & says the lord's prayer.

Disowned Savings

The colours of the candles,
We stream up & down
In the untouched woods.
We kneel before the air
That's the preparation
Of the art. The disowned
Ingredients have found
Its way into the swimming pool.
It is the solution to the meal
Served on the solemnity of
The Holy Trinity. We can't
Purchase the designs posted
On Facebook. The true story
Has come to light that Mohamed hates
Development & always being in bed
With destruction. Look at us,
Night has no home in Dubai
Because of his conduct.

Signature

We studied well in the universe.
Research trekked far & near
To pay an august call on Solomon but
We all know that gold can never be oil.

Bawumtongues has been taught to steal, loot
The pool of sweats in Germany.
There is no an existence of a river
To bring fishes to the dining table.

Banks are visiting the land of ghosts.
The time has told us that if we don't know
Then we should look forward. He loves
To live in the Netherlands because there is no jail.

Suggestion Boxes

We can't end narrating the life
Journey we are about to commence.
Bawuliar is a chief smuggler of life.
Dogs & tigers are aware of the maltreatment,

The custom of penance will bear with us.
Money laundry in the Jubilee House, floats
On the surface of wine & bread consecrates
In the holy eucharist. I can't stop praying the holy

Rosary for miracles in the monstrance on the feast
Of Corpus Christi.
Hear us, hear the other side of the game,
let's play together.

He has emptied all the governmental institutions' coffers.
They promised their destinies on the mountains
& paint the other side of the world sanctimonious
Education. Our land is not like Nepal which doesn't

Have a national anthem. We worship in the temple
But devil has chopped us into pieces & devoured
The confidence we planted in him. The walk around
The China Wall has already told us his empty integrity.

Drink The Red Wine with Us

Time doesn't wait for the right season.
Our sleep on the unwanted bed is not
Ready to rest the customers in tranquillity.

It's too much to allow the young beards to
Burn under an empty head. We run ups &
Downs in the flame of boxes of gold.

Up for the move, never say there's no
Man in the land. You're a man, capable to
Iron out the wrong line, which is kneeling.

Arise the land of sonnet. Peace & smile belongs
To the sea of the south leg. Move beyond the line
Of the brave touch. Let your life proclaim the

Achievement of the martyrs. On the mountain,
We shall strike heavily.
On the sea, we shall provoke the angry waves.

Say no to intimidation, hoot at ill practices.
Away you evil.

Talking Points

Awake from your slumber in discomfort
Arise from your sleep in the time of war.
Yesterday has enjoyed her privilege to her fullness.
I am reading what I will write for tomorrow to announce.

Look at him, our reversed forest will tell us the battle
That foretold us no beginning will speak for himself. I can
Stop finding the meaning of spoilt meat in the soup. They
Can't continue to wear shields at night when the dictionary

Of the scriptures preaches traditions & beliefs. I see
The new day in the fold. Arise on your feet & your life can
Be multiplied tomorrow. Stop the noise in your ears & calm
The winds from the desert on Independence Day.

Vandalism.... Immediately

It is an offertory time.
It is in the middle of the service.
I can't wait again to allow the
Period to slip off.
If I don't hear the sound
Of the dog at the entrance of the gate
Then I will feel the perception. The
Purpose of the move is to wear new clothes
On the anniversary day. Smart to feelings
Count the missing smiles on the celebration day.
Count your fortunes & report them to scanner.
The scores are around the clock.

Radical Walkie-Talkie

I missed myriad calls
Looking for fruitful answers.
The Pacific Ocean will spare
Me if I permit lakes & lagoons
To make noise in your presence.
Do the work assigned to you now
Before the afternoon, reject your
Concern.
Kick the ass of the fog from the
Hill for, the farmland has nothing
For him. The hymns of this small clan
Are played outside Eden. Say no
To this heat, let the voice of the
Fathers resound beyond the lines.

Surgery.... Now

Break the silence, the voiceless.
It needs a blood transfusion.
To talk to the half-living,
Dive in the cold water.
Baptism & confirmation.
In your teens.
Say the citation of your choice.
It is very clear in the shadows.
Free the sentences of the dry forest,
The kitchen is asking for ingredients.
The minds from their cages.
No limitation for the assignment.
For the afflicted in the rain
Cannot sing the same song again.

Rejection In Rejections

I have been famished for a unique food in my dream.
My manuscripts need *p* to start the preparation of the

Meal but the meaning of this *o, partnership to transact*
Business with *e* so that there will be transparency.

What I am complaining about, numberless, tasty food
Can testify at the law court. Not all the alphabet

Can prepare the meal everyone will enjoy.
I must ask for help so that I can pass my external

Exams colourfully. The alphabet describes the gender
That I belong to *m.* The light I need to kill starvation, is

Poem. Light to the candle of *poem* whenever the waves
Of the calculation challenge the breath in the box.

Fire On the Skin

Imagine how the funeral sings in
The hearts of the green life, it will dance.
Check the time, the bell started
Crying loudly. 60 degrees Celsius.
Too much for the storeroom; mixture
Of sunless & brown; lack of tools
At the workplace now.
Root of the poems, your children
Are needed on the field.
At the bank, only waste sings alleluia.
Roots stand in your brain, take back
Your seats *now.*

Theology In Racism

Practice is missing in the cantata
Because the sleeping eyeballs
Is knotted to hypocrisy in the
War time. I should have seen
The practices at the doors of religion.

The tune of the music is sleeping
On the lips. The so-called senior
Journalists' eyeballs have
Been sleeping on their brains & on
The dying lives of innocent folks.

Fear of missing the brown envelopes
At the right time. The plots of
The candidate for the heavy duties,
Are all over everywhere.
I read the teachings of the laws,

Metal & plastic designs in the
Frames of the broken arms. Foundation
Has no respect for the pillars.
Fake products walking into actualisation.
Why the crocodile teeth have no job on

The working day? When did fishes refuse to live
In the water? They have seen half of the water.
The surfaces of life refuse to tell the lifespan of the
Theory. Senses have died off because of nepotism.
You are the brain behind the agony.

Thorn In the Flesh

We like going around the virgin ideas,
The face of the statues, the climate is the answer.

Days in the week; the calculation of hours
In energy. Weakness & stubbornness in reply.

Destinies always talk to the mountains in
The sea, the blockage of success in trials. We

Feel the failures in the flesh. Their ways are the ways
Of the flesh in the open. Pernicious & impecunious.

The part of the hemeralopia. If we are now frugivorous,
Then vegetarians need a move to purge away the

Malicious feelings, for, the rainy season won't permit
The dry season to wear her shrouded clothes.

Invasion In the Daylight

The mirror of the mission; old shoes of the vulture
Dancing on the rubbish in the daylight. Invasion
In the father's house from the main gate, the citation
In the sacred room, the images remain unconcerned.

The first reading on the deafened ears. Calls drummed
To the participation of the mood. Trust wore his crown
In the daylight; debate of the mirror; questions popped
On the skins. As words scattered at the entrances

Of every door, we began to sing the national anthem. We
Trusted the angel & left the devil to escape the dungeon.
We failed the test on the ordination day & reaped for a little
Mouse. Trust is good but control is better to conquer

Gullible acts.

Dying Street in Lagos

Gaze at him, stare at them.
Two lives in one world,
The heat of the street,
The black smoke of tension,
No man's ghetto is locked.
It is for me; it is for the darkness.
A second, the reap of the grace,
I calculate the suns under the clouds.
The birth must be any colour
Of its beauty. The strength at the
Door of hope; numberless & limitless,
Efforts dig the weather in the soil.
Whoever is there, the moment waits for
No excuses at the panel. No teeth,
No sacrifice at the mass for the
Less privileges to crawl at the
Foot of the sacred shrine.
It is a drive in the struggle between
Sunlight & darkness.

Twin-City in Twin-Enmity

The New York City, twin sister of Cape Town
The twin-city from different wombs, born
On assorted days. The atlas of old & new has
Not altered the original speeches. Languages

Hold their vows to their culture & tradition.
These places we live in now are termed many
In one. I can stroll from heaven & earth but still
I will not buy the products which narrate the

Stories about forefathers. They couldn't
Comprehend. Items are more than the
Consumers displayed at the catch of eyes.
I cannot assume these people exist on the

Same planet with me. There are diverse
Features from unknown walks, might in
Crime, tininess in understanding. We look
At the soil, not the purlieus in turpitude,

They look at the soil, not the ashes on the
Ash Wednesday & we don't want to see
Tasteless & artificial. I spend so much time
Within me in studying those birds with four

Wings which no one seems to be very
Familiar with, rather feel lost because they
Can't be named. More than half plus half
Can't give birth to the same twin-city.

Missionary In the Red Shirt

The music in the land has changed
Its navigation. Morality has become
Homeless in his land.

The farming season with the red eyes.
Left & right.
The weight of the blow on the face,
up & down.

Air & rain & suns & darkness
Don't catch on to us. Here & there,
From & to

Are speedily searching for a poem
To detect the catastrophe devouring them.
We were happy

Before the fresh architecture of the village.
Not forgetting routine,
Each day smoothly ran into the arms of night.

We clap for resurrection, for, flowers always
Smile at us.
Now these genetics, this politics on the

Stolen seat, the presence of shame.
There is repetition in how we do the reverse.

First, invite their hands at the entrance &
See whether
Thunderstorms will embrace them.

Chemotherapy For the Climate

If I tell you the behaviour of the
Deserted barrel, I won't hear the
Drop of the tropical shower again.

Imagine a certificateless graduate
Who is boasting that he has a classmate.
Because the dictionary is trying to clear

The mess the bad textbooks have broadcast.
Mountain & hill & sea & river & lake & lagoon
Cannot wait to undress the snake under the grass.

Itching Stool

Nothing is luscious at the bouquet.
Fruits & vegetables will not be bellyache
In the shadow of the wicked. If we
Don't excavate the decay, then there

Is no need for a tried examination.
The discussion is that the beauty of
Entreaty is not in the basket. Wrong
Occupant, the season questions

Shortcoming. Something suffers from
Many worries living with us. It doesn't
Belong to polemic. Brobdingnagian &
Excruciating, no abode for waste.

Stand above the height of pyramid,
The debate in the red wine doesn't
Want to mix with white wine, as the river
Will not allow the lake to say my dearest.

Thesis For Us

If the cutlery set will tell the farmers
The truth then let the timetable of the incoming

Wedding divides the sea into thousand parts,
But I love the sea & I cannot kiss her. I have

Not started writing myself. Plus & minus hold on.
The research on *Naada,* arms retire on heads,

One two three four five six seven, many times.
He has injured the pure hearts. This one, let

The discrimination read out his offences.
I don't know home because of the uninhabited

Morality.

Magnificent Liaison

Bawudangerous is nefarious in white.
I can see him through a black window.
The glass at the main trouble,
History of the century, the agonies
In archives, the jubilation of Lucifers
Under the white carpet; the immoral odour.
I encounter the flog of intimidation, subtraction
Of throat, cease of a flowing juice on the palm.
I stare into a chalice, answers & joy in their
Clothes. Holy Thursday, the weapon to gun
Them down. The affliction in a song, much to
Wash down. The river Nile has already
Disowned him because the black box isn't satisfied.
The cry of the narrow way should be taken into
Account. Up against the leakage in the pocket, now.

Reverberations In Conflict

It is bitter to heart
As if a biology has introduced
New products for unkempt mouths
Or minds have passed through
Shock or the announcement of
A new date to open the wretched
Temple that is towering evil skies
Or let us read out his biography
On his inauguration as the chief
Priest of occult. Let the blood
Flow in the garden of Cain. Abel
Will say prayer or gaze the
Flight of blue birds on religious
Assignment. Let's practise
Seeing ups & downs in the
Waterfalls. Let the water write
Her sorrowful songs. He has
Faded the beauty of smiles.
But have not captured the glory
Of purity.

Philosophy In Doubt

We've ignored the nonsense
For a lengthy period now.
We've endured the hatred
Pains more than necessary.
We've been without eyes
For some reasons but the

Heat in the voices has declared
Her stand in the way of life.
Sit up in your blood.
We've heard about this......
We cannot go & come on the same day.
Effect in this group exceeds

The tower of the Pharos.
In the air, the messages are clear to the
Audience with the scanner.

Thespian & theophany,

Fire & gas will not sit the new books down
To be written under their watch.
The whisper is clear.
Sit up in your wheelchair,
Gold & diamond is shared
Behind closed doors.

How can we step outside to know
The gravity, when we are about
To grow teeth
Under a different roof. It is you now.

Timetable Is Voracious

Evil upon evil, this melody is bitter to dance to.
Bawuevil is the most desperate devil among
The children of lucifer. The darkest archangel
Of all time, the beat of a war drum on the altar.
We dreamt the dream of the seven men in one & half
Bodies. The roar of the skiving half, grief-stricken
& enigmatic & wearisome & trickery & loony,
All his breakfast at midnight. We won't talk about
Misfortune. Week can plot against hours & months.
We won't disturb snow to purchase mansion in
The heat, at Day & Night. We know what is
The Passover, what is behind the shrine of weakness.
His laughter is a satanic last supper organised for the
Gormandizing, saying the Koran four times a day.
For the poor, parched living meal.
Taking to heart, *DNA* result would not bother to
Challenge his flowers at the lips of interrogation.
His knot to a sanguinary, several voices die.
The drum of the ghosts is the winning album,
So, let's sing together.

Afterthought

I must listen to the disturbances
Of the siren.
It is the time I must obey the call,
Not once it is
Written on my forehead, that I should wake strategies
Up from my sleep.
I should tell my soul to push the journey aside.
Push the river now
Back to them, I've tried plenty of times to reflect.
We've to gallivant
Around the runaway to let the lying dogs in their
Sweet dreams.
I divide whatever hangs on the tree. Good to see
Christians & Muslims
Worshipping together in the church & in the
Mosque read the
New & old testaments & purchase all the ideas.
Proposals will stand up themselves.

Dedication Of Blood

First, kick it out of the dilatory net.
I will delegate the rests to the awaited hands
At the centre of many views. I watch the wall clock.
I watch the life of the atmosphere. Steady & study,
Life & lives in the present tense. The heat in the
Offer cannot wait for tomorrow.
I'm beating the huge, numberless drums.
Hear me, the parched drums are hungry of your
Sacrifices in the flames. In the flare we shall climb,
We shall receive the sacrament of confirmation.
Go mad in the desert, the wooden bridges will swallow you.
& I will spit on the so-called burning fire of theirs.

Portmanteau Is Stirring Up

NanaSatan, father of unclean spirits,
The promoter of destruction
The murder of billions
The founder of an empty mortality
The president of a garbage integrity
The user of a fake navigator
The rejection from the garden of Eden

Evil, you evil of the century
He laughs on the respiration
Of the dying. We ask for lessons
About the creation of the universe.
He has already spoiled rich plans a million times.
We learnt to set the captives free from
The constant quotations. The joy of a

Green calendar. Awareness & respiration.
The world hears the true, untold encounter.
The xeric life, the conversation of veracity
Has died off. In him is a turpitude, then we
Ululate at him as the pains in the kidney fuel.

Interruption Of Schedule

On the cross,
I look around to search the missing half of me.
I read the oblique miles ahead
On the edge. The white birds suspire
The steatopygia on the floor.
To begin the behaviour of
Venezuela in Ghana, let's invite rebarbative
Seismic on them now.
The susurration to the naked walls
& the reclaim of the
Raddled pother. The rataplan in the wings.
Let's talk about perfidy
Nugatory & iniquitous
The exact paints for his image,
Not better than a sinner in Adamah & Zeboiim.

Periphery On the Walk

Around a very few directions
A new beat is struggling to dance
On the extremities of the question,
Slow to anger, pity to tiny souls

Beneath tones in the virgin forest.
This tu-whit-tu-whoo in the night,
DJ's observe the disco light of the
Proposal. The cock-a-drodle-doo

Of the machinery, swifter than serpent.
This is the concept in the choice of a few.
The prediction in the missing boat.
The chirp above The White Castle,

The numberless plots in the pant.
We need to sleep with the lights
When the knocks challenge our
Existence. No more nyctalopia

No more noctambulist.

Mathematics For All

"Youthless" village
Unproductive blood
Useless muscle
Let your words walk in the welkin
Your sweats surround the oceans
Preach the gospel when confusion arises
The land of the Leal has no snowy cloth to wear
Blow the fire in the hoes, multiplication of
Flame on their heads; chase poison
Out of Eden. "Youthless" land is
The agony of future readings.

Four-Time Call

A wake-up call,
Yes, a wake-up goal
Numerous times at the gate
Of my life. Come & go (language)
I still witness things falling apart
On the unprescribed channel.
Scream loudly, shriek hardly, gunshot smartly,
Strongly beyond the boundaries.
It is our parts to keep the ball rolling
From the square of standstill to
The heaven unknown to books to come.
Old print will not wait for the new prints.
The new day is drawing near to the departure
Hall for those who are still sleeping in the endeavours.
I print out the interruption of the phrase.
I hold stanzas & verses to the incense.
The burnt offering, the hard decision.

Strike The Deal

I chant to injuries.
I heat the engine.
I cock the shoulders up.
I take them to Mecca.
Then I say your time is up.

Away You Satan

Away, you, looter of the state lives.
You are in hell.
With a phosphorescence, chandelier stretches his neck
Limitlessly & irrecoverably.
Living beings have become something.
Living thing have
Spoilt & decayed on a sale; twice & three beats
Away from
The land of the conundrum.
Chase Naada out of the land of the living now.
White is blue, white is red, is Naada's song.
For the sake of
The intermission; uproot the expired roots
Over-brimmed & immortal.

Evil Mud

Numerous, wicked folks have branches.
We could see the road in endless
Parts. Walk up & down on the borrowed channels,

The sharp teeth of the animations regulate nobody.
The feelings of the evil mud, we jog hundred times.
The number of aches, the disqualifying truth.

We carry the summer trees in our livers. The loss of
Sanity salutes glimpse. Crimes still hold the flag to
The symbol of the wastage. We wear the signs. The

Range of reflection, mud has spread its scents above
The catch of hope & deliberation. The dresses of
The soil: we feel the vapour from the freeze. The

Discussion of the missing surface of the creature. Creation
Can't even half believe the new attitude of a half man.
In the mirror are the results of today's lotto.

Blame The Sight

Hoot at him, them
Chase them from their homes,
They are aliens encroaching
Our treasures.
Run after him, sweep the sand
Under their feet. The weather
Doesn't need them.
The slumber of religion.
We know something about him,
We can tell you their secrets.
If a green colour doesn't accept
Them, the other colours also say no.
We have nothing to say now.
Still, they are weaker than nothing.

More Than the Cup

We've tested what was rejected after
Being landed on the right eye.
Dying for medicine in the exams,
We tune to the wake-up siren of

Nepotism in the stream of together
Journey. We tested what our naming
Ceremonies turned the ground to the song
Of the angel. We can't drink from the same

River with the half features. How many times
Have we attempted to count the quarter of the
Sufferings & the loss of fasting on his way?
It is more than what we expected to arrive on

The day we wanted to describe the symbol.

Don't Look Far Away

Around the start of the walk
There, the faces of the quarter trips.

We've got to start the unending walk.
The motor broke down then all the

Looks confessed the reality. The youthful
Sentences in the streaming. Hunger fired

To cease the flow of failure; disappointment
In the artificial shoes; the burial

Ceremony of the sick words. Journalism on
The run; no flame in the tongue of parrots.

We could weigh the loads left behind. We don't
Need the weak stars in the clouds.

Supper Sight with Satanic Centre

To you Bawuheartless
Who doesn't know shame,
Who licks the sacks of sugar
Of the injury.
Your own words,
The freight in an anxiety,
The clutter & bereavement,
The endlessness in chains,
Havoc conditions
As you thought on your flight.
He has undressed the secrets
Beneath the breakdown vehicles.
Check the wood in woods
Your blind walking stick
Has kicked away the golden targets.

Stanzas In Proverbs

You know very well that
I stand before the crowns.
You have opened to the
Dim glasses. I can testify at the

Festivals of the triplet-village.
On every line, alphabets
Cannot dodge the meaning
Of the proverbs ringing

In the heads of the cutlery set.
I stroll on these stanzas,
The sounds of the feet drama,
Multiple explanations.

I hear them, the tones of a
Newly born laughter in the
Clapping. No reap for the ghettos.
He cannot move the rock he built

Sometime back. He tastes what
Salt can strongly confess his
Barbaric behaviour. I still declare
To the certificates, notes & remarks,

Shadows & indifferent oceans,
layers & stanzas, to denounce the
Red & black attitude on Saturday,
Await the three-third glass of ……

These stanzas in colourless prover.

Verses In Discussion

We are on the rented planet.
Not yet discover the noise
In the throat after responding
To the wishes of the moisture
When the national flag raises
A beat behind the grave of the

Martyrs.
When we can count how many
Facts in history. Library
Will not stop growing grey hairs
At the early stage. Numberless
Places are welcoming fresh books.

When the rich foodstuff of debates
Is exported to a diversity of faculties.
Verses are discovered in inspiration,
When the songs of the true apostles
Are murmured beneath the muscles
Of the blueprint. Through every message

History will still remind us of the diversion
On the sea when the clue on the fingertips
Run front & back on the skins of the death.
When the discussion has not found the verses
When senses challenge the new versions,
When sons & daughters on the waiving boat.

The distances to the nose, signs & wonders
Can now purchase the distaste of double centres.
No dreams in the actions; despair in jubilation.

Figure Of Speeches

These actions in cover, under the itching,
Bring the hidden pot in the corner,

In the light, I stand boldly in the transparent glass.
There is something in vocabularies,

I can open the cup of these words.
Messages are there to carry different shots at

The same time. I should have weighed the
Silvers in the figures of speeches because

White papers have declared her stand on
Mars. I play separate roles like as to

Write powerful poems that will burn fat in
The heart of liars.

Until The Daybreak

If you're looking for troubles
You're looking for punishments
Which are older than your brain
& faculty. It is not new with
Actions we perceived under
The orange & brown suns.
We compare two photos
Standing before truth & deception.
We miss the directions. Photos are
Still on the satisfactory waves. We
Wanted to eat the fruits, rather
Our sweats cooked us & baked our
Hopes into ashes. Yes, until the
Day break we could not print the
Reports out of the products & prophecies.

Intimidation Wears His Crown

These, nobody-people locate nowhere
On the asteroid; capable hands of branches

Don't recognise them, now, because of
Injuries on the little babies they see darkness

As their strangler. Nobody knows their
Generation but their works.

As guns are pointed at my heads,
Indifferent flames reverse their strike.

Sizes of imaginations, faces of the wall.
Memories of the wide path carry the messages.

Voices can travel beyond reaped fruits but
Titles lose their images at the news time.

When The Great Land Sinks

There are games to play in public.
Ideas are now invited to play the games
On the same page of trials. We mix the ideas
Because we commence on the land & in the air,

Can tell us the result on the next day in the
Next town. Practice of things that is not
The friends of the white smoke. We can
Judge the games he plays with his plantation

& his people. The nose, the more gigantic than his
Department. Arrogance has made him the least

Breath among the heroes in the sanctuary. We
Scan the days of the week. We photograph
The errors in the casket. His department
Does not produce people richer than

Themselves. Where to go! We now know to
Crawl in the sand in the mire; the news is
Everywhere to discern the hidden-eyed catch.

On The Same Page

I say every article four times seven in dreams
But I want to calculate the expression in his peeper.

To meet the viridescent fruits rejected at hand, the hours
Ahead of summer, I can meet the target, action

When, what is in him, it is not recognised. It is
Extreme to walk past by. Worse than before,

No balance on the scale, the assorted views
Stand for judgement. Voices sail & fly above

Their level in the sphere. I type the names
& his name appears in numerous.

Where Is the Upper Class?

How many times will darkness advise him
To stop fooling under the carpet? Carry-in,

Carry-out. It started before the right hand felt
Absence in action. I saw NO, Doubts, rejection

Rising from the same hole. From the soul of
Indifferent world; the results of the tests; the

Trauma in assorted confusions in the church.
The lack of the upper class in the warehouse.

Venus can now be perceived on the Jupiter as
Neighbours, if possibilities are combating to be

The answers of our shortcomings. The runs of
Today, there is a shortage of the upper class.

The Weak Clocks as Mouthpiece

I've heard the cry of the thing.
The name is published on the
Unknown, heavy heart of the east palace.

Looking for it, is the close of the trip
Promised to add & minus things.
I have heard the report of plenty of things

Are occurring with the five arms
In Kyebi & in Ashanti,
The ring of the weak clock.

What, When, Where?

What I always receive in numbers in the dream
From the consecrated streams could be the
Questions of a teenage pregnancy.

I ask what they could

Fetch to the noisy, assorted winds, dancing
Around the problems that grow beards &
Moustaches. Adjacent fire, the rains form

New layers on the rented platform.
If I know the clouds will not narrate
The mystery after the knock at the door

Of the rain, I won't have challenged the
Ugliest features of Kyebi. When to
Excuse the wrath of the spring's behaviour

At her arrival of the poor harvest. Turn
Out the tone. Yes, your smile builds hell
Of disappointment.

Where to dream on the safer side,
I look for the vacant dream.
Don't be mysterious on the eyes

Of determination, what, when, where is
Unhappiness in life?

Mad Family in Mess

If the weather will be willing &
Sincere to confess every first Saturday then,

The assignments of the investigators
Will not climb above towers' level &

Spit on the face of shame. The mad
Family in mess, with torn dresses in public.

When children question the
Cause of present poverty & hardship

On the heavenly earth, I won't
Blame suns alone for residing in the

Middle of the computer. As I
Combed the marketplace, I witnessed

More madness in the baskets
For sale, the rejected mess.

Who, Whose?

I've already greeted shadows twelve times
Who're in their shrouds ------- I wished morning
Would wholeheartedly respond hundred times
At the beginning of the crusade that, the heated oxygen
Was stealing the silver seats of the white birds.
Who's who, the image of the white tongue,
The good companion of a variety of sunshine.
Still, I know who is on the left hands am of
Unhappiness. The seconds have something.
Nobody is like an egg on the shoulders of the hill.
The mist on the face of an extremely poor performance.
The screech of the crawling greens, whose right hands
Are in the sludge now? With the help of the shrivelled
Season, their names are mentioned every day.
These are people still wrestling to sail through the
Narrow path. The attendance of the attendees,
Read the world, the skeletons & veins of brand,
Fresh leaves. Listen to the shouting songs.
The honest narration of
The Guiness book has the answer now.

Latest Afternoon

Silence on the telephone.
The comb on the farmland.
I will try to comprehend
The speed of the quandary.
Arrows & spears prepare for
The flight. I will trek as well
If the autumn will predict the
Meal on the field. Fabulous or
Fake arms are enjoyable. I can't rest
If siren doesn't know the activities
Of siesta. It is waiting for the feedback under
The mercy of neglect. I am typing the
Year's reports for the gods to decide
The next life.

Documentation In Theatre

What are the arrangements for the depiction?
It is the exact period to climb above
The towering trees & allow owls purify
The atmosphere hangs around
The wrists.
To sing the verses of music with-
Out notes. Loud & clear in reading,
The moonless weapons flying in
Whisper. It is only thing between
Impossibilities & possibilities.
Pessimism is stronger than optimism
When rain showers cat, when dog
Tries to swim to the end of the
Problems. Then there will be more to
Write about. At this moment, laughter
Is nowhere to locate because businesses
Are closed.

Unprofessionalism In the Profession

Down with blind channels to tunnels,
Paddle the self-proclaimed best yacht

On the gumbo streaming to the sawdust.
Read his memoir in the evening. Supper has

Can fly far but cannot compete with
The timetable for the close of the year's

Party. More to come, the crack on the
New floor: we haven't finished listening

To complain in the law court. I still stand
Here, I still stand there for the next projects.

DreiRad Fahrrad

Hence a bike has become ein dreirad fahrrad then
I have to learn to jog with one leg across ocean

But deserts are hungry for rich vegetables. I can sip
Gallons of water. Come-&-go affection, for us; not mine,

It is ours, & so what! He left the doors of the problems
Before the lakes closed. The mouths of the sharks

Will not spare the beauty of colours on the minds.
I can spring faster than the north winds. The songs of

Dreirad fahrrad are the testimonies in the daily service.
A bike could not say his last prayer in the nightmare,

Rather-----

God created animals & made us senior prefects. I
Can predict that their words are longer than their

Sanity. Things are still talking to breathing traditions.
The accounts are the dreirad fahrrad on the road.

The Sacred Harvest

Also, have you seen what
We haven't seen in the air?
Have you felt the condition?
Gold doesn't see its beauty
Because of one thing. We can
Spell the word & define the
Meaning of silver. Hands can
Fly & the result will tell you the
Commitment of voices on the grounds.
I say it, the brightness of the day
Will wear her white gown.
Yet clauses can't assemble what
Littered in the sacred woods.

Two-And-Half Days

Sorrow in the blood.
Pain here, there & elsewhere
Eating rocks in the mountain.
Around the clock, are the deaf
Feelings from them. I feel ache
In the rainfalls, hot & panic.
Smoky & loud; untold life in the
Blessing of a single street. Here
We look for two & half days; the
Lost in the endeavours, the shouting
Of a cancer, as we sky, that is the
Procession of the worries on the
Calvary. Runaway could be seen
On the heartless river, health can't
Wrestle with his character. We
Encounter evil channels in the fresh
Blood. Naada has eliminated millions treasure,
You-they-we-I, compare ourselves
To the missing heads of the saints. Why these
Crops are rooted in shamelessness?

Is The Chant?

Listener, spectator, singer, guitarist,
Dancer, programmer. Drummer, keyboard,
Microphone, light, furniture. Mornings,
Afternoons, evenings in a unseparated choir;
Their lives are still in the shivering Saturn. I
Salute them & bow to their commitment. Liking
Of the quiet middle age, I will learn how to
Dance to the rustling under the feet. One,
Ears spin in the rhythm, two, love for the words,
Three, banquet for the smile of sweet parents,
So let's start breaking the vows of loneliness.
On the walk, the capacity of ambitions,
The failure of brake from the peak of
Target, the assurance of feet to climb
Any height on the page. Businesses
Set the goal around the circle in square.
I expect what is unexpected
To prepare for an expectation around the
Swords. The studies of the weather forecasters'
Paratus, computers, won't be corrupt like him.
No thermometer is out of duty.
Remembrance kicks out the noisy basket.
The sound of the roaring street. The taste of
Anticipation opens the main gate. I could only
Hear the combat of kidney, liver & intestines
Against their enemies on Freedom Day. The
Telephone calls out, the parts are worn out.

The tones aren't the offspring of jazz but
—- the Moodle of this semester, slap on the
Face of the national slogan, the outline of the engine.
Jazz, ready for a national flag to sing gentle words.

Hosanna With a Black Flag

Smallness, macabre on the screen,
Another handwork of the night.
Liar, murder, looter, insulter.
Future has more results
To publish at the close of the
Battle. The contents in the note,
Rhyme or poetry in the four
Layers for the different places
Of activities. Or he's stealing
The rest of our happiness.
Murdering our unborn babies,
Wrecking our fate in the
Bethels, wearing clothes.
As a wolf in the uniform of lamb,
Unforgettable duties of lips,
Let the blood remain in the breathing
Thing as water can't wear another
Uniform. We've lost our voices to
Sing Hosanna in Jerusalem. No
Liberty for the feet, you know that.

Unquenched River

…… fear to say dear
If I don't know the mood
You're dancing in now.
Your face on the river,
A multiple of plots,
Because the black pot has
Broken into a thousand
Of pieces on my skin.
The reflection on the river
Is the Genesis of the
Endless chapters. The
Agitation of the goddesses.
You've breached contracts.
Trust is donning his mask,
Shameless goat crowns her disgrace.
Canoes travel with a broken
Navigator with results. The
Net reaches a quarter of me.
You're shorter than a canoe,
Slimmer than a river.
Fishing will tell us the outcome
On the dining table. I would not like
Vitamin B12 to miss a comfort an
Abled apartment in my life. I wished
The river would teach me how to
Swim in her life. To dive, hands
Are ready to construct new ways
Under sight. Doubled drives in a
Narrow pathway. To catch the
Hanging victory on the flight.

Influence Of Marijuana

In the evening, even, rocks,
Waters & sands are wrestling
Against each other painfully.
They are complaining to the materials
& workers, upon heavy
Sorrow covering their faces.
Taste & see whether they are under
The influence of marijuana. I could touch
The cold stone but extremely hot for the
Skin to contact in the winter. Articles have
Forgotten where they live & where they
Are sailing to. The effect of the unseen
Lives, no apparatus fits now to handle
Joke displayed on the altar. We want to
Leave for nature. No home for lies, crimes,
Murdering & looting in the constitution.
Remember the songs of a rich nature on her
First-sixth days on the stool. No way,
A new day is born for a spotless start & a
Productive uniqueness.

Fever Performance

Nothing lasts forever in the activities.
In the beginning of the creation
The suns reign for a while
I stare at the sunshine around.

Nothing lasts forever in the heat.
Goodness is wine in the heat.
I tasted the wrong meat at the annual festival,
I weighed the head of the forsaken discussion.

Today is boastful of the clouds.
I'm even ready to drink at the bank of river Volta.
I do like vegetable soup.
The discussion of the medicine.

Crops will read out the results.
Ask for the closing date.
Nothing lasts forever in trust.
Mornings have kept his strategies

Running to the tree.
I count the dry leaves on the stolen soil.
I have a virgin energy. Time doesn't wait
For afternoon to mess

The revolution up.

Achievements On the Float

I greet evening in the stage of his life
In his bad mood, the temperature
Misses the way.
I say recitations on the tablet.
His performance
Ups & downs on the flight
I wash away the old colours
Until the new prints
Reject the opinion of inconsistency.
Remember the rainfalls of their
Eighteenth anniversary
That lasts when the songs
In the kitchen are
Delicious.

His Annual Reports

The voices of the earth.
Shake the troubling seven seas.
We hear the true stories,
Even the continuous funeral
Announcements; pictures
Proclaim the fidelity among
The living voices. Yes, we asked for
Hug on the naming-ceremony day.
Minus plus negation,
Picturesqueness & smirk
On an indefinite sabbatical leave.
We cannot feel the untarnished creation
Anymore at her place.

Scores

NPPliar has passed us by
In times of storms & fears.
Bestiality & howl has come

To reside with silver & gold.
Now, we struggle in the wrath
Of breezes; the sins & righteousness,

& tranquillity & lament cry to hold
The horizontal branches of development.
Our agonies hold the fingers of a

Vertical dying stems in strength.
No hope in the belly of a destroyer
Like him. His anthem on the wide

Scope, disgrace & fiasco; ceaseless
Faults on his forehead, the acidic
Behaviour scores negative zero.

Contaminated Accounting Book

The heat out there,
The fire is cooking the wrong meat
Not often I call some names out
From the attendant book
Responses were not cool
In the swimming pool.
Different features appear

& disappear on the
Hungry surface of the plain glass.
I now see the attendees wearing another
Clothes fit for the leopard in the forbidden shrine
Full of unclear images. Their features
Are longer than their brains. I perceive
Circumstances. I listen to Latin proverbs.

Salsa blood in me. I want to pray everywhere,
Always. On the broad way they
Chant. They fail endlessly.
See how unpolished they are,
Disgraceful trash.
Hamlet will not entertain their illness.
When juice in the village has become bitter.

Restless Moment

Restless moment is needed when resting
Has encroached the full bed of legitimate
Owners. The fight is your fight at your look.
You have been sent out to liberate your stolen
Happiness. Do so, do now, for the sake of
Sorrowful land. Chase out the smell & sweep
Away their footsteps after the shake. Days are
Longing to kick their flat buttocks. unattractive
To play with, have never been the food everyone
Would like to test between life & death.
Come out from their sheds. I can't wait to welcome
The favourite day in my arms. I have dates for their
Activities to mount pressure on action. No! They
Are all calling for a untouched day to wear unfriendly
Clothes, even on his battlefield. Be on the front, fear
Not the talk of the waves.

Purchase Of a New Reading Glass

Hungry years, waste & spoilt have
Celebrated in the rented land.
Chest out the muscles in the coat,
Fly the indolent arms beyond
His territories. I can now travel
Above my height because
I am tired of residing with my enemies,
The people in the enclosure.
We have now seen the smiling glasses
Opening the gates of awareness.

All Die Be Die

I have seen the worries
With longer wide wings.
Prepare the goal that
Hunts move & action.

With all might & ideas
Of melodies that are
Untapped. Crawling
By this time, nowhere

To grab the trophy on
The sail pace. Whether
Reading the book from
The last page & pin

At the start, I must
Count how many hairs
On the aged elephant.
There is no need for a

Beautician to count
The customers in the
Queue at the weekend.
He has answered himself

Before the guns. Don't let
Their offspring, the sweats
Of the virtuous friends.
Look around Synagogue

Survey the inner behaviour
Of parties at work. One
Hand is ill with bloodshed.
So cut the two off before

The Other entertains any
Duty at the entrance of
The mosque. No more chances.
Run after him, after them.

Yes, conquer the night.

Boot 4 Boot

We aren't ill at all .... Have
Been sleeping for while
Not when we've to give an
Account of sanity. For all

The temptations in the beards,
Carry out the assignment.
Don't leave yourself behind the fruit,
Be smarter than shadows.

Lease your boot, bigger than the
Ball, dribble in the hot
Sand, compose virgin songs
Of the fanatics. Waterfalls

In the electricity, flame in the
River Niger, we need an
Excavator, plough the old,
Rough school. Spare not the night.

I weigh the instrument, the
Familiar friends, echo & chant.
Drum close to the grave. They
Belong to the broader side.

If I can do with them in the temple,
Let us read new books
In the publishing companies.
Poems won't spare any fool.

Renovation

Upright from one place.
It is not yours.
We're the sons of the year.
We can interpret the
Withered laughter.

Let the wicked Naada
Answer the questions.
The misery of the feet
On the cursed land.
The depression sitting

In the mouth of the air.
Slow is the dilemma of
Both legs standing
At the two junctions.
Box the chest of decisions

At the time showers are
Contemplating whether
They will be merciful to
The cracks in their youthful age.
The mid-day has spoken

In parables. The meanings
Are the activities shouldering
The calamities on the desk.
I read literature for years.
There is a need for renovation

Of plantation. The teeth
Said “they won’t allow the bad
Weeds to mix with productive
Weeds in Greenland”. We sat on
Tornado. It’s boring to shake

Hands with the branches of Tornado.
Evil & unproductive measures
Want to bring solid towers
Down before joy reaches the
Feet of real images.

Wounds are littered on the
Inevitability of chances.
Heal the scream in the waves,
Polish the old shoes out there.

Nonstop Fasting

Anchor the sinking boat on the tiny lagoon,
Turn the dusty mist to daylight in Northern Iceland.

You're our dislike & toxic in the precious environment.
Remove the obstacles in the dreams.

We sky through the sunless cage, the treasure of the
Stars: throats & words hang on the eagle. Parrots can

Only talk when rain is about to display her talent on the
On the hard soil. Drive nonstop on the highway.

Voices catch illegal intentions. I am holding unto what
Is in the middle of the prayers. Fingers are well

Crossed. Arms like metals in the burning fire.
We shall cook him to inedible stages,

Bring the unborn creatures back to life.

An Eye 4 An Eye

Tooth for tooth, I stand on the unshaking rock.
The lions & tigers know what I can implement.
Remember the war I won without weapons,
The ribs I removed under the sunlight & gave
To vultures on their golden anniversaries.
I am ever ready to break more rods into atoms.
The weight to start the trek is on the cemented foundation.
I am ever ready to run limitless miles on the ropes in the air.
No amount of roar will dig a hole under the feet of
Fearlessness. I'll beat you & beat you well to the satisfaction
Of unfailing gods. Their hands lift the trophy to the
Tabernacle. It concerns you now & tomorrow.
Leave nothing unconcern, for the cry is our challenge.

Memorable Tools

In the matter of fact,
If we go there,
We shan't come back
& welcome you back from work.
If we have the good taste of
The tools on the field, I will learn
Whatever I need & still need
To write null on the paper.
As far as suns were born out of
Darkness so I will turn their
Beautiful dancing into a chronic
Testimony on the judgement day.
As far as weeks are under study
So are sons & daughters are being
The memorable tools to wash
The killing odour on the palm.

Agitated Foodstuff in The ....

This is the day packs with failing missiles
Speed to anger. The failing help is calling

You to be on the ground to say bad bye to
Hardship & wickedness on the jubilation day.

We are dreaming live, seeing yesterday weather
Completely vanished into months ahead.

The atmosphere exists on the foreign land.
I see myself as a borrowed finger on my hired stool.

I eye ahead, beyond calculation, hello & dear has
Nothing to offer this time when things can't boast

Of mixing the river Nile & river Niger together in order
To change acid into drinking water. The virgin smile as the

Wake whisper is on the run. A takeover journey is
Needed to settle down.

No Mercy for The Intimidation

Look for the ancient seat,
At our feet can we recite
Our national pledge &
Carry the plague on the
Shoulder. For all those who
Weep for their loved ones.
Recite the holy rosary
Everyday. The hour of
Angelus, let us build the
Village of ours, our light,
Our love will imitate the
Natural love which cannot
Conjure suffering from no-
Where to somewhere on the
The golden stool. Let us
Sing the weaponised,
Good morning songs now.

Turning Round & Turning Down

How long are we going to
Allow these an eye-saw
Dust to hover over the sight
Of a torch light in the afternoon?

How long are we going to
entertain this volcano in the
Paradise of the attraction?
Enough with these games

Which cannot climb a manikin.
The fabulist is persistently
Changing the beautiful colours
Of vision. To experience them,

We miss the bus that will
Take us to the colourful adoration.
Continuous slaughtering &
Wickedness of ambition, we begin

To add more beauty that
Will ask for more explanations.
At this period,
Whatever we touch in the name

Of the land has responded
Otherwise. I baptised with
Only two words "Yes or No".
The truth goes before development

But zero credibility turns round &
Turns down for the sheep to
Ask him, them to confess before Easter Break.
Going down, deep down behind

The line, he, they live with
Farms & gardens at the same time.
He, they lack the understanding
Of saying, apart from you no taste

& choice is invited to the table.
Turning round & turning down,
Is where we're today.

Still Detritus

I can't smile openly,
Even under the broad daylight.
It shines dark, everywhere.
It throws its light beside

Heinousness. My white cassock,
Not that of a pastor,
Homilies are paralysed. Now, tons of
Snow are in an immaculate conflict.

This is the promise I made with
My first word. I stare at the trees
Billowing me among the rich weeds
That fall at the elbow of interrogations.

Interpretation of the Pentecostal songs,
I vowed to say the truth to power.
The truth is willing to feed the
Constitution when Bawulügner brushes

His teeth well & removes the sunglasses
During harmattan. Norway doesn't want
To come & live with us. Whether the
Dead night is perfect or the knock

Of a sleep on the eyes,
The right statement is hungry
Of the balanced diet, so set the
Right banquet before us.

Sleeping Outside the Castle

Need to water the dry land
In the rainy season. Upon the
Efforts from the mountainous
Pledge to talk to huge trees,

Running for a half of mile,
Ask the plantations in tears.
Left hands of the months are
Amputated, still the body is fit

To defend the rest.
In the home of the ancestors
No place for me now.
If I go to bed as early as possible

Still, I don't have a home to accommodate
My feelings. Food & melodies are
To sing to the dying winds. Castle,
The precious home of haves.

They have nothing in love now.

Empty Morality as Their Weapon

Lazy Tongues

Look at the appearance of their tongues.
Look at the structure of their bodies in the display.
Look at the size of their features in the universe.
Read their case studies before the performance.
They go beyond the miles prescribed for them.
They don't know the directions to their destinations.
They settle everywhere they like to stage films.
Yes, these words are not required on the birthday.
Any word goes as they said on their confirmation day.
The duties of the fresh tongues have been ignored,
The formation of the words has been changed his
Syllabus. The new training has been adopted on the
Board. Now words describe anyhow they please the
Village. The strength of the tongues loses honour on the
Feast days. Lazy tongues do not know their boundaries
Because they are not intelligent & morally empty.

Wrong Channel

There are plenty of roads signing
At us in the dark,
We can't count them in the daylights
When the rainstorm
Is angry at his siblings at work.

We know very well that darkness
Will not allow him to underscore them
Before a thousand of folks
Who are ever ready to reach out
To the fresh fruits on the
Farmlands buy acidic products.

The sound of the thunderstorm
Is full of insults.
The dance of the arms &
The legs miss the channel.
The rhythm of the body
Produces expired products

Into the market.
What they can do better is
what we are living with.
Insults upon insults
Are raining on the saints
& the white hairs lose

The images on their birthday.
Angels can no longer salute
The altar of prayers when
Wrong channels sit on the throne.

Wounded Quotes

Where are the alphabets?
Where is the fertile vocabulary

If a school will go far to teach home
The manners of the weather in the

Rainy season then let's wait for the quotations
Which will appear in their minds. The words

They use against the white clothes, the fresh images
Of the souls in hearts paint themselves the fruits

& the vegetables they are enjoying now. Their quotes
Wear double clothes & they don't recognise who is who.

III Description

What have they seen at all?
What have they eaten before?
What are they saying?
What are they vomiting?

Where do they come from?
Who are their parents?
Which homes were they born in?
Which schools did they attend at all?

If seconds are not familiar with some
Sentences, where did minutes teach them
When the lesson note prepared for them
Are appreciated by hours, even days

Are interested in emulating them.
We have heard them countless times
Roaring like immoral kids. Too much for
The land to belly when the navigations are

Directed by spoiled instruments. They spoil
Everything around the altar. Adjectives
Qualify wrong noun & adverbs modify
Sick adjectives in their talks. This type of

Sayings have started growing wings &
Feathers have grown longer & bigger than
The structures they are tapping their energy
From. We can't believe what the sunlight is

Exposing to the sea light to see. Even fishes
& sharks can't buy them with their ears.
Only the waves can interpret them when
Tornados are angry at the statements from

The unkempt mouths. The checks in the
Different dictionaries, the meanings in the
Holy bible speak the same languages the
Holy Koran will perform his cantata. If

Different non-fiction books could clap their
Hands for others, where come from this ill
Description when there is no need.

Crying Team

They throw their tongues
Here & there,
Shouting above mountains
& hills in the time of sorrow.

The roaring of the winds
In the east coast,
The crash of
Wave & weave

In the air contains
The expression of the
Contents in their voices.
We cannot delve in

The unfriendly sea
Because it is
No more place
Of entertainment

When their saliva
Has contaminated
The atmosphere.
The crying teams could

Not comprehend the seasons
We are dancing in.
The injured could not
Walk because of

Their grimy words
Do not who should
Talk to, when the
Atmosphere does not

Dance to their music.
We don't want to sike
The tower, which looks
Left shoulder of their

Shortcomings, their right
Shoulder is still being
Impregnated with dirty
Voices of the time. Their
Words flog fresh air &
Pollute the drinking water.
Soiled moment of all time.

Slur In Coat

We've heard loud bombshells
Digging immeasurable graves

In the lives of angels who are
Prepared to deliver the promised

Land from the hands of the heartless
Stones who won't bring. The slur on

The infants in the dreams when the
Siesta was preparing them for the

Next assignment hanging around
Their necks. It was a mighty noise,

Shapeless like darkness, corruptible
Like them. Many slurs pack in their

Coats in the clouds of merciless fire
But they were born in the daylight.

Jibes On the Seat

Any word that comes from his sleep
Is full of jibes discrediting the beauty of the sky.
One, two, jibes; three, four jibes; five, six jibes.
Everywhere we go, taunts are winning hearts

Demoting the real substance of life.
They bow jibes in public. They kneel
Before the shrine of the jibes in the sanctuary.
They worship them everyday of their life.

When pens will not allow them anymore
To utter a jibe. Reading today's reports jibes
Have grown immeasurable winds,
Their weights are heavier than dirt in the
Jubilee House.

Yes, everywhere is flooded with jibes.

Chewing Stick

Now the market is soiled with
unhealthy voices in the air.
& they are the new productions

Called chewing sticks, which
Poison the mouths of the saints.
They are planted in the hearts of

The lazy lips.
Their main work is to shower slight
On the unborn babies, bury sun under

The skies. If we check around the faces
Of beauty, something is losing his favour
To greed at work. Something has become minus

In the face of negativity on the harvest day. This
Unusual about the moon in the daytime.
We've heard this type of chewing sticks.

Which ignore their assignments in the rain,
Sickening the green world.
That creates image & likeness.

There are healthy meats looking at them
At the table but they are only
Interested in chewing sticks.

They reject fitting words,
Start selling sick chewing sticks.
Saints are wounded in the sanctuaries.

No place for holiness in the tabernacle.
Grey hairs lose honour on the throne.
Wisdom & knowledge dies prematurely.

Zero Expressions on Them

In these days,
They play only zero expressions on
The radios. No rich content in the tone.
No timetable in the waves. No plan to
Sell the worthy weather to the dying air.
What the atmosphere requires, has been

Snubbed by the poisonous zero expressions.
We can't comprehend the movement of jaws
On the food. They work at the time when
Rainfall decides to disobey his masters in summer.
They are not needed when response to needs

Could not account the missing happiness in store.
They don't obey the traffic lights in their lives.
Their motto is "anything goes". Jaws say
Any word & dance to the sweats streaming
From the peak of the lonely mountain into a

Rejected lake. They injure virgin hearts.
These zero expressions on them,
No point has come from the lake to irrigate
The dry land in the farming season
Rather retire the healthy seeds into a sack.

Misdeed On Air

We have turned on the radios.
So many languages are in the waves

Countless constructions head towards
Wrong directions. The sad news is

That sorrowful dialects are heard
In the throats. Words miss their

Right target on the field. We could
Listen to failed practices on the air.

We are very unhappy about the
Behaviour of the clouds among

Her family members. The tone
Is ill. Acidic & soiled to whiteness.

Bad Sentences

Huge mouths on the way.
They have nothing good to offer
On the anniversary of the land.
Their huge mouths utter only
Bad sentences. They describe
Themselves to the world & write
About themselves. We listen
To the news at 6pm, the threat
To discipline; the worry to culture.
The gunshot to tradition. Bad
Sentences could be heard 24/7
After the birth of the land. Shame
To their huge mouths in public.

Hollow Phrases

They are there
For themselves.
Their phrases
Are hollow when
The sound on the
Lips are not
Polished. We
Could read &
Stabbed our
Eyes in the future.
No help from the
Melodies on air
Neither nor life
In the hope
Signalling at us.

Dying Clauses

The subject of the matter
Not walking from here & there,
Not swimming from river Mississippi
To river Niger before crossing the
Boundaries telling us many stories
At a time. Subject plus verb will
Clearly define clauses in the class.
I can only tell you that I am not
Happy about the noise around
When siesta is knocking at my door.
There is no hope in whatever i have
Been hearing since the birth of
This epidemic. Ears could not be
Proud of themselves at duty post.
Why? because of them.

Poor Selection

If a cooking pot is continuously saying
She is cleaner than a cooker then what
Will fruits tell vegetables at the debate.

Yes, I know my taste & choice & they are
Very nice to seasons that select motivational
Words. I know I am selective, but I won't choose

Rain over sun in time of dancing in dilemma.
North pole & south pole know their differences
But they won't fight over who's who when

East pole & west pole are slowly welcome into
The world. Goodness is good at the time the right
Sacrifices are needed to be offered. Does Where

Knows where she resides? She'll go where she's
Supposed to reside when how is there to
Help her to do what he's supposed to do.

Weak Players on The Field

Yesterday, was that statement,
Today, this statement on the float.
It is too much for the centre to
Hold things together. Strange things

Are happening at the back of the moon
When stars leaning on their beds
Contemplating the reaction of the rains
In the winter. Even water & cement are

On different lanes because of something
Wrong somewhere. Something has
Refused to work with nothing, also,
Anything is not ready to entertain barbarian

On the floor. Everything around him is
Weak. No training before the match.
The weather can't award the rain & sun
Anyhow. The statements from these people
Not seen on the world's atlas.

Blunt Cutlasses

Their voices can't change
The land from nowhere to
Somewhere in the fruitful
Weather. We trust nature

At work when there is a
Need to say words which
Will renew the face of the
Earth. The sharp cutlass

Which both sides please
Products on the market
Are completely blunt.
They can't cut softest object

Into two as six-month baby'
Smile could soften the
Stony heart within shortest
Period. Words are

Words but not all words
Are words when the earth
Is longing for the satisfactory
Nutrition. Their blunt cut

Lasses knife spotless souls
Into pieces, destroy heaven
& earth in the sunlight. Now,
the statues are broken down,

Joy of the sky withers, the
Perfume of the newborn
Babies get dried in the sea.
Truly, things are not the

Way they were manufactured.
Even the birth of the virgin
New breath into the stars
So have you seen some

Of the works of the blunt
Cutlasses in the harvest
Season when the innocent
Rains continue to complain.

Expired Seeds on The Farmlands

We do not invite these expired
Seeds on the farmland in this
Period when already
Rich seeds are behaving well

To the song of the rain. The
Appearance of the expired seeds.
Their eyes look like lifeless breath
On the surface of the angry lake.

We can now define the colour of
Their sentences clouding the
Exposure. Something leans on
The back of backwardness. We

Can now feel the presence of
Uncultured drama on the wave.
Proverbs written on the face
Of the expired seeds are falsely

Operating on the images which
Are worthier than clouds in the
Winter. The air from them.
The walk of the seeds in the life

Of the beauty; the perfume on
The stars are bleaching the beauty
Of the land. The expired seeds
On the farmland has taken us back.

Schlecte Wie-Worter

If a day can't multiply a month
& get the correct result so that
The weather forecaster can

Delve into the rests of the planets
Tell us when summer is allowed
To knock at the gate of a waterfall.

Too much of adjectives which, even
Cannot describe the ugliness of their
Large lips are left alone to keep

Wrong writers are busy on the moon.
The lonely nouns make reading
Tasteless in the competition when

The right adjectives are begging to
Be used in their working days. Seven
Days in the week we can speak better

Than NPP whose writings bring no fish
To the dining table but another beginning
For the sunshine. Their adjectives, our pains.

No Toothbrush

They can talk without permission from sanity.
They can speak from their ass & defecate in the public.

They can piss inside the mouth of the holy of holiness.
Heads cannot purchase the philosophy at the cheapest
price.

The complaint is over brimmed. Ten trillion GB
Cannot house them in the largest castle in the world.

We can't believe what we are inhaling on the free market
When they can easily afford them with the whisper of waves.

The conjure of clapping from their hideout is the shortest
way
To command paradise & palace on the surface of the river.

Despite the fact that Covid has come to dwell with us, our
Senses smartly feel the hell walking on our smooth skins.

Runaway Contents

They always play one-way music
Which is forbidden in the house
Of wisdom & elite. Because of the

Contents, tongues & shoulders
Have become siblings. They throw
Shot at anyone who ask the opinion

Of the soiled features. Their ideas
Are to wait when the dry land askes
Why she is suffering, then they vomit

Out fungi & algae on social media.
They've even insulted the goddesses
Of the land to the extent that no seed

Sow in the land germinate.
Runaway contents are still illegally breaking into
People's abode & staining their spotless reputation.

Incomprehensible Commas

Unexpected vomit is poured on the ground.
The odour blows over life & death on the coast.
The particles from the rejected farms show
How primitive their behaviour can sicken the

Novelty of the invention. The trip of heads on
The rough roads. Humid in the sun; the talk of
The Structures; the vexation of the leaves in the
Rainy period. Notions in the pen; let's find out

The meaning of the action. The calculation of
The incomprehensible commas; similar words
Send a sound of warning to the audience.
Let us calculate the number of insults.

Insults describe their lives in the trash. So many
Things are said in the fall of darkness. They know
How to pollute waterfalls, vegetables & fruits are
Already perishing in the graves. Their question

Marks are the answers with which we are living. They
Have nothing to offer than a chain of stained air.

Heavy Blow

The tune inside the
The different voices on the
Assorted lanes are eager to
Gun down profitable
In his mother's womb we
Have studied these salutations,

No dance is ready to entertain the
Heavy blow. The statue of the founder
Wheels in confusion. Too much
Of rubbish serves around breath.
The church bell tunes. The first, second,
Third readings convey the

Homily that edges only along
The boundary. Life could not be born
Out of noise which was still
Putting the congregation into
A swift slumber. This heavy blow is the scar
In our memory.

Jobless Lips

There are somethings, therefore,
There are things which need attention
In sentences. They have names
In the registers. We can't forget to mention

A stainless Integrity in the department.
The words of settlement; It is a course on its
Own around the clock are flooded
With greener pastures floating over her territories.

There are more jobs than labourers.
Nothing goes inside the paradise, nothing
Comes from the palace in the harvest.
Their lips are unskilled, ruining the towers

Of the sacred temples. They know what to do to
Please the hot weather in the winter.
Jackets & boots speak their languages at work.
Only rainfall can assist them in making decisions.

Even those birds which fly from Europe in winter
Because of the freezing weather advises themselves on
The trip. Going & coming has reserved its comments.
The right information is sitting on the lazy

Chairs that need to be attended.
They do not want to accept the right offer.
There is the need to feed the empty morality.
The lazy lips must challenge the Egyptian

Pyramid on Olympic Games so that everyone
Will know how lazy their lips are.

Ohne Verb Im Satz

The sound in the talking drum
The description of the whistle

Of the colours on their faces
Has multiple interpretations.

They can read every dialect.
They pronounce the words of

Parrots. Speaking the language
You can sell & buy at the inter-

National market, comb around
Thoroughly the assignments

Signalling you. Subject &
Predict will entertain meaning-

Less judgement. Weighing
The stones for the foundations

In the water, let's leave the
Rest for erosion to decide

Who is stronger than the truth.
Even a simple translation will

Read out the judgement that
These folks only know how

Insult but nothing else on the
Altar to be sacrificed

Plenty Of Question Marks

NPP knows only one song
Which produces sadness

An insult is an insult,
Born by them on the acidic
land roaming around circles

& squares of messages.
They are enemies of progress,

The wounds in the liver,
Another colour on the

Skin; their messages
Disrespect resurrection.

The joyful day for suns & skies.
Truly their way of speaking is

Full of plenty of question marks
Knocking castles & destroying

Farmlands from here & there.
As far as the curtains

Are still hanging
Pyramids we will wait until

Harvest season, then we can
Calculate the damages caused

Vacations in retreats. We've
Noticed plenty of question marks

Which need answers.

Incorrect Phonology

Are they learning how to speak like infants?
Can they construct

Two-word sentence at the age of two without mistakes?
What is wrong with

Their tongues in the delicious soup on the public holiday?
Are their lips larger

Than the words which are looking for places to settle down?
Or because of plenty of

Saliva in their mouths for that matter they cannot speak out?
Primitivity is their blood

Through campaigns the south pole collides the north pole
On the same lane.

They cannot pronounce the words correctly. The stench from
Their tummies sends

The folks early into their graves before enjoyment.
The summer & the winter

Combat each other in the ring. Ears could not far before buying

The Meaning of reading

Newspapers four times. We have seen the start when they have

Empty heads &

No plans to sell the products which are to sell the products which

Are lying dormant

Rather calculate simple clauses & phrases in the scripts instead

Of dodging simple exams

& spelling simple two-letter words correctly. because the muscles

In their mouths as

Weak as their brains, as the veins coil in the lips as dormant as

Harmattan leaves in the mud.

More Full Stops

At the round table time overtakes
Something in the brain unprepared
Moment looks for a place to rest in
The abode of nature searching for
The dying fishes to net for undecided
Speech. At every intersection we
Cannot fish out the footprint of their
Work. Discussions upon arguments
Run for their lives without anybody
Chasing the missing stars in their
Speech. More full stops are planted
On the heels of the script sleeping
On the desk of insolence. Going &
Coming, we could only swim in the
River of pejorative languages. Some
Of our relatives have been devoured
By the uncultured drama as their
Daily meals & greetings.

Null Readings

We wanted to research about suns & skies
At work but they were nowhere to be fund
In the safe boxes. The empty morality has
Crowned himself among withered mouths.

The social-interaction grades as null readings
About the constant impudence ringing in the
Hearts of good health. From left hand to the
Right angle, no book is seen in the shelves

Rather the walk of sass slapping each other
At the mercies of darkness. They do not see
The bedroom of our output, they thought. The
Interrogations with assorted clothes; the answers

Are what we are experiencing.

Roar Of Tension

On the radio
Out of many voices eating silence in the meditation period,
Only thunderstorm was / is still eroding the happiness which
Doesn't want to fold her bed & leave for good. The eyes of

Sauce & rudeness quickly look for comfortable apartments
To lodge. If they aren't too much for rooms to accommodate
Rainfalls won't wash some away.

Everywhere we
Go, the sound of seminars staging in both up & lower rooms.
The songs are changing their way of lives, books are being
Rewritten in the clouds. Sunlight has no access to edit the

Products of Lucifer. The chase of rainbows in the silent time;
Questions answer questions 'because of the amplification.

Lack Of Poems

For a very long period of time, we haven't had our
Daily breakfast, our daily lunch & daily supper to

Keep us fitter than metal. We are sweating like he-goat
But there are no poems in the store to restore the

Burning fire in the dry land. All the green pastures are a mess.
To read about *NPP,* their famished library will feed Synagogue

Where have you been poems when we needed you?
People are asking of you & your family. We want to feel your

Presence when our air is ready to arm you when our hearts
Are longing to home & entertain happily. Come now &

Educate them how to speak poems in Latin, speak poem
Of Jerusalem & of Weimer. For fishes are ready

To enjoy the angelic voices of poems in the tabernacles
There are a lot of a thousand of publication walking

From door to door looking for consumers to satisfy them.
But they could net fishes in the mediterranean sea.

Life is empty because there is a lack of poems in the market.
The dictionary of thought has vanished from the world of

Living in the village on sabbatical holidays. They are
Interested in writing trash for the withering cottages

Surrounded by anything-goes people. From up to
Down there are no poems to pump the heart. We

Lack poems in our answers. The alpha & omega of
Poems that resurrect the hopeless tongue.

Blank Scripts

As we began the journey
In the desert of hope & despair
Things travelled far in the liver of
Printed books & landed
On the first page of disappointment.
We combed the pathway,

The bellies of the sacred forest,
There was nothing written in their
Voices because of the empty morality
Flooding the lives of the angels. We
Wanted to read & read to the satisfaction
Of whiteness we are emulating.

No advice to convey to the hungry
Throats rather discourtesy &
Tactlessness is sickening the daily
Products weaving among healthy seeds.
No plans on the sheets so they are insulting
& planting impoliteness every corner of

The sea. Audacity is continuously poisoning
The good name of sanctity. There is despair
To write about it. There are crosses &
Wise cracks that's why we have blank sheets
Looking at the blazing sun for assistance.

Rejected Manuscripts

Trying to climb the highest
Mountains in question
We try to work out things out
Of hopelessness in the grave.

Going there for passages
Spread around the problems &
Troubles sitting with their enemies,
Many ways have opened

Their mouths to answer the five
Exam questions coil our bodies.
Upon uncountable manuscripts
Scattered at the entrances of their

Lives, no salvation has been
Awarded to the noise consuming
The tranquillity dwelling with our
Reputation. Sailing through the

Rejected manuscript thoroughly
We have come across trash &
Sorrow was homeless & was under

The mercies of the immaculate
Immorality. The comprehension
For the disowned manuscripts
Is the song of pure morality.

Endless Statements

When we opened the left-side gate
Of the moon in Neptune,

The moisture was dancing among her
Siblings who were preparing the day

For the earth. These announcements
Opening the doors of tornadoes to vomit

From the other side of the matter. Pointing
At the tallest trees, we can't finish describing

The stems of the matter. We have started
Days before creation, we haven't finished

Reading the statements because the endless
Statements are impregnated with

Brazenness & crassness. They are countless
Before aristocrat, immeasurable like the

Length of sea on your eyes.
We can read them & we shan't meet

The end of the statements.
No glimpse of diagnosis in the melodies.

Forgetful Titles

Scanning Europe & Asia
The oceans jog in the sleepless hours,
Day & night unfold their programmes
On the platforms of the living time.
But there is nothing profitable from NPP
To sell to the dry sea residing with them.
The same tongues they use to praise Him
The same strength they employ to discredit
The beauty of the sunlight in the smoke.

No Eye-Contact

Whenever the leaves on
The branches of arms
Are flying unceremoniously
In the time of no eye-contact
We could experience the
Rattling of vulgarity encroaching

The territory of three meals per
A day. We could hear the
Speeches of bullies sipping
The happiness feeding the
Hungry souls. Word-to-word
Gunning down interest of the

Nutritional meals. The bombshell
From their stinky mouths.
Their faces like those chimpanzees
Defecating in the hideout.
Their teeth are like beneath a
Public waste container. That is the

Truth in the Sunday sunlight.
The guff always identifies
Herself when the weather
Starts to narrate fairy tale after
Receiving & looting booties.
They are professional

Trolls & Butt hurts, even the
Whisper of the ghost can testify
The contaminated debates on
The dais, full of bluntness.
Look at the swollen backtalk raining
& reigning heavily & heartlessly.

Tricky Calls

Every second in their training,
Every minute around the desk,
Every hour at dinner.

Days & night can't stomach this
Unwanted breakfast of mixing
Coffee & milo together in the

Cup of tea. The teaspoon is
Not ready to mix rubbish in the
Chalice. The rainfall of cheeks

& archaic has given birth to
Many premature babies. Every-
Where we go there is a complaint.

Guttered Telegrams

You insult our immaculate spotless
Dresses cleaner than the shrines in this

Kingdom More beautiful than heaven & Dubai
Put together in the hearts of the gold & diamond

In competition. They discredit the statue of
Nature, the family of perfections. We can't buy

Buy these adjectives on sale, not our taste &
Choice. We aren't hungry for old & diabolic

Face in the mirror. For this one; For that too,
No match on the field for games, Their throw out

Out on the Surface of the decency; the slap
On the side of the liver; the oxygen on the run

To nowhere; the bitterness of the drug for
Healthy smiles. The accountability of this time,

Checking the moons residing with unfriendly

Statements on the notice board. Looking is minus &
Negative = character assassination. The ejecta in the

Bone; the sweats plus heat as caution; the feelings of
Wounds on the skin of climate. The ears of the sun have

Heard the worst songs mounting up debates in the
Public. Many insults bleach out the attraction.

Because of numberless talks the rainfalls have refused
To hear the petition knocking at the gate of provisions.

They've been awarded numerous certificates under-
Scoring the existence of breath & beauty in the sky.

Watch their movie now. Listen to their music, and now
Calculate the friendship they have with healthy tones

Proverbs

Your insolence has enormous features
On the stream of homeless words,
Illegally taking the abodes of tedious labours.
The meaning of these proverbs is clear
Which can fetch the length & the breadth
Of typing sheets in the printing firm.

Many are whispered behind the vision.
We could not stop undertone actions.
The billion proverbs disfigure the certainty
Cultivating the hearts of fresh sanitation.
We wished we could scan inside of the tunnel
& interpret the invention of new crude oil in the

System. We could remember the whistle of the
Uninvited novelty of unconducive accommodations
In our midst. The injured reputation is struggling
To come down with the hot season under the
Watch the new commandment. Open the books,
Let them know that these proverbs are uncultured.

Parables Vomit

This brusqueness in the master chair
  That surliness in the news all over
Pointing his fingers at the black sea,

The movement of the uncomfortable lives
  Fearing the seconds ahead of nature.
They do not know the selection breath of phrases.

Before the breath of alcohol in the
  Parables, the audience has been sickened.
The paint of today is reviving the agony

Flogging the green leaves
  On the farmland. The continuous comeback
If we could explain the uncountable parables we

Shan't stop weeping at our birthdays.
  Their handwritings are difficult to interpret but only
Seers & thinkers like us can purchase the

Information they are still transporting to Solomon
  Whose cannot peacefully sleep on quarry stones
Designed for rough roads. The situation in which

We are dancing, the mix of colours smearing the
  Natural forest Reserve. They print so many
Parables which are their true images. They can

Insult like the children born out of trash.
  They resemble the words & the statues
Of their parables.

Letter In Letters

All words go
The chain of them
They know that they
Are still constructing
More in advance to
Stream among the
Angels in paradise.
Letter in letters was/
Is chasing us. The
Titles with so many
Subtitles. Going &
Coming, let's scan
Inner blow again,
Emotion & feelings
Of the land. The
Drive of this script
Is to describe their
Lifestyles in public.
Their halitosis advi-
Ses them to think
Like Sodom &

Gomorrah in mess,
Akyem in the gutter.
Everyday, the same
Composition narrat-
Ing how they can
Pollute the finest

Image that has never
& ever existed at the
Right corner on the
Seventh day. After
Reading the bodies
The harvest day
Will share the report
With saints & lucifer
On the judgement day.

Short Alphabetical Order

There are activities on the tablet.
Dates have no places to sleep.
Daily books have stories to tell
The incoming activities. There
Is the meaning. There are meanings
That challenge the situation we are
Wrestling in. Now, new songs are
Composed, which does not match
To the joy ringing in cleanness.

Mouths In the Muds

Immoral is immorality.
The famished mouth has finally found a job,
Which nobody is interested in. She has given
Birth to numerous children eating in the muds.

Anything possible at their sight, gold or diamond
Signalling at the cool sea. The reflection of the
Cliff at the angels of the matter. The moves,
Anything goes, the danger in the white, assorted

Appearances in the transparent mirror. We have
Seen them in multiple worlds. If you see darkness
They are there for negative minuses in a red coat.
Their mouths are always seen in the muds drawing

Cantankerous arts in the centres of the sunshine.
Truly, mouth in the muds; she does respect the
Creation around the clock. They change the
Duty of features & immorality has become a stain.

No Point of Silence

Don't insult nature in the light.
Don't create the world within circles.
Don't mould artificial waves in theory.
Homeless air upon sick coughing

Has been struggling to accommodate
Themselves in the unqualified residence.
Flooring over the rivers in our limit
Seeing another practice younger than

Their sanity, smaller the upper class
Never & ever rain these words because
The suns & rains are older than you.
You little meats of rejected poisonous

Baby makers, the smell of chronic
Disaster challenging the smoothness
Of smiles & laughter in their paradise.
Hearing the sounds, meditating on

Their passages that travel near & far
We found the immeasurable no point of silence
Hunting innocent joy & tranquillity on the throne.

Intentionally Light-Off

They send telegrams every minute
Belly of audaciousness, taller the highest
Tower on the mountain, with sharp edges

Like cliffs in the Mediterranean Sea
That dig every hole in every sentence looking
For a peaceful siesta at the close of season.

They continue to make calls which are obliques
In shape, anticlockwise in movement to provoke the
Strength of the rotting tongue at work. Their work

As easy as dreaming eating cakes & toffees early
In the morning as the sign of saluting the clouds
In the day-broad light. We wished experts would

Check their body temperatures so that we will know
Kind of madness that is devouring them. They are
Intentionally blind to activities burying the breath of

Imagination, crucifying truth in honeymoon & deafening
Themselves to listen to healing recitations, when strong
Winds are angrily working against the hostility at camp.

DEADLY DANGEROUS LOOTERS OF THE CENTURY

The Most Criminal of Africa

We've seen Naadalooter as
The most criminal political party NPP in Africa.
The most fraudster in the history of the world.
His record still sits on the peak of the darkness

As the UN rates him as dangerously wicked
At the sight of the experts, no debate, no
Challenger. The longer arms, more than
Than the length of sea,

Wider than the size of the earth.
He has changed worthy
Graces from morning stars
To hungry grasses on our faces.

Looking into realm, his vision
Is to raid our arms & legs so that
We could not climb the temple
In the hearts of our strength.

Still, the harvest on our lands.
The products giving us hope.
Blue & white colours have
Plundered at the daylight.

The body parts of our engines
Have been removed. Our moneys
Have landed on wrong hands.
Check & watch how your account

Has been become blank crying
For water & food. He's the most
Dangerous criminal with us.

Lecture Of This Day

Looters.... ooo looters
The merciless centre of feelings.
The envy of the sweats in summer,

Unsatisfaction of the immaculate nature
The erosion of rainfalls in dry season,
The enemy of progress under the light.

They are here to loot our sweats
Before the calculation of assets.
They are there to empty

The rest of our lives before the
Smooth waves stream away
Without notice.

NPP started looting the land the
Creation of the first day land full
Of bars of gold in the naked

Suns & Mars & boxes of diamonds
Before lecturing saints how to steal
From the sacred sanctuary.

Sincerely, we haven't seen such
Looters living with saints in heaven.
They exist to make away our joy.

Robbing The Suns

NPP have robbed the suns
That shine our money pockets.
The shining stars that boast
Our strength looks sad & worn-out.
They have swiped the fresh air
Giving us day & night.

Going ups & downs in the
Rainfalls, the don'ts are
Struggling to overthrow dos
From their hometown. It is not
What we saw yesterday. The
Changes don't match the songs
In the air.

Have they come to stay with us?
Is it true that she is searching
For salt & sugar in the kitchen?
Is it true that the savings we are
Breathing on, have been taken
Away from the tabernacles?

Global Pilfer

Scanning ***Christian Council of Ghana***
In the moonlight, at the bank of
River Jordan, we saw congrats

Smuggling booties from the altars & collection
Boxes from the poor.

Revealing to their teachings,
Their pastors are scamming
The churchgoers who could not

Smile to the greetings
That birds offer them in the morning.

The place is full of Sodom & Gomora.
Suns could not buy the pickpocketing
Flooding everywhere. Because their pastors

Could not preach salvation rather thieving
The happiness portioned for them.

Even the head pastor is a senior mafia
Hijacking their daily bread before the
Holy cross. The last energy that taps

Joy from the summer rainfalls could not
Dodge from the scammers hunting their

Treasures giving them hope, fear the
Future. Travelling far above the entertain-
Ment music, they are there to rip everything off.

Dangerous Mifias

One, two, things are getting
missing in the society.
The owners have been combing
Under the sea to
Fish out the parts of their lives.
Only darkness is seen operating,
carpeting the beauty of the
atmosphere. No sunshine on the
Side of the village. We could see
Senior armed robbers donating
Big money ICGC because the
Founder is the senior most robber.
He teaches how to scam stars &
Reject the poor climate looking
For rain & sun to survive. Around
Him are full of criminals like him
So, watch the movement of the
Moon & clouds at work.

Wrong Payment

From the global report under the scrutiny
Of auditors, NPP is full of most criminal beings

Ever seen in the darkness. They loot the energy
Of the stars & kills the roots of the skies.

State looters ooo, looters ooo, the criminals
Of the sea, the thieves of the valleys, the

Smugglers of sweats at the daytime. Yes
John Agyekum Kuffour laid the stone of

Stealing the happiness of the land. Truly,
He is a state criminal who stole every glory

Of the output. He cannot be a stateman if
He is known as senior mafia in the record

Of most criminals in the moon. Even darkness
& wickedness can testify.

Fake Account

The notice of the ears,
The trip of the nose in
The winter, the snow in

Africa, the result has this
To say to his neighbours
Our treasure bills were

Snatched from our hands.
Our future was shot down
By evil thought.

There is nothing to be bold
Of when the reserved

Forest was sneaked into
Without the permission of
The sunshine.

Open Details

We've been looking for our joy
But the tone in the rain knows
The architecture of the sport.

Not a single sign of a healing
Climate cough loudly to show
Up her presence. Nothing is

There to boast of when the
Day opens her eyes to control
Her assets in the hands of

Clouds. Everything has vanished
Into hands of shadow. The end
Of the harvest will testify.

No Reaping

NPP has forgotten the culture
Of the big streams. The lagoons

Sharing the same vicinity with
Lakes of the hope. We have

Been counting the hours in years.
Hope could no longer trek as

Despair took the lead without
Entertaining the music that

Accompanied disappointment.
We cannot go & come because

They have emptied the world
We are living in. They are swindlers.

Only Blank

I have heard what we haven't
Felt in the bank account. Even
The sight of sorrow could not

Dry up the lagoons sprinkling
On the formulars. Neither the
Zeros numbers could crawl

In disappointment. The eye
Balls danced & jumped around
Figures in order to buy what

Was weaving through hoes
& on desert. Feelings could
Sail through the veins.

The central bank has sunk
Below the earth. Its body could
Not be found in the rivers.

It looks pale & unhappy in
Appearance.
They have removed her

Spare parts. It has lost in
Trades because these people
Have stolen all the monies.

Billions of dollars have been
wired into their private accounts.
The shape of the architecture

Has deteriorated. She cannot
Still stand her feet at all to
Make noise around herself.

Internationally Dangerous

Listen to the fact flying over mountains
Yachting on the angry sea in winter.
NPP is a pickpocket to the degree that
She has collapsed lives on the throne.

Since the elephant stepped in, the roads
Haven't been smooth in the skies. The
Curves are double in shape. Their lips
Are more than necessary. Their forms

Are dismantled. Hear the true information
About the savings in our life. The faces
Of the winds are torn down. The Waste
Of the moon needs the support of a

Walking stick to bring out the secrets.
NPP came to dupe the universe without
Measuring the height of the pyramid at
The heart of the case. She is fraudster.

Abstruse

IMF, look at the affection these people have for crime.
Hear the incredible story of earthquakes swallowing
Our sweats on the desert, on the empty stomachs,

On the crucified frames along the red river awaiting us.
Climbing the mountains in the suns, descending them
Into the burning bush on our birthdays. They could

Comprehend the narrations at the theatre. "There" has
Nothing to explain to "here" when arms have crisscrossed
In the front of day & night, when they continue to loot our

Heart, when they box on to erode the unaffordable joy singing
Praises & harmonies to our destinies in the time of despair
On our trails. Reading into their hands they are preparing

To make away the last hope, which pushing us to reap the
Victory awaiting the joyful hope in our endeavours.
They are heartless criminals. They are weaponised criminals.

Accidie

Euro Bonds, lend us your ears
Dry seasons have many more
To complain to nature. Hear us before
The clock changes her calculations,
Your silence stains your cassocks.

Documents have details to unfold on the judgement day.
Paragraphs are ever ready to read word for word
Situations are not within themselves.
Conditions are losing weight.
Roads are shouldering heavy burdens.

Lagoons are swallowing the biggest meats.
This people from shady cottage, uglier
Than Satan, & their actions are full of bromhidrosis.
They are thieves harvesting stars on other planets.
Thiefooo thieves. The skilled thieves. Things are getting

Missed underneath the sun & water. Flowers, roses fear
To see smoke occupying their territories. For some time
Now, feathers from under branches have grown double
Arms reaching the throat of destruction, yes, they are
The agents of a billion lives. They borrowed over six

Billion euros in the name of a struggling land. Singing
& praising the storms, writing to the noise in the rains
Posting a life video in the midnight, the sound of the
Plane drinking glass exposes the junctions.

Acculturate

Ecowas Bank,
These folks of negative plus zero,
Swindlers of the 20th & 21st generation.
Billions of US dollars miss their way.
Stars & skies sink into wrong rainfalls.
Fruits & vegetables land into a false

Cooking pot on the first day at work.
Their mouths in every food around
Trashcan, in the gutter or with toxic hands,
You don't need a torch light to hunt
A thousand features in one body.

They go anywhere, come in anytime.
Before independence, the mathematics,
The geography debated front & back.
Demonstration on behalf of Mars.
They wanted to stop the existence of

White sea in the land. Zero vision over-
Shadows the candlelight on the first
Day at work.
Their names were dancing in their heads,
On the eyes of patience, their thoughts

Were meeting their enemies on the field.
Even a shark won't shake hands
With rivers & clouds at the inauguration
Of questionable hands. The four arms
Are still hunting their target because the

Season is preaching the topics under
The watch of the wine which changes
Hardship Into blood. They can't run
Away from water, soap, sponge & towel.
Our facial posture will undress them.

Adulate

They deserted Eden in the gardens.
They uprooted all the roots in the veins.
The muscles have been woven among

Hells & deaths of all times. The nose is
Always alive to weigh the strength of

The light in the dark.
They have the smells of their mouths.
Feelings cannot deny the facts hanging

On the waterfalls in the temples.
Mecca in the Koran; Basilica in the Bible.
The vanished weather on the flight,

The sank, honey beneath the reach of strength,
No more sugar in the tea at breakfast.
No salutation at the lips of Niger River,

No more fertile land to wake up the death
From his long sleep on the last day.
Look at the black smoke, breaking

The foundation of the pillars, holding
Might of the air. See the
Character of the useless, huge animals

In the forest.
Memories will not die even if a transsexual
Planet dwells in the palanquin. The centre

Has confessed that the doors & windows
Cannot close at the same time.

Amphigoric

Knowing the mess before the creation
Of mountains & rivers in Saturn, they
Have thieved all the reaping in the glass.

Truly, they are highest mafia in the midst
Of the archfiend. Their names are the true
Symbols of their practices. Near & beyond,

The properties from the 24/7 fear for the
Sound of motors looking for places to rest.
We fear to leave our doors unclose while

Security arm oxygen & quietness in the brown
Envelope. Their motto is to steal happiness
Resting on the throne. They are anything goes.

Anomalous

An armed robber, dangerous armed robber like
Naada in the history of the hard armed robber.
Like a serpent with hundreds of hands longer
Than the globe in the wilderness; a mighty
Antagonist living with blueprints, an opposer
Of friends of progress breaking into their bank
Accounts. He is on borrowed land, stabbing at them.
His family & friends are defined deadly armed robbers
Will not spare green leaves to survive on the fertile land.
The classmate of a wicked climate; different blood group
In the system. The temperature above breathing level,
The face of disappointment, graves at the noses, because
Of constance robbing by Naada. He has robbed both
The beneath, surface of undefeated honesty.

Avid

Perhaps they are strangers
Who have haven't seen bars of
Gold & bauxite littered on the street
Of the poor. They combated over

Hells, death, storms, flood, poison
Before the suns open their secrets in
The dark, Russia have smuggled out
The red wine in the cold store. This is

The start. The whisper on the flight.
They have found life accommodative
& conducive. They're immaculate
looters of all seasons, plus looting

The hearts, meal of the scorching
Flame in the castles. As we knocked
The head of our assurance, it sounded
Empty sorrowful in the ears of wisdom.

Atrabilious

Between 2017 & 2024
Is in the arms of thousand fingers,

The gangs born out of rocks & animals,
With immeasurable necks like that

Of crocodiles looking for innocence.
Merciless brains ransacking the hotel

In the hands of joy & wealth; the confidence
Of the earth & faithful asset on the lane.

The senior cartels with a lot of degrees,
Popular than the powerful cartel in Mexico

Statue of elephants destroying the beautiful
Literature in the library. Searching for the

Hearty documents I could feel the absence
Absence of trust & presence in the

Tabernacle screaming for rescue in
The flourishing period of walking. I start
Again to count the remaining drops of water & life

Swimming in the saver, but hope challenges
Reality. They've really emptied the sunshine.

Bacchanalia

He spirits money from the sole & harena.
Investors comb the sand on the skin of the mirror.
The balance of the powers tells the
Lifespan of the joyous praises on the hill signalling us.

She creeps fishes in the waters. The labour under
The curses of the dying words of the gods. The
Watch of the watches fly beyond miles & reports
The collapse of renowned history. The reality of

Bigness is now wearing the smallest size of a shoe.
They ghost the pride of the lands. The soiled image
Is laying down like a doormat, like spotted clothes
Of the Uranus, the Venus must fight her life because

Many errors hunting other features of the sphere.
The glory & honour has deserted into Jupiter for safety
Without the notice of the daily camera arresting the human
Traffic, these active bandits have ruined the ups & downs.

Blatherskite

Hold yourselves before
The wicked ghetto
Kidnaps you on the

Reaping day, before
The vacant apartment
Says hello to the talking

Drum before the sick air
Speaks undertone to
The walls which are

Ever ready to gossip
You count the hours
Jogging around the

Table. Everywhere
We go, we will hear
The broken-hearted
Stories of looters.

Crooks

Crooks ooo, crooks
Crooking the surface of Mars
Crooking the face of handsomeness,

Destroying the original skins of gold &
Diamond in the glass. The barrel
Sounds low before angels at work.

Smugglers ooo, smugglers,
Smuggling liver & kidney from the
Sanctuary in the armchair of purity.

The subtraction of the good news,
The crawling of the truth in the race,
The disgrace of plenty of letters.

Going there on time, we are already
At post, they are natural & gifted
Crooks with criminal ideas.

Bouleversement

There are a lot of activities
Breaking the heart of the city
Ears could not sleep without

Enjoying the words swimming
In the red sea but the muggers
Are there operating effectively

On the edges of life. Waves
Have photographed their criminality,
Ghosts have traced their footprints,

They have robbed skies & rainbows.
As we were studying the mess
Pouring at our doorsteps' souls

Cannot be proud of themselves.
Left & right sides of the palm,
Front & back squares of the triangle

Fear could not stop eroding us into
Graves & poverty. They are
Professional muggers hunting

The glamours of the year. Trillion
Of US dollars have been wired
From life to death. Lost upon

Vacancies are reigning in the pockets
Of sleeplessness. The voices of the
Saints have already confessed.

Braggadocio

The vicinity cannot boast of her presence.
She cannot be independent on her own.

Music roaming among us. The panic air
Knifing the fresh bodies, the words dancing

On the lips. The NPP's hands are immeasurable
In nature, because they are pickpockets by nature.

The cry of the state account; the redlight catching
The view of the images sitting on the floor. Nowhere

Is safe in the hands of healthy arrows. As the bank
Accounts are asking for customers, moneys are

Wired from one account to the other in order to
Pour soil into the eyes of the light. The dangerous

Pickpockets living with the gods & goddesses
Of the productions & provisions in smile.

Brummagem

Are our businesses safe?
Why are we skiing into the deep sea?
Where is the legacy of hope?

The pirate reads the movement
Of the moon. He reads the movement
Of Mercury among her siblings

No freedom of movement of
Businesses on the fertile land. Tornadoes
& the earthquakes have been wiping

Away our proud fruits hanging in the
Garden of achievement. We cannot cruise
On the living water. We cannot taste

The sweetness of the water we enjoyed
During baptism. Yes, they always take
What they did not sow. They truly pirates

Looting our happiness & sweats, cooling
Our hearts. There is nothing we can see.

Cache

Almighty robber
Before the clouds started
Forming behind the skies,
We knew when they would
Be born among the chosen people.
We knew how they would look like
Among the beautiful ones.

Their behaviours do not surprise
The planting seasons nor the suffering
Of the pregnant woman.
Yes, their weapons are famished of
Knowledge to change raw materials
Into production. They rob the interest

Of the wisdom, & hallow the creativity
Of the soil. Going & coming is an effort
To speak to imagination. But leaving
There in the care of those whom you
Trust cannot fetch you the cold water
To quench the scorching throat.

Life cannot go with love & come back with
Joy. The roads are not motorable. Human
Relations are still holding unto fear. No
Mercy for safety & honesty inside & outside
The camp. They have come to rob arms,
Ideas, environment & nature which is the
Friend of solidarity.

Cajole

They are the gods & goddesses
Of sniper among the lands,
The antagonists of finished
Products in the exhibition,

Greed on the borrowed environs.
Therefore, there is nothing here
To count on for the survival of the
Discipline. They ransack the red

Wine & the bread on the altar.
So let us ask the suns for the
Answer in the temple. The
Unlocked gates need patronage.

Scanning the skies of today
Counting the missing fruits
At the sight of whisper,
Reading the body temperature

Under the heat of the unfriendly
Input & output of them
They deceive the holy hearts of
The fresh sand. Things fight against

Wrong materials on the brain. They
Sweep away the flowers of our joy
Crash down the hope, which is
Keeping us alive. We are deserted.

Cantankerous Swindler

Where has the flood of our smiles gone?
Where is the joy ringing in the winds?
Where the stream of blood is answering
Our daily calls?
Where the strength of the storms
Determining our lifespan on earth?

As the engine was telling us different stories
The body of the weather could not welcome
The sounded whistle roaming up & down for
Heaven & Eden together on the lake. He could

Talk to his heart to bathe in the ice as a sign of
Baptism. Monies trailed off from air corridors
Several times. Still, the cameras are gossiping
To the daily looting by *NPP*. The redlight in the

Account is struggling to survive on the dry soil.
Everywhere is as empty as darkness in our lives.

Casuistry

This negative-minus people
Settling behind the earth,
This zero plus zero people
Living with trash because of
Their behaviour. Their name
Baddie is found in the Guinness
Record Book. the red star in
The book of double hands.
We did not pay attention
To the note of warning
Struggling to overcome the
Music in the thunderstorms.
The chain of nightmares
Subtracting the peaceful
Sleep after putting the ends
To meet at the banquet.
Truly, they are enemies of
Savings & Savers.

Cataclysm

Baddy

Where are our profits in the market?
Where are our achievements in the stock exchange?

Dangerous smugglers, diabolic smugglers
Poisonous sneakers, pirate in snakes

Scatter on our face, the disfiguration in the
Image of serpent. We search for our production

In numbers. Before the day renders its full
Account, the night has disheartened the smooth

Lane in our veins. Full of regret & hell in our sun.

Wound in wounds in the energy,
Pain in pains running in all corners

Of lives to rest on the peak of hills.
We can't stop crying day-in & night-out.

NPP are making away our bars of gold &
Boxes of diamonds. They are thieves with

Sharp hands, hungry of stealing & empty
The happiness ringing in our hearts.

Smash To Pieces

The most wanted devil in the history of the land.
Land. Now we see Venezuela in the land,

Beelzebub & fiend.

The prince of darkness, no laughter on the boat.
The shameful side of the news is that

Eyes have trillions to tell ears

At the court. If the activities of yesterday & today
Are fatigue of the meal served at the table then

There is no need to look for a beautician
To polish the glasses. Service to mankind,

Zero on the floating; sloshy & slushy.
We snivel every second, the outcome blights.

The count of one. He has reserved us to
Negativity. He has smashed us to pieces.

Thousand Times

Enough of this Cain, your misdemeanour &
An amphigoric art; read your own scripts. Non-
Identical colours have the chest to
Spit on the face of the night.
You live with double characters. If the
Testimonies refuse to trip to Mecca,
Vatican City must fly to Afghanistan.
When did he start this journey?
Where did he take his lessons?
How many times does he want to lie?
What are his goals?
What has he achieved?
Where is his integrity?
The unbearable exclamation,
Malicious & Machiavellian
Our hypocrisy & duplicity have
Exposed us, have afflicted us.
This is our achievement.

Evacuated Power

We look for the gifts
  We received them on
Thanksgiving Day.
They could be anything
  We asked & arrived at the time
When our inevitabilities look
For the items of the gods,
  Part of us is missing in the circle.
It rains nonstop in the

Lives of the ghosts &
  We cannot sleep because of the heat
In the blood.
  Evacuated power is a kangaroo.
Opposite & direct.
Plus & minus; No addition can
Change the footsteps

In the night but the division &
  The multiplication can speak
The same language at the
  Conference centre. I have thought
What I had long ago prepared to
Adorn in the temples, but

They were not found in Saudi Arabia.
No power to kiss on
Liberation Day. Our tears cannot
Cleanse the dirt but the affliction
Looks forward to embracing the
Wickedness of a religion.

Graceless Leftover

We could only hear the trailed
Off voice in our kismets.
We are human beings &
We can't pretend to be
Angels without guidance &
Guardiancy at post.

We don't want to answer
The mail in the account.
We read novels to delve into
The results of the day,
But the rest of the hours will
Not wait for the sunshine

To die just like that. The dry
Leaves give birth to
Many outcomes in the woods.
The period is wearing
The most torn clothes
On her wedding day.
Present gifts are our thanks-
Giving words in speeches.

Impairment In Trouble

Before the ditty prays to talk, we've known
Many times, Bawuwicked has changed the
Stand of happiness. We know the calculations
Have no time to shave the heads

Of the thousand tones. We can sing
However, we can't sing the same song
Of the Old Testament. We listen to the voices of
Birds singing the lyrics of the virgin forest.

We cannot count the wounds on our skins.
We take the measurements on the ground,
Then they are bigger than the ocean.
Billions are lifeless. The castles in our lives

Are Poland on the eastern coast.

Non-Identical Materials

The knock at the gate speaks different cheeks
& only the talking drum can interpret the dialogue
Like what occurred in the senior room. The scent
In his mouth is like his anal region. Neither can we
Wait for the three miracles nor the four trials to test
Our faith on the day of lifelessness. We wished we
Could sail miles on the rough sea when lakes are
Ready to challenge the existence of rivers on
The fasting period. We are witnessing what
Our favourite books will fall ill off. These different
Materials aren't what we are spading into the abode
Meant for another pasture. The taste on the lips of
The liars will not confess their sins when the
Ingredients at the market are prepared in ways of
Their dreams & choice. Different materials know
Their consumers on the feast day.

Black Beards

After telling the black feelings the truth,
I played the guitar in a lonely place.
There are numbers of lies written
On their faces, heavier than the red sea,
Stronger than their strength. I heard them,
I am still hearing many times, making
Ill noise in the ears of the reggae.
Bawuliar could lie as if he didn't feel the
Fresh creation of a spotless affection.
I listened to the energy in the talk &
It was as weak as his age. I tried the
Spirit in him is as powerless as a devil
Keeping a watch at the church.
Black beard is the younger
Life of accumulated experiences.
Try me has become lesson,
Wickedness & die early. Black beard
Is a big brother of an immaculate
Duplicity. Even on my dying bed I will
Shave all my black bears to restore lives.

Worst Food

When I was famished on the first birthday
I counted the promises he made to me
When I was in my sweet mother's womb.
The storms threatened the contact I have
With the sweet sacrament. His lies have
Eroded the sincere path to the smiles.
Deception has stronger wings than the ideas
To create a new village in the chapter.
Worst food has fed the farmland that requires
Fumigations & reformation on the crucifixion day.

Caterwaul

There is a game of deception winning small teams,
Which, they don't know where they belong.
They don't know what they are doing with their lives.
We don't want to study with them. Their lessons buy

Goods & they are being rejected at the international
Market. We ate their food, we died outside.
This shame could not correct the mistakes in the new
Testament. I always figure errors out in the
Performance of the vultures. The more

They lie against their destinies; the eviller & more
Destructive to feelings. 'because of their fruits we shall
Know how the fruitful land has painted them. The bad
Smell on them creates another ill atlas in the land

Which means retrogression, the pain in pains.

Bitterness In an Elegant Garment

We've not been with ourselves.
The inner listens to the wrong voices.
There are many problems littered in
Every corner of the pages.

The input reaches nowhere, then,
The waters change their attitude.
Bigger than the brain,
More wicked than hell.

Look at them, the enemy of love,
The greatest foe of comfort.
We can no longer pretend
That the so-called heaven

Is with us to measure the rest
Of the activities waiting for the
Beauty & babies to count the biology,
That lives in their talk. We thought

We'd conveyed the healthy materials.
The lessons on the zoom,
No time to climb the mountains.
Things around us have

Become the dreamed failure.

Amorphous Article Multiplies

As if feelings were not fair to taste & choice.
As we found it difficult to comprehend the
Methods applied in calculating the approach
To the system, we are now tired of not seeing
Water in the desert. The transformation of
Rivers & hills on the borrowed land should
Wage a civil war against the attitude of criminals.
Nature is creation. The use of heart, the missed
Road, the beginning of the authority in hand,
The direction turns the winds to Russia. He has
Misled us. The lost vision.

Vilification

Spare us the dirtiest duplicity in the air
Spare us the immaculate antonyms,
The atmosphere of today in the store.

Spare us the sign of the cross, praise Him
Will not renew his mind. It's a deliberate act.

Spare us the family & friends whose desert
Requires Dubai & Saudi Arabia in their lives.

Spare us the multiplied faces, behind the
Garden, the reserve in the head of a few.

Spare us, he always wears a new pair of shoes
So, the news is everywhere. The walls have heard.

Spare us the million promises, more elephantine
Than your astuteness. The destruction & the hell.

Spare us the sport on the sea without feeling the
Rough wrath, the fishes have dodged the real game.

Spare us the hope in the cross. No little help will
Will fetch Gold & diamond. The more efforts on
The lane let's wait for the outcome.

Spare us vilification on our confirmation day.
On the campaign periods many things
Unfolded at the sight,

Spare us the unproductive heat on our birthday
The blood flows in gallons,
The pool of red sweats on the skin

Spare us the weakness of the day, grey hairs
Cannot bring food to the table they are
The friends of appointment & disappointment

Spare us the lack of trust in the administration.
Dogs bark at him, vehicles hoot him because
They are immorally bastards.

Spare us the world knows that he came to kill,
To steal & to ruin
You smell badly like your contagious lies.
Spare us the sight can see now.
Spare us the nose can inhale now.
Spare us the tongue can taste now.
Spare us the finger can feel now.
Spare us the ear can hear now.

Dead Bodies in Realm

This is not our choice said the death.
Bawuthief was gambolling on the holy ground

& then the evil spirit invited him into his abode.
Here he is now. Another interpretation, not

Found in the Holy Koran or in the dictionary.
I prefer reality to belief. During an offertory

Only dead bodies are brought to the altar.
It's not an obligation to pray four times a day.

Things have travelled from somewhere to no
Where. The wheat feeds only those she knows.

The real story is around you.

Always, Always

I'm doing these things so that
You'll remember me, said Gabbycriminal
Before morning finishes her work,
The waves are being troubled on the shore.
Fishes cannot relax at their abodes &
Make a joyous noise in the ears of sharks.

His appointees like a master using the wrong
Ways to produce disabled products. Our land
Is lost on the map. Images wear vulture's designs
On the run. Like pigs don't know the difference
Between sanity & secrecy. It's so now. The
Hollow integrity is their honour, The blueprint &
Statue; reflection & result, it's live to witness.

Uncertainty Celebrates

Behind every story, there is another & another.
It is difficult to understand the solemnity of the
Most Holy Trinity. One multiply by one by one
By one. It is missing in the picture.

Crusade on air loudly, propaganda & campaign.
Still rivers & lakes cannot meet at the banquet.
It's their time to count the stars in the sky & look
For cures to cancer. The disgrace

Of the supreme court judges in Ghana, emptiness
In the upper ghetto. Garbage is living with humans.
Befouled & cataclysmic, treacherous & infamous,
Ask for their responsibility in the land. The dance

Of the wind, listen to the phrases that need medical
Attention. Uncertainty should be the certainty on
The keyboard, now. They will remember the founder
Has become the loser.

Lethal

The photo of the clouds,
The full image of backwardness
Let us start revisiting the occurrence.
Today's mathematics is false,
Unacceptable. Totally villainous.
One message for you
The evil & injustice
You berate in this land
Where is justice?
Where is the equity?
Where is the fairness?

Lost Treasures

Where are the better eagles?
We're all human beings
Not an animal like you.
We do not compromise your evil power.
Your toxic authority or anything with
An acid, with power
You're worse than a beast.
You don't consider the joy of the moon.
Stars weep for the clouds.
We cannot stand such evil acts.
Our heart forever is in pain.
Your wickedness makes us cry,
But we have a message for you.
You're a terrible monster in human form.
Your highness has become a commoner
It's forever lost under the bright daylight.

Comatose

Your tools are toothless in an account.
The sand in our eyes,
The colours are the same.
When the bags are full.
Let us fill them. We run here & there.

Let's begin the assignment.
Still the lips are craving.
The sweetness of morality.
The rain showers in the rainy period.
The anniversary of winter is on the calendar.
Read me & never forget the bluff on the tree.

Stop deceiving the ghost of the night.
The drinking cup is wearing assorted colours.
The holy words are on the float like the erosion
That always misses the right heavens.
The soil knows the seedlings on the borrowed soil.
You are naked under the sun.

Lethargy

We are tired of the drama of dissimulation.
Everything, falling apart. Here & there are
The same theatre. This is the time to
Inhale the burning sea. We can run faster than
Kangaroo in the sand of the camel.
We need to listen to their vocabulary
With thousands of meanings.
Alternative & opposite.
The suns have gone for an assignment.
Too much for the incompetence.
Before the degeneration commences
Her life must be out of the cabin.
Contumaciously duplicitous.
Metamorphosis & peculiarity.
The earth has confirmed it

Burning Fire in The Rain

Run for the medal in the fire, your skills will serve
Will serve food on the table. For the living dead.
Read the sweats of the voices in the inland.
I have already denied the greetings. Come now,
It is your turn to hold the vigil candle.
Minus the tornado, multiply the gentle rains
In the oceans. Heroes will hold the fire.
Start something before the cry will overtake
The sweet laughter of new babies.
Don't sleep on the left arm & allow the wicked
Tree to fall on the ice. I whisper to the breeze
On the inauguration day.
Something to start something now.

Articles For Sale

I will not wait for the day to
Slam the door of the ghost.
Time will not answer this
Call when the oxygen has not
Confessed to Hello. Your own
Is smaller than your silver.

How many times will they
Disturb nature in her prayers?
I am struggling to kick the ball
Rolling from hardship to hell.
I must afford the articles in
The small sack. The budget

Is spinning around the plans
& for sale remains where it is.
Not everything is needed in the
Kitchen to prepare the cheap
Food. I will search for the quality
In the hidden Uranus, the

Look in the Venus will study the
Tests set for the flowers at
The balcony. Machine & medicine,
Players & prayers, the
Rests of the items declared
Wanted. On the skins, taste &

Choice. The percentage is equal
To the normal days being
Outside. I am still thinking about
The lifespan of the spring.
The articles are for sale, smile &
Sorrow, on the wall, no life.

Unto The Voice

This is the day. It is the day
After days in the week.
The seven days can reply
Every question set in
The voice of the wind.
Angels can surprise saints.

On the knees, faith flies
Uncountable distances.
Voices still don't observe
Their boundaries.
Whistles echo in the whisper,
Twins are non-identical.

Who belongs to the good
Friend of archangels?
Time will tell the cross,
The problems that are
Homeless in their bedrooms.
Back to the scripts.

How many earthquakes
Are there in their voices?
The answer is that the weather
Cannot vomit on her palm.
What is inside the nails on
The cross? Teach us how

To say the lord's prayer
Without dancing before
The three junctions.
The voice of the poor springs
Over the restless sea.
They touch the feet of the earth.

Basket Associations

In the day I could greet afternoon.
If I knew what I needed in a friendship,
If the hours ahead have good news
To proclaim then I can say good

Afternoon. I haven't finished reading atlas,
Knowing where they come from. It is not too
Late. Often it is good to be on the way
& the work is at hand, not as many

As the people on the wide way. I have joined
Associations & I can identify the basket
Associations. Whenever I ring the bell to
Meet, only deserted tone is echoing behind the

Waterfalls. Since I have been throwing nets in the
Wilderness only basket associations are found
On the lake bank. I could only hear the song of a
Unproductive friendship.

Paroxysm

The freshness of the evening is the
Beginning of what I have not seen.
I stare at the pictures on the wall
& the old statues are newer than
The fresh born ones. True or false?
I see things as same as the trees
In the garden. The size of the stem
Is like the energy behind the move.
Moving around the clock in the
Living room, I could not experience
A sudden depreciation consuming
Meat & fishes at the marketplace.
I can boast of quality presence in our
Amidst. I read reports to the dump &
The deaf could not believe their ears.
Yes, no control in the eyes of debate.
They came like the arm rubbers in
The daylight, yes, from
Generation to generation.

Power To the Right Land

As I woke up from the other side
Of the village, plants & breath
Could not smile at me. In the shadows
I cried & I am still weeping for losing
Crown for the empty throne. What
Went wrong is what we are struggling
In now. I learnt how to drive in the realm,
In the names, indescribable, calls are in
Many folds & unfolds. False response
From fake, unskilled professors. Their
Results are drama without cantata.
I work seven days in the week, I climb
High above the level of skies, glory &
Honour has been strangled in their youthful
Age. I ask soils what I am looking
For in the offertory surrounding me.
I can see, you can feel that the curtains
Are drawn to cover lost in the vineyard.

Wounded Tradition

Something is wrong somewhere, there, wounding
All the hearts of traditions- right at our noses-falling down.
For the elders to perceive the heat circulating
In the sand. Black clothes white. Yellow clothes brown.
Mouths open wide & long to reject conditions.
Water is water & alcohol is alcohol on the altar

& their taste cannot change truth which has been
Starved for a longer period.
Words are more than teeth in the cabinet. While
Conflicting images wear war clothing to narrate
Live stories to the oldest stool. See now the
Upside-down practice. The pictures of disappoint

Ment compete with the skies. We are severely
Slapped on the face.
New tone on the phone falling deeply.
Darkness makes a joyful noise.
Conversation threatens our existence.
Flowers at the background feeds us psychologically,

Selling expired products at exorbitant prices.
Alarm echoes & echoes again. Black smoke
Overwhelms layers upon layers. Dirt spread its
Territory over & over. Now we've woken up
From our slumber. Pool of tears drips & drops
In our oceans. We do not need walking sticks

To climb mt. Everest to see Saturn. Images have
Been washed away because no elders' hats to
Protect the light. We blow sirens & the world
Cannot believe the maltreatment of the people.
The wounded tradition is crying loud for protection.

CHRONIC ILLNESS IN THEIR BLOOD

Deceitful Atlas

There could be many lines, representing
Streets & roads, pathways & paths.
How many?
Counting them will cost lies but favour truth
Before the second coming of Christ.
We don't know how many

That will cost virgins. Before we start
The journey we know there would be no
Miracles in clapping around belief.
So, we meet the wrong train at the right time.
We shall taste it,
We thought. We met triplets who looked

Like some of the streets leading to
Another direction, longer &
Shorter than the length & breadth of the
Arctic Ocean. We calculate the hours
In the suns so that moons will not slip

Out from his seat into the angry sea.
Closer to the most powerful shrine in
The town we witness
Negative changes. the language on air.
We cross the rivers in the eastern corridor
& River Densu is not

Happy about the studies of the wasted crops.
We know very well how to swim.
The cliff remains the strongest
Man in the sea. We cannot fight the climate.
Final erosion has come to liberate us
From the captivity of night.

One of the richest cultures & traditions in the world
Introduced by our forefathers has failed
The gods & goddesses
In the universe. They have been now
Adulterated to the extent that their
Beauty, value, significance

Has been reduced. Their pride has visited
The gate of no resurrection.
The land of no return. The Horns of
Of no sound. Ears run to cemetery,
The land of bend down.
The mirror in our bathroom reminds us of
The beautiful dance Agbadza.

His Excellency Our Trash

The sick shepherd breathes
Into the green images.
Now full of joints
Unusual walk,

Downs on the floor completely-
Resting on the shoulders
Of the mountain, on the edges heavily.
We don't see things well
As the air in the middle told

A new time around the clock.
A close look.
It's too much
(immeasurable waves)

He roasts corn in
His stinking mouth.
Airborne diseases.
We can read many violent
Lips at war against sanity. His

Words are pregnant.
Undefined. Full of injury.
Strange at the scene.
His sick breath seals mouths.
Our voices have swallowed us.

We eat words which should
Have cleared the air but guns
Are pointed at the back
Of innocent notions.
He ceases our breaths untimely.

We count the fruitful seeds,
Not enough to net fresh fishes
Purchasing ideas; a wasting time
In the white moons.
We are watching our death live.

Minus Negative Minus

We've received telegrams from the world
To be created, which name is written on
The foreheads of unknown folks.

As plenty as problems on the coast
The browser is divided from heads to feet.
We now calculate minus negative minus.

A lot of numbers are missing in the hairs,
Physics plus chemistry, another matter.
There is much deeper to dig into affairs.

We see minus negative minus persistently
Netting out our fruits without care & concern.
Care & concern has no authority to fight their

Assets, because we aren't part of the game.
Our tongues cannot plug their grown wings.
We complain hell to the heavens.

Our grievances spin around like armed,
Prepared armies who see their toothless
Mouths, still, run for their lives. They have

People but we don't have any
Weapons. Everything looks like minus
Negative minus because of another

Entry at the back, the almighty saver saw,
Being fixed in one of the reservoirs in the
Chamber of their secrets in the sacred room.

The storm in their holy temple washes away
Dirt on the surface of the earth. The
Jubilee house has become the home of

Sodom & Gomorrah. Their architecture is floating
On the eyes of many. Problems have conceived
Troubles & given birth to minus negative minus.

Addressing Them

Candidates have questions & answers before
The exams. They ask themselves questions.
We ask them questions & the tricks around.
Activities going on, on the rise in the mud.

The litter of unkempt smoke puffs in the face.
A heart attack asks too much of salt. Blindness.
A wounded weather. Doubts have taken their
Seats currently, sitting on the thoughts of Many,

Worse than previous pains & worries. We can't
Buy what is being sold within us. Not the at
The price of madness. Or rejected stones.
On the lips play words. Curses. Wrath! We listen

To the toothless address, no head, no tail, no hair.
There are eyes to see more damages Nadaa
Has caused. No lips to confess his sins. He has
Hardened the climate & shot down the sun.

Hands have become homeless, retired from his

Legitimate job, bellies pregnant of illegal Stuffs
Unprescribed moves. Broken protocols, every level.
The package: *deception. Fabricated Integrity.*
They haven't laboured. No fruit. No honourable

Under the sunlight, still with multiple stains.
Animals!
The complaints are in multiples, bath with acid.
No confession at all. Healthy ears like that of rabbit

Have heard the sorrowful maltreatment & the sharp
Tongues have stopped clearing the plantations
With long hairs that are planting illegal seedlings.
Now snow is heavily showering in the wrong

Place, at the wrong time. Climate is importing
New crops. Markets are ever ready to disown
Wrong figures. The folded arms resting on the
Chests will unfold very soon.

Talking About... In The Forest

There could be anything = uniquely unique.
Talking about....in the forest.
Talking with the air=good
Dancing to the horn of a rejected
Vehicle=trouble.
Feeling empty, feeling worthless

At the wrong place
Cannot excavate the hell in the
Soup at the table now.
The disowned songs in the
Virgin forest=homeless
Full of tears. All the drawings

Have their=unique languages.
All ears=alert. We walk in the
Forest where young trees live.
The visitation of *Nadaa* in the
Forest=curses. Ideas pump out
From their cabinets. Resurrecting

The moment, we thought.
The strength of the collapsing
Branches=shocking. The dance Of
The weak branches of mango trees
Tried to conveniently convince him
But he still clings to the clap of dry

Leaves in the wind. He takes
Home the talk of withered trees &
Celebrates over.
There are subways leading to
Conflicting directions.
The entrances resemble =

Good exams & meaningful lives
River Pra wants to enlarge its
Kingdom but its strength cannot be
Maintain. We could not believe=
The manner the guard are
Misleading=regression

The inhabitants, instead of
7 years, it's now 2 years.
Ill-structure is mounted.
The syllabus for the death
Is being prepared for the living.
River Oti could not embrace=

Disgrace
Arms of the falling village are broken.
The light on the farmland vomits=
Putting
Poison on the face of the folks with
The clean hearts are consuming them

Up.
Read & understand =a topic= has
Become=the shield of the tortoise.
Sick materials are=on the marketplace
To chase out=the healthy ones.
Regret will never sleep until =the
Healing honey= is dripped =on a
Famished tongue.

Entertainment In the Desert

The heat in the rainfall invites/
More heat than life in the sacred land.
Much more talk, we look at/
The top of the roofing sheet of the new houses.
There is/ a lot to tell/
The weather, his relationship with the inhabitants
Sauntering on the edge
Of the agonies with the inflicts/
On their souls.
Sounds outside in the rainfall,
Have made/ us not to enjoy/
Bestselling novels.
Behind the tallest wall, we could count/
lifeless activities struggling to emerge/
On the surface of lakes. Walk/
No feet, many footprints as huge as the sizes
Of the African continent. The land/
Needs massage for the cultivation of cash crops.

We/
Run to *entertainment in the empty market/*
No smile on the sand about the sinking
Entertainment. No heads /
To make population census/
But voices are heard without bodies.
A new scenario /is running on. The tribesmen/
Place their wrists on their shoulders of the
Weak. Elephants cannot/
Counsel themselves. They/
Follow the made-in-character of their
Jungle with their smallest arms. Mount Afadjato/
Underscores their presence.

Wasteful Elements

Before the right season, we don't know yet.
Wrong items have already begun their noises.
We can say thousand times because the day will
Be annoyed & go into hiding. The noises in plan.

Let us listen to the wisdom of the market.
We tune to our favourite radio station
& our problems are on the plates
Clearing the air, feeding the good listeners

With the most nutritional ingredients.
The arts on the walls of Athens remind
The novel I read several times because
I found what I needed at the right time

The true history of the know-how of the thinkers
Trying to be disciplined & law-abiding.
The very best friend of forward ever
The song of the day is I'm above the law.
Even in zoos the animals are law-abiding.

Investment

For innumerable calendar years now,
A mixture of red & black
Acrobatics on the feelings,
A homeless truth cries for a bailout.

We haven't experienced fire before
A blanket of darkness is the king of kings.
There are rumours everywhere,
Even under the sea, in the pocket of the water.

Even poems of today haven't been heard.
No, they have heard them many times.
Even walls of the most powerful shrine.
The yearly report is being tempered.

Investment reads the flight of issues.
Help from them- no help from them.
Investment currently, not our notion,
Yes, our notion/our investment in the sun.

Ash Wednesday

Use it anyhow
There are businesses within actions, performance
Bends down running up, we meet dissatisfactions
& downs in the pollution. We don't want to do
Businesses with *him* but we need to do businesses
With brains, not buy & sell altered destinies.

Don't mind them
Night refuses to attend to its guests who want
To write down the reports. Fear is to face the
Panel of an immaculate conception. Say the
Holy Rosary so that the earthquake will digest
Your disgrace. Too many pens to shoulder the

Labour of an eraser
At the point of questions. We need to make the
Heat up so that we will not buy anything stupid.
They're smartly doing their things before owls
Resume offices in the night. Time has been sadly
Swallowed by a heartless

Earthquake. The interventional hell,
We are doing so many things which the Holy bible
R*efuses to sell to the customers* who want to test the
Muscles of the so-called men of *God. "Weaponless"*
Vocabulary, shameless toys like him.

We know our right
Attendance books are sick of the direct sunshine.
Its arms have been crucified at the mouth of the year.
We can talk well. “Youthless”, useless. Falling apart.
Cry loud in your ears, no pillars in the ground.

A very good friend of indiscipline
By the absence of the chair there is no word to
Import into the book of life. The heavy storm has
Exposed the cause & we aren’t above the law.
The words aren’t the actions, but the words are
The verbs in the commandments.

Are we the folks who are going to do it well?
He’s still dancing to the music his relatives planted
Some years back. The brown Jupiter has assured
The soil to put on the apron. We know what made
Us & we know where we shall return after our efforts.

The rising of the sun
Till the settling of the sun & the sleepless knife
Has dugout the spoiled elements of the period
Under the skin. Night, out from the world, no rain.
The sun reigns. Eyes out there.
The clap of the feet & the shine in the secret.

Destructed Periods

Side by side, no fresh air behind the pictures,
Sieving them. Cobwebs settle on our eyes.

So many actions are unfolding, folding them
Behind our heads forever, yes computers live.

We know how to read & we read the music note
Circulating in our blood, body down now.

It's taking ground smartly at the wrong time.
Effulgence washes the shabbiest parts.

More to come, day at work 247 live.
Days cannot overtake nights, we are independent,

What when how why where which
No words now but noise in the air, yesterday.

We motion into the centre of the town.
Look into the eyes of the young flowers,

Collection of poems could not believe the words
We could not hold ourselves & photograph the disaster.

To survive, then, a package of questions starts
To rain on biology. Answers from nowhere to

Pump up numbers from the above like how
Manna drops from the sky. The years of no use.

Fruits & vegetables could not answer our plea.

Depression

Why?
Is
On
The whisper of the dawn birds conveys mighty
Narration, the preaching of the years. The keys
Of the principal doors are missing in the advice.
The chase of warplanes' gas reaches zero land.

Chuckling
Deeply
GabbySatan does whatever he wants to please Satan.
The words, darkness, like a tropical shower &
Bridges lose their image. Examination could not
Prove the capability of the students, *chief injustice.*

Quantify
My
Belly
On the holy land are tiny lives. The lifestyle on
The waves from Chicago to Norway, the perfume
Along competes with that of Africa. Things are unhappy.
The sign of regression. Shame!

Fear

For

Children

Forwardness sees the shadow of the ghost.
The dream of Dubai is eroded. The oil in the
Land is being looted by him, by them.
Smiles cannot be boosted off its lifespan.
The very good comrade of stagnation,
Always, the redlight on the way after them.

He

Careless

We know that we're doing the right thing.
Lines behind us, oblique dying
In summer. We cannot spend as much
As we want. Their thunderstorm
Roars at length. The foundation of the
Agenda is unshakeable. He smiles.

All

Die

Be

Die

Gallons of blood of deception are
Mixed with pollution. Ideas of vision
& mission cry. The affliction of the land is
The promise he made to them.

We

Not

Interested

He sees Christmas in the middle of his mouth.
The bank account of the beginner tells us
The budget on the table. Present sweats haven't
Denied us happiness. Funeral should be
Organised on his birthday.

You

Can

Die

We've missed the gold & we have met
The talking drum. Overflow of the rivers
To the city calls for burial masses.
We can't cry the whole day but
The smile of the first child feeds promised
Us the resurrection.

Vegetable For Sale

Back in the days, the sizeable pot,
Bucket, full of substances.
The vegetables for sale
At the throat of the forbidden wood

Has been finally found.
Time has worked out labouriously
& tirelessly & it has broken
Into pieces. A knitting machine

Couldn't knit the problem
Surrounding his necks.
Glint is still roofing over some, from
The direct sunshine. Outcast

Less than outcast of today.
Dislike a balanced diet, lacking
More sea sand. It is too high for
Kangaroos to spring over fire.

To carry homeless ghosts
In her womb, saints reposition
Themselves to the white hands.
Hardship from nowhere to somewhere.

He is now chasing unborn babies so
That they will be delivered prematurely.
Neither Tema harbour
Could export ill practice eating up

The good fruits that boom the
Promised earth nor inviting the ingredients
That paste a broadening smile on our face.
The sick lessons are introduced into the offices.

Nose cannot welcome the scent.
Hold on to the failure,
Uselessness, recklessness & unproductivity.
“They don’t deserve to see themselves

On the throne”, we said.
The brilliant sharks in the camp.
Restriction of yachting on our territories.

We wear red & black clothes because
We are out of the shell to read out
Testimonies, for healthy seeds want to shine.

Reckless Intentions

The move on the heel, faster than wind.
The move in the mud, not welcome at all.
The cheaper disinfectant, expensive for the rich.
Darkness is affordable for evildoers.
He, they, all of them.
No beauty, no life in the system now.

Lips are hungry.
Upside down on the throne,
Injustice plants everywhere.
Door entrance. Political judges,
The exchange of reputation.
Clock harbours many narrations.

Novelists couldn't wait to script
Fiction upon nonfiction because
They don't read the skies.
Feed the hungry public library
With the truth. Things are occurring
Behind doors. Supreme court,

Inferior court. Useless occupants.
A new day is dawning for all those
Who weep day-in, day-out.
Reckless intentions are our cross.
The outcome, no honour clothes them.
The speed of the minute hand is

Reminding the people in darkness.
We scan backwards. Thoughts. Ideas.
Lack of wisdom at the desk.
Truly *mboa are at the wrong place.*
The guests are eating what they never
Planted. We throw a great light in

Delight but sorrow & hardship smile
At us countless times

Antonyms

The wrong seat has encroached
On the liberty of silver jubilee.
The opposite of the opposite,
Antonyms are synonyms.
The hosts have regretted it.

The land is so fertile, but it has
Given birth to sick foodstuffs,
Down-looking ones.

Other planets, neighbours are
Jealous of it. They wished
They had one of these foods.

Some of the spring-ups have
Given birth to whom?
In the upstairs corridor are paralysed

Upstairs of conflict of interest.
They look abnormal. The face of the
Water is the harvest. They have sprouted

Winter colours. The tasteless colour of
All souls. I'm even blind to it.
Their interrogated characters alarm

In every yard of walk,
Even the biggest tree in Akim Oda
Hates them. I am proud of you.

The biggest wishes they should
Emulate is genuine seedlings,
But they took ill channels.

Glints of the souls will liberate
Us from a dry pot.

Rationale

Thought touches some parts of
The errors swimming in the lakes
& we know that Bain has so many
Rhythms to dance to.

But there are swollen issues
Hanging around our wrists.
There is no need to make comments
When some of the words

Are enemies of today's sentences.
Defining the words,
Insulting dictionaries, hearing
Some words, scorning lessons

In the Law school. Dictionary
Means another conflict with jargon.
Some cases have surpassed
Being careful. Match with evil.

Before the hours, the house is
Tormented, strolling on problems.
The design of the ceiling interrogates
The culprit, because of power.

Our intelligence brushes out the
Nonsense, the polluted decisions.
The slogan (patriotic) opens fresh
Chapters & pages to the cottage.

The songs in the background
Repeat & alter the destiny. We
Challenge the look of
Aluminium, the gold looks at the

Results & spare us the rests.

Now 10+10=18, said the political
Supreme court judges. They have
Serious hollow knowledge. I wished
I would know the manufacturers who

Manufactured them. Salt tells *Bawudieb*
That she's more delicious than him.
They behave like professionals whose
Heads could dig gold, because of their

Foolishness & their dance to money, booty.
Thousands of websites close their doors
Completely because of the 18. They don't
Deserve the planet mercury (keys in the saver).

The existence of gold & diamond does not
Pay tribute to their ancestors. The threat to
Wage a civil war against partners, no way.
The duties of computers in him, in them

Affect Covid 19 leading good things to
Lifeless camp, he says, they say.
They quickly import viruses from nowhere
Onto the healthy land. Pandemic, epidemic.

Was it the vow he made to us?
Not at all. I'm bold, he thought.
He's a shameless liar by any moral definition.
The sizes of their corruption struggle to carry

The bellies that are stuffed with lies & looted
Booties. We farm & the seasons change
Their attitude to their workers. The immaculate
Truth cries for her right. Oppression grows

Wings. Fresh becomes old at once, say the
Gaze of the greetings of the evening stars.
It's not completely dead. The resurrected day
Has posted new stars of victory of John D. Mahama.

Sick Receipts

If there will be—-a surprise
Looking for a settlement,
Our palms welcome
Without——-asking for a
Blow——-the cut in hope.
The WhatsApp text
The phrases—--foul
We read——-the winners
Of 21st century's poems
Touching—--on the titles,
Some remind——-us
Of the green life.
We are diving——-in &
Out of the span.
The sick receipts
Have—--4 noses & 3 eyes.
The sentences in the prelude
Match———with the vision
Of the greens & pinks
On the land, in trance.
We reserve—--virgin wood
For tomorrow——-protecting.
——-Unborn lives to smile
———with the gods
But the drive——-
On the ground
Conflicts—--with many occurrences
The fishy carpet lays——-on the untarred road.

We fall——---millions of times
——---attempt to reap—our labour
The reflection of rivers
——---washes out
——---The kilos of pepper
———---into our sights.
The earth is clearly open
——---- to us.

NATIVE AS AN ALIEN IN HIS OWN LAND

Obituary As Fashion

Things are turning against us
Left, the unstable signals &
Right, the ocean laughs at us.
The soil of yesterday revisited the learning
Materials in the minds of the audience.
The surface tells the stories of chameleon
That exist in the world to come,
Already in existence–different forms on the leaves
Prophets discussed the issues of yesterday.
Mix of feelings stands aside to watch
Incoming games—unfamiliar faces coming up.
We hope our tips will overtake their ideas.
Even the inventors could not answer why.
Rain cannot promise strategies that cried for
A job. We need to walk now, night cannot promise
Us a day. We take days to the end of the trip.
As a professional builder we do not know
How many particles of atoms participate
In the preparation of the new paradise.
Churches continue to deceive the sacred.
Opposite songs play against advantages,
Everywhere the floors are shocked &
Turned their backs to days & night.
Dogs begin to bark at obituary as fashion
Undress the village whenever they
Step on their toes. The presence of pinks

On the platform speaks of paradise.
We weigh day & night in our hearts
But the constant cry knocks at problems,
The highway traffic lights stay red.
On the land yet to be posted.
We aren't ready to read
Evil letters. But the first downpour
Exposes the castle in the air.
The angry crocodiles have come
Out of their horizons.
The pull out of the stainless horse----
Good to be clear & right.

Flog On the Face

The light in us is greater than the curtains
Use in decorating a new elected king,
Down in the mud.
The look of the life–let's start to
Count the twelve stones
In the cathedral, continue to throw
Its light at an immeasurable length.
The meaning is unknown to us.
The start to the close is known to each other.
The information; more to be read. More
Explanations needed to catch the minds.
The earth can't contain
The *flog on the face, anymore. We can't describe*
The twelve stones. But the mystery
Around them; we don't remember, leave to them.
The stream of tears floating on the contoured line.
Plug down the immature fruits, try your luck. Time
Has been in its disliked clothes. Its attractiveness,
No more. Tension, chopping
All the reaped fruits are on the dining table.
Bones & skeletons fight for a nutritional position.

Only poems,
The genius does not understand the cantata.
The cantata in nine minerals looks worrying.
The score bends down
Because of him, because of them.

Beautiful Empire Falling Apart

We have heard much about what we do not hear well.
We haven't heard from the toothless mouth.
But every tooth can bite & chew beyond his strength.
BawuLair is running after a job he doesn't
Deserve to feel in the sweaty world.
We have seen his different kinds of photos.
We have read plenty about him in our nightmares,
In private newspapers & magazines.
We aren't satisfied the cooks needed to add
More supplements. Research centres
Are lazily working on projects. We need
To know him better. The information around
Could not feed two pages. As we caressed
Him in his both ears, horrible news. Horrible news
Reflects in red wine. It's so sizable; more than
Atoms under specific close look.
That the wing from nowhere could not attain the
Same size. Wing from somewhere
Will have to know much about it before pulling out
Its muscles. Kindergarten is still
Waiting to direct to baptise us & relocate
Moonlight in our lives.

Hell Plus Heaven

We have heard about folks
But we have never perceived
A–the town will soon write
Biography about him.

Dangerously selfish, we are
Seeing what is taboo. The air
Has confessed. The sunless moment
Feels it. The sun is muscling the time

Or he wants to have the world
For himself. To himself on the golden stool,
To us he is a vulture, no place on the planet
Say hello to him. He divorces from human progress.

We can now feel the hundreds of tonnes
Of sand from a cloud of smoke
In our eyes, in our mouths
Making us believe in a cloudless globe.

The rest of the village is looking

For the missing substances. A huge pothole
Has no time to swallow them.
Ahead of us is time plus time= more strength,
Rich ideas to be called in.

A new trip, with an efficient navigator.

The verbs require cement to hold the other words.
The other words need refinery machines to whisper
Intriguing statements into their hungry lives.

A dense dimmed blanket occupies ⅔ Of the lighting
Sky, we fish out a clumsy immaculate wood,
Nowhere to locate *the hell plus heaven.*

Angry Golden Stream

News, the news everywhere
The world cannot survive

Without rumours,
Without its siblings, gossip.

The world is hungry for rich information.
The livelihoods lay on a solid foundation.

A bad rhythm is swimming
On the lost roads

& the lack of water has
Become an angry *golden river.*

News, the news everywhere.
So many things are happening.

We must chase the news from the hideout
It is said to be consumed live.

I grab information that has been
Hidden from the touch of gossip.

As a journalist, specialised in politics
My responsibility is to conduct

An effective interview & feed
The famished ears with facts

& updates not like biassed journalists
Like some who are working with Peace

FM & Metro TV. They are married to
Incompetency & money. Their work

Plugs the community into chaos
Because of lack of professionalism.

Fresh news is still awaiting.

Under The Sea

A

On the left fallouts are taking place in numbers.
We haven't set sight on them before.
We don't see them well. Where are their origins?
We ask the mother of the sea.
Another home with different images there.
Lips have already testified before the panel.
They cook their special meal for us, but we do not eat
More to say, the moment confesses the startling truth.

B

In the realm, we notice that they could be hard stones
Or a length of leg that has missed his journey. The right
Hand cannot prophesy to fish. A healthy table missed.
Accidents are sweeping us away. We say *no no no!*
Weights are losing their abilities, fade skins today,
Shocking sweats cook; arms on the heads, hmmmm.
Laws without liver; constitution lacks kidney,
Vacant heart; *he they our life span*
Is calculated every day. Why what how

C

Slips in the hands of wrong people.
For a paradise cries for the saint on high
To dwell in, to sleep in peace.
The conservation room is situated,
At the front, black & white. The odour,
Stronger than a dead body.
The entrances have been unlawfully blocked
& the inhabitants are dead.
Under the sea, full of questionable ugliness.
The old people are still planting the ancient notions.

D

These crops are keeping us in prison
Of the rooms reserved for them.
They have taken the land back.
New things have rotten irreparably.
Living things have been deformed & disfigured.
Their ghosts continue to chase the culprit.
They refuse to say water is water, alcohol is alcohol.
They refuse to sing the songs of little children.
The new grasses are struggling to be graceful
So that they would be planted on the fertile soil
& boom the wretched situation.

Drought Notion

The bag is full to be transported
To the rightful destination.
He thought quickly.
They believed confidently

What is inside it
Is unknown
& nobody knows it
Or know their love.
It contains one & more
Confidential.

Our dreams wire the contents.
It contains moneys
Contact documents
& cheques.

Their assumption, laughable.
The nose of the wild dogs
Will further open their ass,
That is our drive.
I wished I could scan their crux.
The behaviour fishes out
The contents
As easy as possible.
The waves on the aerated sea
Will soon invite a raincoat.
One day monkey will go
To the market & he won't come back.

As the day has plenty of "undos" on his head,
They are not able to break bones of the day.
Evening has opened its arms to embrace
The labourious labours where
Their activities please the burning essence
& dead looking for Elysium
To rest in peace.

At its right destination
& It contains letters
But it gets to crooked hands
& the contents are air-ballooned
With stench facts
& dead ugliness
But beauticians have the answers.

Oily Mouth

Twelve- month pregnant rumours
Have given birth to headlines

Snatching the attention of those
Who have been assigned to other duties.

There is a solid confirmation that new seeds
But as old as the birth of the earth are being

Taken care of by the most poisonous chemicals.
The threat of human existence on the right place,

He supported their thought.
Its seedlings have already geminated,

Uprooting the healthiest natural resources
Sleeping on beds left unattended.

Martyrs have owed to dig out
The kind of ailments reducing

The stainless image of the century.
Erosion is waiting for its season

To expose the impostors.
Your Kingdom Come

Owls' eyes are polishing
Useless shrouded clothes in the package

.

Something is happening now & then.
It has become an epidemic in society.

Upon the heaviest weight of fumigation
It is still taking huge roots in every community.

It could not bribe the deadly illness. Thunder-
Storms could liberate, shoulder up here, there.

Daily Bread

We have a very important appointment
At 9am & we do not need
To miss this gorgeous platform

Ordained for us. Our diaries remind us of time.
We flip & read through
The lion & elephant skins.

The main junction has uncountable arms.
Greetings read from the movement,
Good day but we did not see anything

Assurance about the day yet & even. The
Combination of praises & curses reminds
Us of our first enrolment in a sacred society.

The myths surround it, mysteries signal us
Seven times in the scorching afternoon.
The fight of the white birds coils around problems.

Daily bread, artificial stones at the last supper,
Walk ups for a daily bread, beneath
To the desolate mountains & down, sweats

Construct its lanes within life, before panels.
The mooneye has a clue for the rest of the day.
We hope for hope that the crown would be

Among the thousands who are smelling.
Its delicious melody has lost its charm.
Not reachable. U1v2w3x4y5z6=non poem

But we could not enjoy it to its satisfaction.
We could not see late afternoon hungry, angry
With us. The shining smile of our charming

Daughters question a package of assurance
Drumming in the daily bread.

In Abundance

Now, time fights seriously against action,
A dry weather has conjured heavy rain to

The heated atmosphere. The expectations
Have gone to bed without giving us rational

Reasons. Things are still unfolding & that
Poems wished they would come to their doors,

Knock loudly at death & the sleeping
Visions. We light the candles of poems in both

Day & night *but we could not see one district,*
One dam. Neither could we see the parents

Smiling at their domestic duties nor inhale
A trade of insults hovering in the area. The

Ghosts have thought twice to resurrect on the
First day, their promise to us. That almost

Six years now, there aren't dams here to
Resurrect business; continuous power-cut in

Every second. Poems create powerful stanzas.
We listen to the breath cruising beneath the

Stanzas of comfort. Numerous difficulties weave
Between curve upon curves, hotter than 700 Celsius.

Endless lies that shut the vision of those who are
Ready to stand up from their sick beds.

Rivers & lakes in some districts wished they would
Shine more than the starlight.

Many productive uses but now in the grip of reckless
& merciless developers. The districts are seriously

Hungry of edible beauty but one person who can
Rescue the situation is the nation builder.

Overwhelming Knowledge

We can only touch a carpet of shadow that has
Refuse to allow a fresh day to dawn for all those
Who paddle in discomfort. They have laid down
Their skill of assistance & creating underworlds

Instead of mounting up Eden for discomfort.
The actresses & actors don unfriendly
Friends, appears worn-out. They could not trade
The items in the concert. In the 21st century pupils

Learn under their foes, combating for comfortability
Against pets & snakes. Children ask the deserts
Where are 350 new schools promised by the
Blatant liar, an enemy of children. Pupils pace

Forty miles for future & return after the curtains
Descend finally. Hell in the net. Traps have
Been set for them in the 3000 dilapidated school
Structures because they are chasing their dreams.

The searching net could not furnish them the
Furniture, accessories & learning materials are
Struggling with lifelessness. They zoom at
Enemies close to them, & at friends on distances.

Their targets will be attainable when the nation
Builder returns, they thought. The birds sing so
That their tears would turn into a joyful dance
One day.

Crippled Solutions

We are in spring; feelings cannot caress the air.
The land has embraced an unwanted air,
With sharp knives

The earth is struggling with funerals.
The agony laughs at comfort.
It is knifing the innocent souls into pieces,

Blood paints us.
We have favourite makeups
But this red & black

Does not appear in our mirrors.
All the renowned museums
Walk on them scornfully.

A natural beauty, healthier than medicine.
Hearts are soaked with painful sorrows.
Plenty of holes are dug in souls.

All the leaves on the virgin trees are
Wine & cry. No fruits at hand.
Vitamin c will strike mercilessly.

Nature will look for laughter.
Lives are now calculated &
Measured on *mars.*

Mercury & ocean have plans.
Ends can meet their zero. The intervals
Are imaginable.

365 days can better explain.
People shoulder *Russia & Ukraine*.
The land still has the worst indices

Of poverty & hardship.
Rain is heavily showering on the ground
But the soil is harder than *Nadaa*.

The first father has a stoned-hearted heart,
The children said.
The children persist to caress him &

Hostility emerges on the skin
With acid. He is a tyrant & married to
Tribalism. Whenever children cry then

He dons white & sings hallelujah
Happily. We are still the green of the morning,
We are pillars of the days & our tears will

One day curve into overwhelming joy.
He is playing the greatest degree of insensitivity
In managing our hearts' rich diversity.

The chime of the bell, our solution.

Everlasting Injure

Guardians know what good keeping day is
& night gladdens. Sunday school is always
Awake until savanna stands on his feet.
We learn to know that *apples are manzanas*

Vegetables are legumins; neither words can
Escape the truth. There are a few people who
Can hear the latest music. For us, no
Difference between a crash & angry wave.

A match does not match fuel & fire
Has vowed not to sit in the same boat
With him, yes neither cannot we marry liar nor
Thieves like this family & buy friends at the cheapest

Prices. Thunder strike will not miss her chances.
Horrible results have shown its decayed
Teeth. We need oil, says an *Everlasting Cure.*
The partner of a unique uniqueness rejects the invitation.

The soil is in pain & the job laments. We do not sniff
Factories & companies around them. Knowledge
Lies fallow, below. We still throw our hands at

Length & they land in fire, behind. Now we're ill
Sitting with death, says the time. Certificates are
Longing to sell notions, gloves. Knowledge's
Hands are tied behind him. Strength in the casket.

Unemployment in the honeymoon. Population
Not the atlas. Mercilessly worried & the
Goddesses of the joblessness have refused
To remove their birthday's clothes. The waves

From the Volta Sea will provide you *a smiling cure.*

Prostitution's Phrase

Abundant/curses & threats.
Machinery/on the other side.
Anytime we wake up/from sleep

We only/hear one song
Promise, promise, promise.
Thousands of promises/have

Been travelling/miles without a smile.
The outcome of the research/has
Shown/that songwriters & composers

Even death has/heard & its head
On the left/arms completely
In spotless/doubts. Why?

But they don't/keep to them,
We could/remember that they
Promised/us an everlasting happiness,

Billions of gallons of honey in our mouths,
But nothing has given/birth at the matured age.
The continuous, many lives he lives & leads

Have/sickened us.
The environment & words have laid/us on a
Sick planet. They feed/on duplicity for energy

To survive. They are/habitual liars, like he-goats
On an assignment. The outcome/of the research
Displays that they are/morally empty. It is

Better that they/don't count them as human beings.

River That Cries

Almost five decades now, this essay is
First-time put-on test & all the candidates

Fail to the degree that the sea overflows.
Because they were knowledgeably blank.

Nadaa is one. Bawumia, worse than a toilet.
They could not answer the questions they set them-

Selves. We could not comprehend the apocalypse.
We could not read well the parts of the engine

That's rudderless & with spoiled signalling aids.
It has come again & we the students are expecting

Revived approaches to tackle issues.
But we dive through them. A slap of acid travels.

Familiar faces appear in the rain.
& friends select to play the side game.

Nepotistic & narcissistic team in a known history.
He promised to exclude devil & Satan in the game.

As birds could not complain that they don't have
Hairs or why an elephant is not behaving like a lion.

The annual results have testified that they are
Ignorant liars. The thick cloud has blanketed the sky

& we are expecting heavy downpour to effectively
Erode nasty practice that is wrecking us.

Flooded Earth

Stay & watch.
Stroll around the shrine of the king
On the peak of the roof is the network of bees
Walk on the surface

Open of arms
Behind the wheel are extra spare parts
But the look of owls has something to tell future.
Strew in

Have to emptiness.
We know it is easy to sail through.
We have now bought as a few as we needed
At very costly prices.

Put us on the stone.
Eat us.
We're going to have tasteless dinner
Like a vulture munching anything it finds.

Sit us on the scale.
Tell our souls.
Stars of heaven read the report to its siblings
Because of the Good Friday's rain

We have been waking up from sleep.

The Bend Down Love

The walk of river Mississippi, Mississippi,
Tell us the story.
The surface is sometimes colourless.
Fishes don't believe this.

We try to find out how many friends
They have so far. The close
Friends whom we can share our rips
With have many clauses.

Dying for us? Ask the sunshine.
The combination of their beliefs &
Practices in their dresses give us a
Lot of assignments to discharge.

They look somehow the same
In the public. Their modelling on the
Street of New York City scores
Different points. It's not a mistakes.

Of their make-up, the thousands of
Mirrors in their rooms furnish them
The correct fresh babies. The
Beauticians question their know-

How but still the weather tells the
Debaters' stories about the creation
Of the earth. It's good to know
But it's better to understand, to eat

The food which you know
The ingredients. It tastes bitter more
Than death, but does it contain
Vitamin to confess at all?

Soursop is there to boom your immune
System. *The bend-down love.*
Slow rough bare. Under the hairs
The calmness tells us the deliberation.

The economists have prepared to try
Their luck game. We haven't met
Our interests at all. Yachting is our hobby.
Sailing from one angle
To the other, don't fetch the answers.
The waves weaving through
The cause & the paddle of the canoes
Tell us the warning of the water.

We cannot imagine the territory of the river.
Metres board from heaven to the earth.
To the earth. There we get the bigger
Problem in our relationships, it's not so

Dangerous as others see it if the reflection
On the water will disclose what's under their
Clothes then we will brush our teeth well in
Order to kill all gems before telling our fellow

Friends to wash their faces. We know that but
There is nothing we could do to change the
Colour of the blood. We will wait patiently for
The new creation. Alleluia, we shall sing.

Worse Than B4

If a lot of ideas are in the freezes,
Then there's no need to ask church's
Bell to remind your assignments

Dancing on your mind. Cartoons of
Meat prepare the way of an action.
There is nothing in the house to applaud for.

Although we are hungry of love to the extent
That starvation is warning laziness.
Listen to the conversation, friends & enemy.

We want to be completely satisfied so we
Are waiting to munch on our death & dislike.
The health of our strength is the brain.

We looked through windowless house
& we saw the brownness of the lungs,
Full of problems & conflicts

Littering every corner of the hospital,
But we could see & feel the salvation,
Our part with the Solomons,

Hiding in the nails, we called for a
Division of labour
& they uprooted them from their holes &

Joined the combat. Now immaculate
Victory awaits us with a distinctive joy.

Starting From the Close

Wind in the ears. The homeless wind on the tree.
The strong wind from somewhere, wait for his
Achievements. Blowing from
The assorted areas of the Christendom,
Somersaulting on the surface of the altar,
Especially from the mountain. In it, many songs

Are crying countless times that they
Trail off & conflict with others,
Like trying to create human beings that
Neither on Mars nor Jupiter. The mathematics
Refuses to rest for a good purpose, like a
Medicine man conjuring strategies for a politician

To win a presidential election. *A big shameless fool.*

It's a shock to feel the air & the pollution
Of the sitting leaders. We have innumerable nightmares
& wake up in the arms of *the famished road.*

Deteriorated Tuition

Outside the circle, the smile behind truth,
& outside knows the babies inside the womb.
The belly admits to all the clinical misfortune.
The move of their scent, come & smell now.

This is not the outside we kissed yesterday.
Folks are flooded around their issues,
Metres away from the reach of its tail. The body
Is headless. Twins, triplets, parallel

Heads to heads, like black sand
On the coast of a new world, like
A stainless powder uses to exorcise
An evil spirit. With the help of view, it is

Easy to identify the unborn babies
Who're sniffing the smoke of uncertainty.
Identity of the look. The truth on the search
For a wedding gown.

Greetings have the answer. Sensitivity has
Already sneaked into the mall & selected
Its items. If not the stream of brown
Envelopes unto the writing desks, under

Designed clothes, no designer wear,
On their bodies, eyes cannot sleep,
Neither could sentences stop gossiping about
Long speeches. Many debates rain on the mind.

Winner or loser dodges each other.

Volcano

If a tiger is always a red weapon because
He isn't satisfied, so let's tell the whole story.
Now listen to the birds. Do research, we're
Your research. There is more to read,
But they are the skins of useless elephants.
The innocent ones, which lay restlessly on

The hideout, the heat under the earth breaths
Unto the surface of the Pacific Ocean,
Then the others see him as starving. He's
Being banished from others & being married to
An isolation & shame his features, the least
Particles gathered to represent some statue,

Are incomplete. As it occurred to Sampson in
The Old Testament. He stalls, takes tough
Measures on matters that favours loyalty,
Like heartless stems feeding their children
With hard stones. In the kingdom, people are
Soaked in trillion packages of fear, like racists

Poisoning another folk with a drip of acid.
He might run after babies who have started
Learning how to crawl from fear to courage.
Outside hasn't finished his narration,
Collides with wind & condolences. He roars
Like a tropical thunder that has been sent by

heads to eliminate his challengers. His
Tongue trembles, airing out malicious words
Of bomb & injection of poison into spotless
Faculties. His eyes flicker like a trafficator
In his arms, which is policing his disfigured
Features. As he was deciding for his bank

Account, another knowledge was sealed off.
However, we swim in thorns. Our freedom
& happiness is struggling to survive after
The Lent Period. A wake up from the
Rising sun to its settling. A new, half
Chapter bred pieces of information.

Ink On the Sheet

We still stroll towards the backwards ever.
Why?
Words are still dancing on the nails,
Yellow leaves bend down.

We do it every third Wednesday,
We're the earth,
But not ashes. We shan't return
With an ambulance.

Of the year as remembrance,
Of the birthday of the Atlantic Ocean.
As we zoomed billions
Plus, hundred metres above

The Southern Ocean, we saw the hungry
World spread everywhere trying
To eat into the Mediterranean Sea.
Scan & x-ray, a brother & a sister

In the same boat.

The results & reflection as an
Accountability. The flow of the sea to
The shore, your photography,
The patients who are suffering from

Unknown ailments like head
Swimming in the questions for a perfect
Settlement. We delve into the mouth
Of a wild shark. We read the energy left

For the goods out there. Truly we fail to
Read history & understand it well.
The engine breathes without a break.
If a green world is easy to create

In a twinkle of an eye, then silver &
Gold could be littered on the skin.
Exploitation of the engine & strength
Without all the parts in the music.

Our left arms land on the red plot
& we mirror the heartbeats of vultures,
Life in a kitchen. We do not mind the
Signal demonstrating. We remember

The story of the angel who feeds the
Land of the ghost who is homeless
Because he's still looking for what he
Does it, what he wants.

Notice

We struggle hard,
We walk through the flame of an endlessness
Like dancing before the gates of water & acid,
Like the laughter of a lion who kills
His only brother for a money ritual.

Fruits & vegetables fight on an infertile land.
The blessing of truth & the sacrifice of lives
Is the understanding of the talk of little children
& its teachings. We crawl on our stomachs &

Cripple on our shoulders. Strength speaks to
Wounds, wait, minutes are still immature.
As a dear never slept & built Paris within
Fourteen days after getting independence,

From tuition, resources are looking up to
The composition of snow. The same folks
Take a remarkably close look. Heads up, tails down.
At its performance we take notice.

All The Way

From period to decision
More years are calculated,
Are added to age & we
Grow old & behave like

An adult. We pray for
A package of wisdom.
Many are added to our
Faculty, sharper than

Computer like a mother-water
Ruling the fishery kingdom
Together with the nine planets.

Seeds germinate in the water.
Others land on the hairs.
We grow pale, blue.

We clothe ourselves
According to the tone
We value beauty.
We decide.
We talk beers, come out.
Birds respond with their feathers.
Snakes warn the world
With their tails.

We are mature.
We dance opposite to the new melodies.
We need to construct lives
For the rest of the land.

We are keen to come
Out of the shell
Because inside is uncomfortable.
Our brains are restless.

Our legs have finally found the way.
Our hands have started creating the
Unfamiliar world in paradise.

Crusade

Middle of the market, there're
Plenty of old sayings at the stalls.

Anything, anytime, anywhere.
He knows that they're aware.

We cannot believe in the anthem.
Paleness, roughness expires in the statements

Walking into the library,
We admire the queue of notions

Willingly to sneak into the
Promised hall, both good & bad

Ideas signal at the tabernacle.
Something has fallen from its throne.

Crude crusade needs backup.
Lessons play around

The lessons we have in Philosophy.
With the help of the case studies

We get solutions to the problems
Crawling in the farmland.

Fake Features

In the presence, it sounds like
Naadaliar & Bawuliar completely.

Chimpanzees accept his look.
His odour is rejected by fresh air.

We talk, trees chat with us amicably.
His talk kills the living soul. He gets

An admission into a zoo. Then we
Escape into an angle of research,

Remembrance. Not one, not two,
More than fishes in an Arctic Ocean.

We drive into ourselves; we don't
Want to divorce ourselves. Freedom

Has glamorous look to cloth us
Because we have been naked before the

Birth of trees & rivers. It is cold, we are
Withering. We are forbidden to chat with

The air. Our questions have the key of
Keys to every lock. Try the red eye.

We don't want to repeat the other side of
The stone. Spread before the Pontius Pilate.

Only *fake features ooo! fall, fade, fault, flaw & foul*
They could glance at the road they could not

Cross. because we glance at the back, still serpent
Wretched, not accommodative like prison, poison

Good for him, for them. We do not need telescopes
To delve into their sacks. Searchlight does not lie

During confession. Beliefs are crucified on
Valentine's day, like ours. Time has told us

Their output. Our capacities 10 + 45 = -25000.
Their behaviour has told us the truth that has been

Buried, trillion feet deep under the tongue.
Cough in the night clears the mess away.

The dirt has endangered the whiteness of the
Images built by nature. We stare at the mountain,

Count the stars in the sky & fly through them.
We are crying, the unfurnished pockets on us

Preach with tears. Tears stain out white clothes
With *fake features ooo! Ungrateful agony.*

Finger Lies Around

We've lived with them before.
We've sailed through continuous power-cut

Before electrification stretched its arms.
We've come back to continue the

Journey that lashed us severely
Where did the engine go off?

Yesterday was better than today, says our feelings.
The designs of spiders confuse the earth.

Travelling here & there in the sky,
Connecting a metaphor to an introduction.

The footprints on the mud, not dreams
Of a simile in the canoe, but his, theirs.

They've been born with nothing unique now.
Roofing with a luxury life, with an accumulation

Of failure bottle of honey & oil is packed out
Of affection. We see serpents as their match-

Makers. Their lives in the garden of
Crocodile, richer than a virgin wood.

Its drip on the blind sight wakes up the veins
Up muscles. Our eyes, feelings are crying

For a glamorous island.
Their fingers lie a thousand times

& bury us alive. The muddy nonsense.
Now, we assemble a might knowledge

To excavate nepotism, first class upper mafias.
We kick off without waiting for motherly love of the

Day. We pace briskly forward. Hills turn into houses.

Culture

We're now reading novels we vowed not to
Attend to. The temperature of the forest
Asks the goddesses of the sincerity

Not to read winter's novels in
Summer neither can we read Quran
& explain the texts from the bible.

Bodies travel anyhow without respecting
The presence of chemistry which must decide
For the biology. Fingers move miles away

Because legs are there to defend them.
We all know that only justice can give birth
To peace. Knowledge laughs at an impunity,

Only baptism asks a driving mirror
To convince an impunity to sail into the river.
Jordan. Smartphone's news is a bombshell.

We do not know what to say to the brightness
Of the side mirror. We do not want to wound
Culture but tradition is watching him.

A stoned-hearted elephant continues to live in
The mud. The money melts into gallons of honey
That drips, springs on the fake minds, on the

Faulty plot of land. In the west of the river.
Our culture remains a tradition. We will jump,
Thoughts will teach us how to sing

Comforting citations.
We cannot dodge our pride; trees stand for us.
We hold our culture to the stars.

We get the right thought for the runaway.
No time to fly under the sea.
No tunnel in the atmosphere.

We still eat from the bowl of genius,
Still no balance, no life at the table.
We still need a kiss.

A sip from the pot of vision.
Culture, our image.

Formation

The art on the wall
Sign of the cross on the foreheads
Appears like
The blacks in United State of America

Different arts are showcased
In another pyramid
The treasure in the drawing
Extremely dear

Unaffordable to buy
The argument surrounding them for
The understanding is very far
To catch up on the field

The pictures in the rooms
Of the kings &
The ministers
Of states as the objects of worship

Or the protection in their lives
History is still alive
Like a flus of blood
On the sight of globe
Part of life to

Remember to build on
To live with
Raising head in hope
We find love for art
The cure to psychological sickness

We cannot delete our wives' image
On our memory, true saying
It moves from left to right
& we tap the richest wealth

Genesis Of Devil

The beginning, the word. The word is the beginning.
We can say *Hail Mary* about the beginning
But the word has an answer for destruction.
We see things, life, life after harvest.
Feelings under temptation, already tasted.
We haven't thought of it, it has thought of us,
Simplicity. For real, now. It is true. We are hungry,
The nightmare under the stainless altar cloth.
Still hungry for a healthy apple.
They could not stand trial anymore.
They could not read how long an intestine is.
Not at all or change its position.
Why this? What is the matter?
Where & where on earth?
How hmhmhmhm? Whenoooo?
Seek & search isn't ready to get pregnant now.
In the marketplace, the drum of the wallet.
Where possible! Tens, twenties,
Thirties of courses, schools, colleges,
Universities, both renowned & shadowy,
On the field, not yet clap. Smile on the
Church's tower, snowy owl; the seer.
We rest fake weathers in summer, we say
To them, heavier than original stone, more
Troublesome than problems lay before judges.
The Prime Minister of Israel. How many lives?
Many ways are there,
Untapped, fresher questions in the palace.

She has tested it, white on the snow.
Green, go ahead, bitter than truth.
She has experienced & even impacted
Knowledge into innocent ones.
We have been sighting categories,
Grade in grades, universe in universal,
Convincing us. Harvest time, hard work delivers.
Plenty of products, what to bring to the house!
It's a big problem. No scale. Type your name now.
Rich product can market without stress,
We thought twice, then we gave a trial.

Drawing To the End

There was an obscure look
Behind sunglasses of the clouds.
We catch every image beyond
The reach of healthy affection.
We can only tell our noses
To relax, study the mouth.
The lips are ready to gossip.
The drives of the pale desire
Of the malicious intentions
Snapping the wrong feelings.
Every two seconds of gloom.
We tried to finger out the real object
Which was hiding its identity.
The real object plus the identity
Tell us the answer. Study them.
Nobody knows the images.
All the colours on the planet.
Come onto the stage
Brothers, sisters alike.
Friends not like family,
Neighbours from the same roots,
Their actions our sorrow landing us
On the battlefield.
Walked past by problems
Signalled
Danced
To show their best, half alive.

The language sounds
Like a parrot communicating
To new recruits in their black uniforms
Thinking about the challenges ahead.

Readings Of the Week

We reach the middle of the conversation.
We touch the
Subject, mine, another name is nominative,
Scholars say so.
Auxiliary verb, we help the main engine
To function well.
Verb, the principal motor of the frame,
The strength of the motion
An indirect object, I am the dative of the work,
The receiver
A direct object, the game of the day,
The accusative, the alcoholic name
In the middle of the book so many chapters
Are found at the genesis
About him, about them.
More to walk to you.
Dangerous, friendly.
Open the envelope now.
At the revelation of lives, death.
Thousands of pages are littered.
We must start what we finished.
On the watch of the land.
Many problems blink continuously.
The tables in the sanctuary are
Full of contaminated seeds.
God is everywhere & He sees everything.
Forget about the church, full of scammers.
We know them. However,
It's a chronic, ironic illness.

Earthquake

If we've dreamt, we've dreamt of falling
Into an immeasurable hoe, not a promise.
In the confirmation of holy sacrament.
We can decide for ourselves. The smile of
The day is the promise we're enjoying.
24 hours will bring
The best performers on the platform.
The content is colourless.
Prediction plus wishes.
Disappointment sits in the palanquin. We
Will study the flow of the ideas moving on.
The type of communication wiring on the net.
The rose at the parade salutes a deserted
Assembly. The stores are closed in poverty.
We have been purchasing our favourite items.
We don't have feathers to fly even
A noticeably short distance. It's not far away to feel
The broken promises.
It's time now to fly with our might.
It appears very costly to afford but
We don't need money,

Say *no to hardship*,
Trees *say hi to comfort*, *smile now.*
Money cannot buy happiness.
The object catches heat.
The heat never loses temperature to winter.
We see the Kremlin live in Akyem.

The ghost of shadows on the dais, cankerous,
Capturing, depositing the spoils in the public.
The design of today does not speak of the economy.
The rivers are restless above boiling degree.

Blind?

We visit books in the state libraries,
Comparing to ours in the Mars well
Decorated advising problems through others,
Measuring the sizes of the ideologies,
They remind us of the first days
Examination we wrote in our lives' the trials
Of trials wake up senses in our moonlights.
Lessons standing out in the climate. Many notions

Slip into the basket like fishing after heavy
Downpour, like after the truth has finally seen
Daylight. On the silver jubilee, shameless.
The real sound has shaken the state's house.
What we wanted to see. The dream of the land
Broke into pieces, was not seen in the life of the

Folks. Still, the wound is enlarging its territory,
The odds could not heal the worry in the land.
The contact with the spirit has been broken.
No light travelled through the flame. No cloud
Has been formed. Which is which?

Smuggling In & Out

We stand now above levels,
We feel under our feet Lucifer,
Penetrating our territories.
We do not know where
We gather the ill fruits.
We still stand above the
Sea level in the mid light,
Throwing the telescope beyond
The reach of a heart-desire.
Imagining how fascinating she will be.
Light does not conquer. Her appearance
Changes, wearing nature,
Plus which could not be designed.
The walking speaks
Words of debate which questions interest,
Happiness. The steps raise doubts
But does not land us in dilemma
Us in dilemma. We don't want to lose
The pink to blue. The competition is tedious.
The work ahead is uncountable.
Many ideas chest it out passed by.

We weigh methods, emerges from experts.
Mathematics will soon teach physics &
Algebra statistics. We remember one thing.
When was your happiest day?
The map of daily routines, macho ideas.

After Sweats in The Heat

If you've dreamt, you've dreamt of a nightmare.
A deep hoe under the bed, the hours before dawn.
Not ready to chest out.

We look at the desk, different assurances.
Families with the same smile, voices out of the
Main rainfall but there are plenty of cases to study

Everyday. Figures are more than the spaces given them.
Calculators disagree with stars commanding miracles.
Hands are disfigured in holding to the fact.

They leave their jobs for hell.
They look as if we don't admire nature.
Don't weekend's confession.

Creation before planning the positions of
Mountains & sea on the fifth day.
We shall not grin together. Contact your enemies

& study your friends. Watch the game
Very good friends of a chameleon standing

Behind a plain glass. Salute transparency!
We tried them like we tasted a thousand
Eggs of serpent at the banquet.

We die before our births. We aren't lost on
The channel to solutions. They're almost the
Same. The trade of Satan & witchcraft in

The same size, but they are prescribed to
Different ages, they are neither easter eggs
Nor birthday kola nuts in the mourning period.

We haven't finished searching. The room
Is still vacant, fuller than before creation.
Nowhere to run to, blanket has come to stay now,

The taste that could give birth to love, a tail, a head
& an endless happiness, has hidden from us.
The grey hairs on us are announcing the time.

We came into being or the Genesis of the year.
No season has told the truth behind the
Division. The rainy season is far away

From the disappointment. If summer had told
Us the productivity at the end of the year, we
Wouldn't have rushed to purchase a charlatan

Spoiled maize & brought to the market. The
Heat in the house isn't conducive to fasting
But We will look up to preparation. We hope

A new season will journey from
The start & the healthy
Fullness will be at the point of readiness.

Negative Plus Hardship

We cast eyes —-- around,
Beyond the reach of description.
There can't be there —-here looks for here,
Half brain dulls.
Not a single blanket of beam on the palm of a leaf.
In spring, although, there's continuous shower

Pouring normally, joy & sorrow cannot
Settle —-- the —-- differences.
There are what —--- in the drugstore
But we cannot predict when
We shall walk to the point, finally.
Consultants are actively at work

Selling ideas to their
Clients at gold/diamond prices.
The machine hasn't hit the place.
The right place is not found.
Meanwhile we've started the walk
Sometime — back— when we were

Responding to many calls at
One — time but we were able to answer
All as —- we were instructed by
The wings of angels. We could
Remember what my lecture said
Go, add more —- to them.

These aren't enough to depend
On, to live with, to survive on.
The soup for the last supper, no date.
The Saturday all night cannot revive —
Broken marriages, last week was fresher than
This week. We can't crawl — we can't walk

—- We can't jog — we can't hop.
We can't jump but we have feathers to fly but….we
Must learn how to build broken bridges without arms.
A long distance. Not even — within the sunlight of
Their lips are rather above sea level. Over a forbidden
Land, if an object can feel — conflicting reactions,

The secret makes it.
The image appears in Mephistopheles/lynching.
We pray that their stomachs
Will face east, his hometown. We feel the method
Staring us, we pray to spell —
The catastrophe.

It is a lesson to have. The end has told
The beginning, the third, there's no leg —
Running here, there,
Chasing closely, we believe it isn't the
Correct oxygen for the time. X-ray gossip
Systematically. Siren announces functions

In the belly. Silence tries to envelop — our voices.
The spot depicts green,
The right tool screws. It touches the engine.
It wakes us up around the accident.
A new tongue composes. A new sound echoes
In the ears of the forest — nose alert.

We're down in mortuary. Sorrowful.
We've started the war without fear/favour.

Keine Antwort

Face there, to face the sky, face bends down,
We fancy the nakedness of the sun,
Running from dislike to a hideout,
Then from where?

Water, tell them now.
We resume.....
A hill to an oldest cemetery in Jerusalem,
Then we see the true ugliness of

The world situates alone with only hoaxers,
Real life dead, sometimes quarter,
On another planet.
There, we think at once. The wind from the wings

Blowing heat; no difference between presence &
Custody in the world to come.
It is 1000 degrees Celsius.
Hearts have lost spaces to hatred,

The glimpse of worries. Some exercises
Went past. It was very cheap to approach
But difficult to tackle, handle. Should
We compare the spotlessness of angels?

Pourquoi Nous?

Many exercises on the table awaiting a
Vast contour line.

Tell the Indian ocean which's in the shape
Of the European continent. In the office

Are plenty of adverts marketing themselves
Like the prices of human

Organs in the Arab States but affordable
To plug within the shortest period.

This music always sickens us. Smile,
Smile with him, them, you, because of this music

Knocking at the doors of those who are
Spinning around the circle constructed

At the front of their problems. We are
Finished. Outside, they are

Uncountable modelling on the grassland.
We do not search to know what we have missed.

Truly, we have shadows in the light.
They have nothing to offer, confess to

Unborn babies—all of them.
They know that we need health to buy health —

Justice to buy peace–where're……?

Dry Hour

We bought our favourite CDs
To understand

Message,
Hope,

New paradise to come with pillars.
Castles in the air

Cannot afford water,
Blood affordable at the table

At the weekend; not our side
As the weather asks for.

He did not come with the real tools
They did not penetrate the real world

Needed now. We are still
Matching to them. On the face of the listeners.

No roses in the hands of the young ladies
The promises are withered under the helpless sun.

There was neither rain to feel life,
Nor smile to straighten the broken afternoon.

It's not beautiful anymore.
No good news from the sacrifice.

There is nowhere to embrace words.
Half weather, zero move in the light,

We walk miles a day,
We smoke day's fruit above us,

Reverse to the starting point.
We Kneel on the sharp stones.

Same brain, many jobs,
Hands wave black birds.

The faded hope sits on their interest.
But the piercing owl cuts the despair.

The Date

Words are thrown hard
Behind them
Stench,
Sad,
Ill,
Dead,

We don't need such ammunition.
They have no teachings to present.
Not plus,
Negative 0,
To stroll

On the lonely land,
Witness the disaster.
Nature hates that it
Does not want to be disturbed blueprint.
Its pride streams rapidly
To everywhere,

The principal engineer of the devil.

Actions of the rust, eyes meet red.
We can no longer endure the agony.
His words do not bear good fruits to adore.
We met him on the sixth day.
On the seventh day, their arms

Only embrace polluted air,

Evaluate it,
A laboratory result,
Not a pregnant test,
See around round
Feel a touch, touch
Tears on the contour line.

Restless Moment

On the front cover,
We could see the activities on the reading glasses,
Wearing the mask of the sea on its questioning days,
Behaving like a romantic lake receiving

Presents on its unique performance, like welcoming
The prince of peace into a heavenly
Kingdom for the first time. Eyes run after
Images, objects will never stop

Transforming from one art to design.
It isn't easy to stop stealing a glance at questions.
Always plus one, plus ten, never ending points.
Its colour, it needs studies but it's inexplicable.

We can drive further, furthest but we don't
Need to count sanities. We have seen what
We're diving, we feel the red light.
We don't need to sieve beans.

Seen Reverse

We look at things well on=the trees.
They are–
Anything from nothing on the matter.
The branches calculate=the fruits,
Results do not know the fruits,
Questions are different from results.
Let's face the stone.
The length of the day tells us=the plantation.
Hours are not ready to ask seconds.
We have asked minutes what to do for hours
Complains are too much,
Their tongues travel=any distances. We've ended.

We've to start
At the heart of the course.
Hearts bleed=pools of blood, blood pressure swims
At our nostrils
We feel it badly, our walk is ready to confess now.
The stairs challenge us.
We weigh morning, afternoon keeps=the sales.
Your money is what you sincerely worked for.

Dream Outside the Net

We move to rejection,
Temperature scares earthquake
They do everything like they are
Animals, more wicked than death.
Even if there is a man in the world,
We shall climb the cross of Jericho.
No tree is taller than us, they know that,
For sure.
We aren't expecting voices in thunder crying loud.
Season buys plenty of disappointments.
Scandals countless.
Our lives don't excavate the wall of Jordan.
West plus west, creation by heart.
Extension of worries. Even nature is bitterly
Angry of itself; they don't have pillars.
Is there anything to invite apart from
What is not there?
Are we hungry? The sound of drums.
Nobody knows the stars
In the morning. We must lift heavy, down.
The evening does not know what to
Say about unfinished jobs.
What we have been seeing cannot
Supply vitamins to the body.
The season has not come to live longer.

Facing The Wall

We have brought him to the house.
It did not go round well with the clock----
Already the trash is full, eyes could
Not take the polluted breath

Walk to him here----see them.
Talk to them there---- we can't end today.
Take to what, as empty as where for what.
Make to that, nothing in the faculty.

We've sent them back to the origin
There're numerous there, breathless respiration
Catch what now?
We salute foreign

Reply to the *Pentecost say*
Understand him follow them.
Buying their stuffs,
Song on the floor

Believe in God
Tail Lucifer wholeheartedly, committedly
Not a single day have we not received
Blow from him. His branches, anyhow anywhere

It can't meet, it can't talk, it can't be itself
My life will never be the same.
We can't hear the killing voices
Of the desperate devil.

Praise to their trash mind & adoration
To their stoned amicability.
Scorching & drought satisfied them.
Their belief not ours.

Neither Salt nor Sugar

Today is the end of another season,
We've already started the conflict of the seasons.
Taste, unfriendly to us; unexpected with this action.
We have learnt what we did not want to.
We are experiencing nebuchadnezzar.
We're now hearing war songs.
When we were breastfeeding our mistakes
Crawling from the entrance of worship,
Say bye to hardship,
Wall to wall with the help of the love
Ones. I thought I would never be a man,
To be on the feet & sail the boat,
Meant for special folks on a unique planet,
The colour of the roses calls the register,
Empty barrels. The age of the roses means
Questions then multiply them by the
Death sentences. It does not look
Attractive & presentable but still useful.

A Hungry Man Is an Angry Man

If we see the movement of the seriousness,
Seriousness edges
The feelings. We don't know
What to say in the daytime.
We hear the drama.
Life leaves falling metres from us,
High above the skies of a plane.
Then if we feel how
The blood is actively circulating
On the eyes of the lion
Pumping gallons of sweats,
No production as a credit.
Our skins on the grill; China Wall,
Preach the true gospel.
How healthy & strong we are.
We look younger than what comes in,
The face in faces.
We've seen him now & we've noticed
What's about to appear.

Spare Not the Rod

We talk to bodies
A body answers without questions.
We can touch the weapons

Not knowing,
Touching them on the heads.
We aren't hungry for what's ready on the table.

It needs green, the real food
To live with. The food that can
Revive the beam of the brain,

Pass the exams not set for him, them,
Rests of nutrients on the
Other branches of the body.

We've to talk now
Not what we studied
Whisper the wind moving in a different direction.
It is extremely dark.

We don't see ourselves anymore, but.......
Within the middle.... plenty of

People around the clock,
In some corners, there,
Darker as-----falling apart
We can't finish today

Rotating/washing
The surface of the darkness----
Pairing the singles. Finishing not now.

The torchlight of Lucifer to send....
Bring folks in the abode, he said.
Voiceless, talking drum on air.

Disinfection plus medication needs job
Attend to them. They are the healers
Said the clean water from biology science.

Instability

Whenever we perceive, today,
Yesterday has a lot for tomorrow.
We pace to fold the curtain up.
Culture,
Tradition,
Music,
Dancing,
Beautiful ones are not yet born.
New objects as old as he, they.
It will be nice to see them, it'll be nice
To tell a liar, a murderer, hypocrite, a thief,
Religious, like Bawubugiardo.
We feel drained at the eyes of rainbows
Before vultures come & eat up us, for so
Many years, we have been looking for protein
Which we needed badly,
We could only find it in summer.
We know what penance can offer.
The eyes are paralysed of
Many beautiful things,
Beauty beyond human description.
Heart never sleeps as she searches
For comfort in the right comfort.
See less, tell more...... grievances, failed.
The skill on display. It comes out
Itself when it is needed.
See how birds are at work,
Their talents carry information.

It is good to see the potentiality in you.
In the huge house, there are very
Few rooms in the faculty. We see it
Or we fell into holes we dug ourselves.
Here is much more evidence.
We feel it or darkness laughs at dirt.
The real objects… turn back,
The true colour. No complaints.
The real choice, confession everyday.

Is It a Curse?

If the baptism's suits on the nails,
Which we wear on the
Remarkable days of St. John,
Then the question is,
What are the names of the suits?

If we know the errors.
The names have no impact on regret.
The main colour has four siblings &
Without them people cannot

Identify twins well. The souls need to be
Greeted & they must trip to the end
Of the start of life. Not what green
Vegetables assured us.

In the kingdom, no space to stand.
We need to provide our souls &
They must shine among
Many stars who are walking on the red carpet.

To be loyal to your feet, open the universe.
Serviceable to the natural resources
In all endeavours, let's see.
It reminds us of her appearance.

The dressing stood out from trees in the garden.
The many who were combing around to net
The right fish for the best soup,
Admire the style at the back.

No Implications around. The ways
Are two but we want to taste the difficulty.
The front view has no problems.
The branches at the front view, talk to us

Earthly heaven, full of perfect interests.
Life within lives. Glory knows owners,
Honour to be deserved. We live for life,
Worth & for living. Buy one & leave the past

Hot

We have a particular drive.
Definition known to the drivers
We love most but.........
It does not shoot out the beauty we want.
One or two are boring.
The best is there or
More can shoot out the natural beauty,
Which is lacking in the kingdom of fairness.
If we're experiencing a very
Heated oven in harmattan,
Then I must look for black shirt or
A black shoe to match
To other siblings. We do not see
Other substances superior to others.
One is better than the other or the
Most beautiful in their kingdom. Day
Does not see herself better than night neither
Star can clothe the moon, throwing her
Birthday party after accepting her mistakes.
They wished there were many, even much
More than hairs on the head.
It is always nice to see the sun & rain
Praising each other. They try to finger
Out the difference but their activities say
That one cannot stand alone rather more as
Million or billion folks plant in every corner.

Brown Boat

We used to have maps for directions
We've tasted all the roads.
Highway, endless run to temporal gain,
Under the sea, activities in the realm,

In the air, without feathers
But numerous looks
See the future of the land,
The cry of the grace,

The limitations of the youths,
The fall of the unborn visions,
Foreseen in the dreams of the saints.
We've immense targets sitting

On our programmes
Bigger than all the nine planets
Combined.
Richer than tonnes of gold &

Diamonds mixed.
The savings inside the black
Box have died off.
Beautiful ideas are locked up.
They are being starved.
This man, Naada gazes

Into people's eyes
Gaze into our eyes again & says
Stupid people, you
People of empty brains,

Insults have become his chewing stick
Sticks & they live on cankerous
Words to achieve their goal.
Their sentences could not polish me, us.

I'm tired of the school because
Their lessons are knowledgeably empty.

X-Ray

The definition of 21st century could be
Best found in the dictionary of madness.
The answer to every life,
In circles, in debts.
We are now living on a
Different slipping floor
Which we didn't dream off,
We didn't think about it at all.
Truly!
We are now seeing the ugliest
Side of the globe.
It's raining normally but the ground is
Harder than three daily meals.
More poisonous than mercurial ground.
Emptier than the upper part of the feature.
What a terrible shock!
My mirror snaps me horrible pictures.
My present health confirms the result.
He promised us an amazing love
That will alter our destinies from
Homelessness to entertainment
From negativeness to freshness
We're sitting on money,
On his polish behaviour
We are hungry because
Of miscalculations
What have we done?
Where are we now?

The Mediterranean Sea
Has shown its sharp teeth.
The surface of
The red fish could not stop
Nodding to the waves.
The pressure to press
The lethal out of
Boats sailing from
East to the under
The matter & north to
The conflict with slow motion.
Elegy caught the air.
The complaints of the
Ghosts on the streets.
The silent feet in match.
Arms talk to the wind
Ahead of the departure.
Necks hold words for the
Feet in the swamp.
Gods accept every
Word like tropical showers
On his birthday & organises a
Grand party on the seventh day.
Study the present situation.
Neither ask the moon
Nor sun their lazy days.
For they're tired of
These primitive least citizens of the land.
Our days are numbered on their foreheads.

The True Gate

Read me us
Dive into every liver.
Hope you can swim
Above the cave's level.
Read & read the walk in the dark,
It is not finished at all.
Devour every substance
Nothing to live on,
Apart from pain & duplicity.
Read & read intensively
The water of the baptism of the first lion.
No fear can close the true testimonies.
Digest them
Different taste & choice.
Reading is good.
To know what to read, ask your homework,
Library doesn't lie to hard work.
To understand what to broadcast,
Information doesn't die.
Comb here, there......the season restless.
We've to learn about the sea.
Whatever we've read, nobody knows.

Forbidden Fruits

We've to practise
What we do not feel for.
The right policies.
Smile on the face of cloudy light,
At the right time.
Tongue will sleep peacefully.
When the cake is equally shared.
The life of the land is the constitution.
The vision & the mission of the land.
Looking backwards,
We haven't farmed at all.
The gods & the goddesses
In the mourning.
The participation &
The cooperation of
The land in the casket.
The guide & the guard of the land.
The effective navigator sleeps
Under the mt. Everest.
The joy & the happiness
Of the land is live buried.
The matchmaker of justice & peace.
The security & the assurance of the land.
Fear isn't in our dictionary.
The hope & the trust of the land,
Moves the mountains, pushes oceans.

The love & the care of the land,
No difference under the moon.
The food & the drink of the land,
Plenty of interrogations.
The home & the hospitality of the land,
On the street.

Poisonous Stuff

The whole body cannot move
Into the same.... body,
Legs behind, love ahead of the games.
Continuation into an uncompleted goal.

Tired of responding to this song
Heads down, shoulders chase responsibilities.
We can only see the breeds of chameleon
Holding the national flag

The anthem.
Poisonous stuff to their system.
The pledge.
No help from anywhere.

When the internal structures are
Afflicted, ask for knowledge.
We remember how previously,
Happily, we enjoyed the songs we-feeling.

The past with one another, it was a honeymoon.
Now everything is ruined beyond flood.

Feelings have been wounded.
The world has turned against fortune. Bitterly.
The breath in the paintings outside is untrustworthy.
No element of breath could save a blanket of smile.

This man, these folks persistently spraying
Dust in the eyes of outsiders, breeds dry, breathless.
From generation to infinite, countless tongues.
Fake prophets of the dark.

Shark In the Net

This is the time you will invite sleep
& sleep will make an appointment
With you
If we have had
A phone to call mums
On her seventieth birthday with her new
Plans,
The angels will be the best agents
To deliver the right messages through a
Misunderstanding between teeth & tongue.
The tones in the phone,
The favourite tone that spits
Cooked Satan & composes
New catastrophe.
Then there is no need to write
Wishes in birthday cards that take weeks
To reach Singapore. Around her are
Full of cards. It is good to write curriculum vitae.
Buy & sell skills. Glad to receive
A million cards per day.
Receive million cards per a day.

Thoughts & designs, marketable.
Thousands of strugglers knock one another.
We must thank the motherly affection.
You're one in trillion.
Not like hardship, not like affliction.
Shameless animals.

We will rest setback & heal tomorrow.
Words pave the airspace,
The plans & reserve shake hands.
Youthful features in the Olympic games.
Periods of time cannot sleep.
Our sweet voices on the piano read
The book of apocalypse
Greetings to the dying trees.
The noise in the wind
Rings our bells, *the regret of our*
Thumbs for him, for them.

Single At the Angle

There could not be/there/
If there wasn't there....
We've felt yesterday &
Today have not spared us
Pictures but/there are......dust
Memories won't be/there if/
There was no yesterday.
You tell us/you're still sleeping/
On your insensitivity
Nothing new about/tomorrow
Winds don't tell lies like him, them.
We don't doubt/
The flight of vulture, more will be unveiled.
At the angle,
Don't close/your eyes, for,
The nightmares are going to breed/
Unhealthier world,
We cannot erase/these pictures.
If the tension cannot lick out/the pains,
The true pictures of/
The centuries are gallivanting on our sights.

The album is open to......
Even the wind/will assist to flip, flop,
It is/horrible to have/
Second creation around the neck.
The mirror in the corridor,
The sound/accompanies,

The vowels & the silence on the
Same platform, unbearable.
Ice & sweats from/the above to ease conflict.
In the war zone. It tells/the truth
Nothing but the ingredients/that wafts
& renew/the throat of/the earth.
In the gardens where the fruits
& the vegetable/live,
There is/life, life within/the cage.
Look how romantic/the sea is
If it's calm, it's rough in decision taking.
We need/one now.
Justice & Peace,
The protection we want to live with.
We need to wear/smiles & laughter.
The promotion of we-feeling
Is on indefinite holidays/& the unfinished duty.

Israel & Palestine in the mud.
Let not here be there.
To be/there search for start.
We need to see/great look,
We love to drive through/struggle,
Size of the product, determination
Listening to/their songs & messages
We need to say the Lord's prayer.

In The Cage

The red colour.
It doesn't say anything to ice.
& nobody is
Interested to know
How an elephant is misbehaving.
Shadow is working hard to shield
The activities of
The side of elephant & his small boys.
The whisper whispers into
The ears of deaf & share
Ideas with mute. Sunlight
Exchanges with darkness.
Demand does not know supply because the
Alphabet & the numbers dance around
Church.
Hands fight feet every second
Over a best performance.
So wretched at
The examination of those who have four eyes,
Twelve fingers like that of lucifer
Virgin Mary, mother of Jesus
Doesn't Want to see her children suffering.
In the cage, limitation plus handcuff
Is the hospitality of the day.
Stretch of the atmosphere,
Accident & singleness,
Often & always has its seat
Plenty of photos confess

The sins of the Akyems.
More than
Sand at the burial ground.
Feelings say,
Horrible plus indescribable
We've missed *JM*.
The air in the atmosphere
Is *a flight of Mephistopheles*.
News in news, a prevaricator.
He, they, fly with fallen angels.

Eye In the Eyes

We see unseeing in the angle,
Spying at the triangle.
Jogging around honey lives.
Ashes to flesh to ashes to ashes.

In the beginning it was on the undeclared planet
But the beginning didn't narrate
All the springs of Oasis
Give birth to the sea, resurfacing rivers,

Mountains minus lakes cry out.
Today has much more to tell live to unbelievers
Controlling the small world.
Eyes remember hearts the pain

They are sailing through.
Full of interesting unborn babies lose
Appetite to come & taste the Earth
Worries to see spring in misfortune,

Winter in divorce.
Lies disgrace out of the courtyard.
Their siblings playing with challenges when
The days are still asking the meaning of drum.

They wake up from their siesta under the scorching
Sun, which their bodies decayed in cold water.
Plus other satisfaction, questioning the law court,
Which is a secret to them.

But they want their caretakers to salute nature.
Fishes will visit the last dinner, life cannot afford
& answer them wholeheartedly
So that the authorities will quickly labour for them.

They can transform clouds into everyday star,
Which will brighten in the sanctimonious houses.
The bright honesty has uncovered the covered
Pot, is like a missing life.

Eye in eyes migrates more than her
Covering telescope. You've witnessed them,
Yourselves.

Ugly Lips in The Honey Pot

Nature asks herself several questions.
Whether she is the true mother

Of the empty-hearted children
Who refuses to arm stars &

Skies together on their birthdays.
You know what I mean.

No cannot argue with Yes on
A blank answer, which cannot

Be seen in the dictionary.
I will sink them when I see them

Around me, says the waves.
No number of words can

Conveniently convince him.
The rainy season protects the soils &

The hard-working tools
Respond wholeheartedly.
In summer, ugly lips in the honey pot like

They sow bronze & they're now
Harvesting gold, diamond, crude oil.

Heating The Engine

His story............
Hmhmhmhmhmhm.
Your story.........hmhm
I can't finish the morning circle or......
A lot of stories awaken the dry trees.
They are in their libraries.
It seems like we're lacking

Hands & feet, which we don't know.
Whether black or white,
Rainbows will separate us.
Green or yellow, whether we're
Young or getting faded.
Red or blue, problems will never stop
Floating to the wrong ghettos.

Brown or silver, they've to confess
To the daylight now.
Define the meaning, what it needs
Before travelling to the ancestors.
Moment of time.
Debate on the missing smile. The calls in
The dreams are many. We do not know
The titles, I wished I could know how many
Teeth still in his stinker mouth & their meanings,
The answers are the rhythms of the economy.

All parts of the economy are spinning around
Medication. Even no number of injections can
Wake the land up, unless new seedlings are
Sanctified on the ordination day.

The Best Food

We are watching what Jupiter
Will do to clean prostitute water,
To wage a war against the earth.
It isn't a part of the game.
We aren't interested in the cantata

We can't play.
You can play.
They are playing dangerous game
Extremely more exorbitant than health.
Indeed, money cannot purchase peace,

But it can be hired.
Lamentation. Nonstop crying.
The pool is full.
Everybody says we're
Sincerely hungry for laughter.

Good to smile, laugh over
What will alter your destiny.
We forget our hobbies
Because enemies of justice & peace
Are now staging plays everywhere.
The sun shines, she sits on her gold,
Words are missing on our lips
Because greedy teeth
Have eaten solutions. Conquer has

Smiled at us. The waves are rough.
In the reflection on the surface of the river,
Ideas bubble out.
We don't need to see the doctor again.
It's time to be youthful, not "youthless."

Honey In the Mouth

We kissed the wrong weather,
this year at her feet.
Unknowingly, she will assist sorrow
To gloat to shroud, blacker, red.
Cool pot has melted down
The ice in us in winter.

So, there is no need for a pullover or
A jacket to reign. Leather is to mock cotton.
The oven to construct what is falling apart at
The wrong time, at the wrong place.
The hospital cannot hold her breath, no way.
To hear, nature is ever ready to show

You the true smile or set an eye on
Catastrophe. Listen to the songs of
Rain on the hard soil. We are very sad
Of losing sky to clouds, like singing
Hallelujah at the funeral ground, like
Vultures devouring your carcasses &
Drinking your blood on her birthday.

Day Break in The Darkness

There could be motion, there,
Pacing now into a new world.
The goal plus minus, we don't
Know why this smart walk.

We can't live in the same apartment,
Darkness thought, a bad idea.
The sun has nowhere to live apart
From sharing the property left
Behind their parents.

keep the eyes open so that snow
Won't turn into salt in summer.
No bed to entertain your laziness,
Interested in what is happening,

Streaming into all directions,
Sorrow to witness that, want it to box on
Without limit. It is an open floor,
No checkpoint in the voice,

All in the instruments.
A lot of activities, going on in the
Jubilee House after phlegmatic
Days & nights. A wide broad

Dissatisfaction designs on his face,
A shadowy smile, the glimpse of confidence
In the missiles, the act with thicker pullover
Designed for mafias, chasing one

Particular contract that may
Net fortune of million lies restlessly in the
Safe box but it knows the owners with
The half-sun mirror, & the cruelty wakes up

Early in the conflict. Try to cut its way
Through judgement, contemplation
& transaction is equal revenge.
Business with criminals like him,

Them, is a premature death.
Retailers who're Itching to maximise
Billions of dollars, their songs, let the blood flow.
He multiplies many times & wickedness

Teases generosity. The depiction of the work,
The voice of the people.
Run but the records tell you the clean labour.
About one thing, it's a masquerade,

It's not good for social media. We don't want
To be ugly like them. Half of the sun weakens
On the way. A strong wind prepares the way.
Chapter one is opened & the pictures are as

Dirty as them. The stench consumes us.
Draught crucifies us mercilessly.

Honourable In the Dustbin

How many times have we seen
Honourable in the dustbin
Comparing himself to a
Dustbin in the public?
Many times, at the sight
Of the wink of winds
Reporting him, them to a plain glass.
The fresh snow laughs at him, them loudly.
He swears to the constitution of the land

They take oaths of the land but
Now they have faces of character.
Rainbows dance on their
Lips at the call of footsteps.
If life stands before mirror
& dances around
Then, there is no need to ask
Rain to fall in the desert,
But if their lives motion a
Little distance then
We must ask them to
Go into river Jordan.
We have heard several times
About promised land,
On hungry ears, the beauty
Is eating in the dustbin.
He doesn't deserve to be seen
Among *who's who*

Morally empty plus fabricated
Integrity plus fake piety.
Light within lights uncovers
The ugliness. Of

Inconsistency in the addition,
In subtraction. The fasting
Eyes cannot leave its post now.
They are not fed with,
The healthy food, also not enough
To satisfy august castles,
We have decided to sightsee
The uncovered earth,
If the horse is going to take us there,
Then the real life,
The journey starts now.
The junctions along the way,

We will firstly take the thousands
Of curves into account,
Then we must test it now,
It's on our minds, gorgeously
Sailing from happiness to
Grave telling horrible
Lives of the NPP of Ghana.

Separation

The argument behind the lifestyle, nowadays.
Challenges
Nature to send for the result of *DNA test*
Of him, of them.
Belief has the skills to dribble doubts anyhow,
Anytime but the control has
The upper hand to check the
Blood group in the bank.
Comfort is getting ill
& fears that the enemies of progress
Will disorganise the unity reigning among us.
The result is that
She cannot house the fallen children.
Ask them whether they deserve to live with
Unctuous pharisaism.
You know that in them there is
Different blood circulating in them.
Nature can
Still separate herself from manmade.
We wish she will enlighten them
So that
They will know that she has saved their mess.
How long will
It takes us to undress them to the world?
We've started to walk,
No question about the training.
No complaints…there are
Complaints about vomiting out.

We’ve prepared, combat is to
Face any confession
Ahead of us. It’s sunny,
The other side is talkable.
It’s raining cats & dogs,
Their lives are smeared with who’re you.
Its future hangs precariously in a balance.

Immaterial Ashes

We've seen a wink of black smoke,
But we could not greet the news on air.
Black smoke & news going in the same
Direction. Owls do always give information,

Division & its friends, errors.
We have worked, many lives still on the trip.
Scan is our witness, ask the witness in the box.
We jog faster than the wind, the thermometer

Is temperature. It is written on us. Genesis,
Act of the beginning of everything.
It passed along the road, more narrations to
Preach. We read & read the skin of a cow,

The novels of the scriptures. To chew & pass
On the board, inexplicable forgetfulness,
Finishing hours. It is a hell for a house,
No news hangs on the air, to accommodate it,
The mistakes of the world, the old men.

There was a place, not the map of human beings.
In the belly of an elephant, let's measure the faults.
That wanted to be housed, in the father's house,
No home. We looked at the time,
It has taken us years back.

Again, in the blue murder, halitosis in our lives.
The entrance has wings, the gobemouche as
A watchdog opens red & sad.
The ground told us thoughtful stories & red dying
Flowers stole a look at us. It was another home,

Full of why & how.

Your Bucket Is Full

A billion buckets are full of downs.
We're extremely empty of
What the mars needs
To attain the position of Neptune.

Beginning cannot meet triangles
& Circles cannot link up to her taste & choice.
We are working labouriously to catch up the lost
But he says no……not at all.

No criticism, more illnesses than before.
There is need to fish when
There is no fish for your health.
They see it & brush their hairs once.

They don't see anything wrong
But they see many things
Wrong about themselves.
We don't see any reverence.
Moving mountains to desert to mud.

We are missing what the *Holy Order*
Refuses to tell on *Holy Thursday.*
What the lips are created for,
White be, black be

Article Of Food

Eye, open the rest of the eyes,
Sense has been bribed under the Sunday light
You, scan their stems of the dark forest,
Indeed, the season is dead.
Funeral overflows the gutters.
The horns of newly saloon cars went into a ditch.
We comb everywhere necessary to do my homework
Before fowls start to say good night to their loved
One. The drum of the footsteps in the communities
Resounded in the bellies of the concerned citizens.
There is nothing new to feel now, if we
Wanted to enjoy the everlasting life. The words of
A half man have shuttered down dreams of energetic
Muscles. Because his words are larger than him
And his faculty is as useless as himself. The dogs
At the posts would not stop hooting at him because
He has smuggled their lives out the cages. He has
Long hands that break prison yards. The pandemic
Of the century. St. Peter's Mini Basilica cannot
Stomach his wrongs. The overflows of the illnesses
Are on the blood list of the pain. Good things have gone
Missing but are found in the wrong hands.

Walking Alone In The Forest

We're already there,
There is much to say to your tasks.
The talk in the rallies.
A bad time around the neck.

Time cries for a bailout. Dust flies.
Desert lives in our bellies.
Nose travels far beyond the world
But Catarrh catches it live.

Touch the problems chopping us bitterly,
The problems will not spare any oxygen.
Your goal over the mountains,
There are commandments,

Sweet vows, many views will answer
Questions & explain difficult matters.
Ideas walk into the right angles.
Everywhere sounds like the awaited

Prince is about to be born in the home,
Which is full of women who are not entitled
To the crown. Another commandment is painted
Somewhere, taken away the happiness from

Those who worked hard for because of
The earthly law, they are being denied their rights.
The good friends of wisdom have inhaled poison.
That has let lamb & goats play
Their dangerous games.

It flows from cat to dogs but the heavenly gate
Opens up to us. All the answers have thrown
The questions away. We used to
Walk on the golden grasses
& they were steady, reliable & I never fell.

Little problems have bred thousands.
No touch, feelings are there but cannot function.
Cannot depict at the sight of the famished ones.
At first, I could smile but now I cannot smile.

I cannot laugh at all. All the little particles that
Make an atom eroded by the trying weapons.

Watching The Time

Load of loads, heavier than
All the six continents sitting
In the ice, even as heavy as an egg

Reserved for the unborn child for the
Day of his appearance.
There are so many illnesses

Eating innocent folks
They deliberately don't want to touch them.
What has water done to you?

How many times do we have to complain that
We are hungry & that our land needs to be fed now?
You've seen it & you want us to expose you.

Living organs are hungry severely.
They know the living words to provide.
They know the living actions to take
Without fear, favour

But....

The tower in the snow & yachting
On the stream during Tornado when many
Cannot understand natural phenomena. Still

Fresh and succulent in the winter. It looks
Easy, even, at the sight of snakes. The ground
Requires chemistry to charge physics. It is

In the afternoon & biology doesn't comprehend
Why she can't read medicine. Pros & cons can't
be cured with the same medication.

The tools are angry
Because they're hungry.
Why silence?

Why is the land hungry of saints?
It's our father's land. Let fire burn them now.

Not Knowing

The throats are thirsty of hard voices.
Oceans can't kill the deliberate devil.
Weaponised words are still running
Away for life,

Unable to reforest the empty heads.
The substances that have kept
Silence on the fertiliser
Refuse to let the living River Dormi overflow.

There are names that are living-dead.
Don't have places in the sky. It
Needs a physiotherapist to polish
The tongues of her clients before

The oral examination. The preparation
Is going on seriously but there is
No symptom on the lives of
The candidates. Nothing is scripted

Under achievement. Records show
That no amounts of chances will be
Given them & that they will surprise
Their loved ones. The paints on them

Have not visited a washing base.
The temperature is speedily rising.
The metrologists are predicting the next
Lifestyles of new products.

Back Entrance of The Royal

Message on them. The awaited
Message arrived at the time,
When the part of the town got
Missing on the world map,
When hope was nowhere to be
Located in Holy Eucharist,
When the sky was looking for
The elegant cloth to burn in shame
Before his master resumes
On the next undefined day,
When singles were thoroughly
Searching for the perfect fruits
On matchmakers to search into
Their souls, when fire was set under
Bear yet to be discovered
Because of its richness in natural
Resources. It needed to be extin-
Guished as soon as possible,
When draught was reigning as
The king of heartless kings
& that life became lifeless,
When people sneaked their dirty
Hands into accounts that did not
Belong to them, when so-called
Men of God scammed the gullible,
When the land married to
Sodom & Gomorrah. Indecisive
Answers in shame, stream into

Human blood & along white,
The coast of remembrance,
The Apostles Creed, belief in
What we don't know. Where
Were the answers
We chased after? The solutions
Were dancing around the start.
We are still the pathfinders.
Only JM can be our answer, cure.

Within The Ring

We have been trained to iron out/
Not staring into a despair &
We know how to put/the heads
On the dais. Feelings are hurt

When drums/are still sleeping.
We thunder like/the roar
Of a full man/on the half
Stool who is/still shorter

Than/a cooking pot.
The null sound is/bringing simulacrum.
The stertorous sound echoing/in the wine.
Nothing good from/souk.

The height of/the strappado
Flogging/us. The heat cooks
Us & changes/the plans
To be executed/We have noticed

That the consequence/would be
Driving on/the same lane. The
Interpreters could interpret/the
Sound & conjure/life & death.

There would be/no need to call
On the seers to guide/us on
The journey we are/almost
At the tail. we do not know/how

To dance/to this rhythm. We weren't
Not born to be present idiot
Like/religion leaders,
Rather emulate/the footsteps of the great
Poets/The arts on the finger.

Tips would be/tenebrous to be born
On the paper/The forsaken walls
Would be glad to sell/the sorrowful
Mystery at the close/of the production.

Independence In the Gutter

How long will some minds sleep in
The mephitis when the huge floods
Are driving us into deep malediction?

We've allowed wrong faces to
Coruscate under our watch. Things
Are reversing rapidly, which feelings

Can't belly them anymore. Minds
Still fight against his lips bitterly.
If we cough, they say *we're littering*

Rubbish on the holy ground. If we
Peel a finger of banana they say
We're making cacophony

& security should arrest us. In winter,
An air conditioner is on summer
When the room heater is 247 Celsius.

It seems we're in the borrowed land
& we can only respire from our annal
Regions. The paint outside has traded

The folks at unbelievably cheap prices.
We're dancing to the
Imbroglio we vowed

Not to hear her hubris in
The flight of spotless
Birds. We're still slaves

To a homunculus.
The previous voices are
Sleeping with the dead &

Our hands can't reach
The delectation of the flat.
Still in the land of captivity

& malevolence.

Talking Leaves

We did not want to climb a withered tree
Because years have confirmed how
His performance would be. His pens have
A balderdash to tell papers-upright in the face.

Not the one of nebuchadnezzar at this
Civilised period. Because the leaves don't know life.
Forest in agony. Gardens have nothing
To deliver to lawns. Span of branches.

Upon our acuity, there could be an atheism in
A theism like studying weaponised stuffs that
Strike the world. The stems have already told us
The turpitude of the roots roaming for survival.

A place has been hanged on the lifeless ghyll
For him. Pique & saints, they're aware.
Lucifer mocks the holy bible plus the pilgrimage
To Mecca. The perfidy in a time of need.

The complexions of nympholepsy. The
Brownness of the mistakes is waving the white
Clothes. The sounds of the talking sycophants.
Feelings of the susurration have changed his

Response. The answers to the questions fail
The season we are struggling inside.

Germs Spreading

The oil on the face has dried up completely.
The juicy smile that makes the aged to

Refuse to grow old, has been taken away
From their mouths. It has vanished into a

Malicious abode. The true game of integrity
Has crippled out. He has broken the promise.

You can feel that conscience.
The awareness to tension; deliberate motions

Padlock the conscience—truly true.
Thought of thoughts floating from Tornado.

The deadly germs have cultivated in the soil.
I hardly hear the microphone

Transporting the hungry food to the sick.
The young ones have become depreciated

In appearance. Integrity & knowledge has
Been battered because the tongue tasted

Disappointments, it tasted like failure. So
The ingredients would cook the soup,

Algae-to-fungi. *You can talk loudly.*
You can talk; look into a mirror

Look into the mirror at the heart of…….
Your conscience: you have several faces.

Your nose, two & half noses
Your eyes; countless but under watch,

Folded arms on the head.

Who're You?

We see you on another planet.
Creation of quotations, scan them closely
In the x-ray like him like them,
We don't know you in this world.
Ashes will bear with us.
We challenge you.

You are running from yours,
It remains yours——--with you.
We can't tolerate you on the continent.
Who sent you into this world of ours?
See things as they are &
We can describe them. It's hard to

Wear them. We have different
Meanings — no head — no tail.
Understanding flows through thought.
I buy some & leave the rest for the climate
To decide the state of interest. How it
Looks like & how I feel at once.

Who's who? The register—names.
We salute them.
What about him?
No words can feed the *USB.*
Things are changed after the arrival
Of ugliness. Invention laughs at the
Maintenance. Wings grow longer &

Bigger than the veracity. There could be a
Thought like elephants walking on the sea.
They believe in themselves &
Hurt the commandments.
They create *Saturn* —
live on earth with fresh air.
We look at him in the realm,
We read them the activities in the cooking pot.

It is uneasy to climb the slippery mountain & he
Witnesses how desert is
Forcing onto the world market.
We listen to voices, nightmares
Stream through paradise.
Destinies alter. We don't have the world.
We don't know him, says the earth.

Tears Of Wounds

At 2 am we greet dawn through the window.
Glasses do not tell us the future
Of the farming land. Neither the gossips of
Fowls on the mahogany trees

Envisage the mathematics papers of the final
Year students. The scorching sun cannot
Read the temperature of the *tears of wounds*
Flogging us with a broad of smile

On his face. Heads travel far for diagnosis but
Still the throne of snakes laughs at them.
Feelings collude temptations before the
Holy tabernacle & we share our pains with

The martyrs of the land. As I turned right
Counting the welkin who are inviting us, we
Feel the poet blue embracing us with an
Everlasting touch.

Once Upon a Time

We see things around us.
But we do not see him
As for nature.
Come.......

We read a book &
We see him as a history
Who has been a place
In the satanic kingdom.

He dodges a traffic light
& edges along the
Pavement. He comes
& lives among us.

Signs & wonders
Never dodge us. The
Storms open its doors
At half day & false

Products sneak out.
Even though
Sweet words are hating
The walls, no baby

Face is seen preach-
Ing the good news. He's
Evil because he comes
From a world with wide gates.

Sick Texture

Something is saying nothing —
About mouths,
Extremely busy, fully hollow.
There is something somewhere—
Missing strength - at the front - of a mirror.
What is behind time? What is behind life?

We've to walk along/every day/
Red sea–to–Pacific–to–ocean–to–Jupiter.
The beginning of the trek/will be answered,
When the navigator – alone – knows the way.
Before the pregnancy of this time.
The angels have/already announced

Its preparation on the day of conflict
& there is no better - time than brown - time, he says.
We follow the artificial move, fully - deserted.
More texture, still naked; blind - to - deaf - online.
Tell us that you are neither blind nor deaf
& that no number of waves will wake you up

From your slumber.
Time comes unaware like him,
Operating on the broad day.
No, we never thought that
There are as plenty as lost voices.
Shocks like showers that fill river.

Flows beyond conundrum, makes
Its way into the ocean. It's the time.
We must mould hearts before mirror,
For the journey,
For the assignment ahead. Looking into
The forest, the breathing leaves have

Commenced dying like they have been
Affected by him. Lives are being
Gambled in at affordable prices.
They're no more tales to kill sadness.
The somersault of features; breeding a
Ugly nonsense. The drama of praising the night

During the heavy down will not change the
Present hardship slaughtering us.

Clock Runs Out Now

As we stole a glance inside the Cathedral's church,
Culture wore another culture. Water, fire see each
Other enemies of forward ever. originality has tied
Knot to artificiality, the United States of America
Cannot blame China. *Clock runs out now, forward,*
Angrily, sorrowfully dead. We run rapidly, backwards.

Images' heads down into the mud.
Moistures have clouded the sight of the glamour,
Completely. We see the world, unfair, rude. The tune
Of murmuring reminds the rips in us, savings accounts.
We don't think about yesterday rather than the muscles
That shine at the workplace. We've reached the tail of

The sea. With the aid of the telescope, we could not
Wander in the moon when her siblings can't stop
Darkness but allow tornado to reap fruits he did not
Labour for.

With An Effective Filter

Time stands behind, *Venus.*
Although there is a toothless space,
No yellow on the platform.
She reverses her steps, innumerably.

We have covered every
Walk of lives living ⅓ of it for action.
A lot of participants in the business
Leaving upper parts of the stratosphere, naked.

Although it is extremely difficult
To knife into the heads. Their tongues
Are hungry of speculation because they're lazy.
A pool of river *Volta* courses down our checks.

We cannot trust teeth anymore because it's
Allowing the throat to swallow illegal products.
Taste at the wrong kitchen; the ingredients
Sicken no life in image, in the heads.

Plots seedlings sprouting speedily.
In other words, many clothes are worn
In the daylight. Churches on the floating river.
Silence wears her white garment,

& again & again in chain of worries
The questions knock down all the inter-
Changes. Sail down the earth many
Times. The answers pity the sweats

Of the tireless muscles whose aims
To climb the mountain Everest
& weave their flags in the woods,
Build houses on the rivers & eat on the

Altars. Create new kingdoms that will
Sweep away the layers of dust, now.

Not In Our Lives

We've come to a junction,
Three eyes, two & half noses.
What are we seeing now in the world of dispute?
We look for another ground in the circle.

We could jog around river Niger
Climb Ash Wednesday, descend safely
Days are no longer interested in
Weeks because weeks could not give

Good account for months. Hours are
Paralysed for not understanding spice.
We plunge into mining holes.
The level of projects slumps us into public

Toilets. We wade through to the end
Of it. There is no time to waffle. A
Snatch of dialogue injects ideas into
Implementation. The odour in the speech

Is more acidic than before. Birds
Disappear into a so- called heaven.
Because they deliver perfect services on
Earth for that matter they deserve

The highest award, we thought.
Today, NPP leaders are like vultures feeding
On carcasses & sheep without faculties.
Doors behind are narrow; perfect; sad, hard.

The path is missing likewise promises
Are dancing in the land of the dead.

About To Conclude

We don't want to remember anything out there
The seasons, still with us; why?
The meaning will explain many breaking marriages,
Then we've to count the stars in our pockets.

But we know how many seeds in pawpaw
When the war of life begins to undress.
Already at the workplace warming up like salt
Doesn't want to recognise the existence of sugar.

Newspapers will not tell us every birth, every death
But tongue has failed her duties, negatively, completely.
The tongue lays dead. They've to brush their tongues well.
Some countries are found pulling out of their shields

& we could not buy their images as rainbow colours
Challenge new invented colours wanted to snatch
Their glories. Prediction, we mock it.
I listen to voices flying along the rockets.

Many times, in the day, discussions settle
Consequences on the sinking boats with
Imitated navigators. With the wrath of the waves
The arms touch the wrath of the shark.

The legs could not win the yachting.
The Pacific Ocean has decided to announce
To the winner because iron metals see themselves
As stones in the debate. We see the eyes of

The muscles, no hope in the Pacific Ocean.
Spirits thought she could empower
The rivers around her.
The results change. We studied
The atmosphere closely,
Notions cloth with muddy clothes,
Slumber, full of pain.

Their pots, full of algae, ailment for sure.
Before the fresh herbs, there was no
Existence of old herbs.
We haven't seen this type
Of Rwanda yet in Africa.
Originality in the pipeline.
Leg have travelled far
Legs have travelled far.
Half still on the hanging valley.
Many places have become blind.
The head on the waiting list,
Falling apart with a deliberate walk.
Silence sits in the palanquin.

Somersaulting On the Way

We compare ourselves to morning.
In the garden of Eden,
Let's close our eyes now.
Start now.

Mention the items.
We've to know how to count rice.
Salt, sugar, & sand will calculate themselves.
We know

The road well, not the many
Streets we stand on.
The dance on the toes to the floras in the vessel.
Fresh vegetables

In the backyards joy mocks us.
Beauty & handsomeness quickly
Vanishes from marketplaces with
Their strength & knowledge.

Behind us carries booties,
Ahead triplets walk on nine lanes.
We looked for a blue land, but we found
The joint

Globe.
We were born in the light, grew up in the dark.
We are being published in the deceptive
Sphere.

We fly with them because of the failure &
Disappointment chewing the rest of the bones
On the table. As we sleep on our minds & souls,
He has the match.

Blast

Commotion. Intention all over the rivers.
Lakes spreads his might, a stretch of arms
To the waist of the mt. Everest.
The respiration of

The Blue Nile could not catch the neck
Of the two metres in the Olympics sports.
The length of Lake Victoria has become

The pride of Savannas in the continent,
The jewellery shops hang around their wrists.
The millions of factories in its pain. We want

To go & search for life after. Labour in battle.
We follow the gospel explaining the next
Talents but clouds block the chances that
Open their mouths

To swallow us. Friends & myself out in question
But the short devil pollutes environment
& blessings could not baptise us. He needs

Baptism in the river Ganges so that Dubai &
Germany will appear in his dream.
Where are we now?
Where are we going now?

Not Words but Missiles To

We trip around to embrace what
The world has scrupulousness. Beyond
Worries & measure, we do not

Accept the gifts in the dream.
Neither do we eat meat in the nightmare.
Deadly illnesses knock doors.

Mysterious problems await
No real faces; another feature at work.
To say it, time does not wait for

Reservation, but revelation goes before items.
Bring them out; they're trailing off.
To feel them, already - feeling - the heat.

Becomes agitated. We know where
We're trekking to, so we follow the echo,
Communicating with angry paths.

Unknown place. Thunderstorms die off.
Challenge silent voices.
We don't buy the paths at all.
Words fuel the division of lives.
Threat plus death.

The shrouds of wickedness,
Wind of Fire, weakness of strength,
Days of incompleteness, troubles on
Enigma on faces, cry in tunes, all bend down.

Our Land Apart Completely

A sharp knife. Inexplicable
Breath in the wrong soil.
His soil is inedible. Not the handmade—of Him.
The first born; not one of the ten.

They have two siblings & their parents are about
To give birth to the tenth born. We aren't ready
To welcome him. with a smelling smile.
A shabby heart onto the throne. This is because

He is interested in retrogression, the paradise
Looks worried. Ruin the paradise, he thunders.
Leave nothing to smile at, they say. They know
Us very well that if we speak, we spark heads

Will knock one another & comb for the real
Apparatus to work with. We're the blood at the
Marketplace that gives strength to the collapsed
Bridge. We're the white cloth in the night. We

Shine; we've to shine like our performance,
Shining among the stars in the casino on the
New planet to be discovered. because of him
If we jump on land in mud. Threat already there.

Taste has been chopped off. Choice struggles
In the dustbin to cross the lagoon, waiting to
Show us heads on the sea.

One Plus One Is Minus

If this picture could be a statue.
It is a triangle in the shape of a
Formless circle. We caress it.
It has no ears.

Go down & eat the meal sets on the table.
The appetite in the mouth dies off.
The scream in the breath does not hold
The matter burning the skins that needs

Gallons of water to grow young & fuel
To move the heart. We feel the emptiness of
The statue. But after his medical check-up,
There is a result that he does not have heart for.

He doesn't read the behaviour of souls that
Visits another village. So, one plus one
Is minus. We see it sharply reserving
itself into a ditch. A terrible shock.

Worthless Goods

If the river we always see after work,
Cools down the hell which has come
To stay, not like his, which generates
The hot temperature,
Then the odd brownness

Clothes on attractive body which
Is new designing false medicine for
Our conditions, we need to exercise
Pink patience, full of green, succulent

Heaven. The name, John sounds healing,
An indescribable nature,
The sunshine can't wobble
In the north pole in the afternoon. Soil
In the daylight is weak, not even in

The daylight of a resurrected morning.
We gaze into one direction & we must
Wait for the birth of a new season.

Inside The Glass

We stab into the glass of many features,
On the battlefield of the war of wars.
What is going on now?
The puff in the left angle now,
There are answers written on his forehead.
Many marks identify them.

The oxygen deflates black smoke over,
Shadowing the news of the day.
Shoulder to shoulder; we have crossed
The red river. The sweat of lakes
Never brim the empty barrels.
The loads are too heavy. At the bottom,

It is dim. Much work must be done
To polish the newly bought shoes.
No help has come out from the belly of an elephant.
No answer has served the consecrated altar.
We haven't begun the journey but a careless whisper
In the air revealing things into his heartless home.

Alarm

Nowadays, we can't dress gorgeously
& appeared in the form of a peacock.
Because we cannot arrest the weather.
Today can't be in a race with yesterday.

The combinations of these periods
At the throats of each other. They find
It's difficult to sail in the same boat.
The household of a fresh globe tries to

Invite assorted dialects in the house,
Like thousand legs that are able
To saunter on the mud to her destination,
Easily in those days. Today has donned

Her wicked dresses & her only colour is
Cry & failure. The enemy of the innocent.
The knowing does not know the know
In the system. We could not wait for

The meaning. Encyclopaedia is not ready
To lecture now. It is
Too much to swallow heaven & hell,
No room to share with.

They're too huge for Sahara.
Our studies of visual art will
Definitely explain the
Meaning of Satan & devil like him.

Their surface is like them. Seas
have grown wings. His name
Is put in the saver for a morning dictation.
We can't under-estimate the billions

Of the deceased in our eyes.
We cast our sights in a fresh
Direction & the song goes

No more to them
More to say about them
More to explain about them
More to clear them away

Hungry Sea

It has been/a while.
We notice that time.
It isn't/happy with days
Likewise, nose wants

To kick/out eyes from
The kingdom. Inside
The glass, we read
An unknown/too inquisitive.

We have never spoken/about
Anything/in the blue-black box
Yet. We know/how It looks like
In the bank account. The contents

Dribble/among the sanities of
Believers. Our throats are/thirsty
Of/spotlessness. The very good
Friends of entertainers/dead.

Chests are ready/to tell arms
That they're ever/prepared to strangle
The neck of the egoist.
Because the piles of untruths/cannot

Be saved/on an Apple laptop,
The Apple still wants/to protect her
Images & pride. All white shirts.
Under the light,
Cream colour/with the tongue of a serpent,

The faces of chimpanzee's families,
Their tongues, see no eviller.

Within The Town

Over the streets, spread from
Imaginable to immeasurable definition.

The cottage, the new cottage on the float,
Full of untold narrations,

Sink beneath honesty & light.
Day & night has retired

To their various hometowns.
The thick dust has snatched

The principal contracts from water
& darkness. *We've become*

Joblessness & the pillar care less
About the intensive erosion

In the community. Early in the morning
Desperate wickedness will always

Work & sleep. He has no dream rather
Thinks about wreck & affliction

& his unkempt families whose hands
Are immeasurable. They love to punish

Spotlessness. The temperature
Now signals us

To look for elsewhere. We can define
The meaning of the ruin sitting

On the golden throne whilst crops
& water look wretched.

Orchard

Periods are very essential,
Our feast days tell us whenever
The hairs on the heads are speedily

Changing their features. The ages
Are still roaming among the youths.
We know but not everyone around

The clock has noticed *Naada*. We love
Light behind the wall, to be cheerful
To perceive the inward activities

Speculating around unhappy destinations,
Dumping individual spirits, closing
Doors to rainbow-colour- mirror. Homes

Plug into problems. The pollution, ugly like him.
The discussions of the birds in the flights
Interrogate the scattering of miles

Ahead & the lack of drugs for
The sick. Why the cottage is unfair
To herself? The two-faced dwarf

Should answer us.

Sharp Curve

The watch of the global village at
The Alexanderplatz in Berlin.
Gossip helps us to enumerate the
Days we have spent in the alien

Vicinity, the garden we farm
Before setting off the journey,
Post on our different exhibitions.
That was correct said

The itching lips. Things don't
Appear perfectly in the mirror
He promised, treacherous.
We accept the birth of truth on the

Fields. Things have become
Older than before & we fear
That malicious elephants will
Continue to jog on the precious

Voices. Honey & gold in the dirty
Hands, comfortability banishes.
The first father of the globe owes us
Truthful explanations, clarification.

Owls & cats refuse to say hello to the
Crucifixion. The assignment of the century.
The ravenousness of a persistent
Conflict of interest. The combat for the sanitation.

The smile doesn't catch a glimpse
Of summer in Africa. The talking drum of the day.
The smile of smiles preaches hard to mouth,
A message killing us.

New Turn

Time will never finish narrating
Her stories in the funeral grounds.
Audience haven't stopped
Asking for more papers in the examination hall.

Listen to countable true facts,
Pictures bigger than your brain,
Imagination on the eyes, crawling to hell.
Notice what cannot degree with the meaning.

We can't trade what we buy from behind us.
We buy tasteless choice, a honest lesson
To pave the way to durability.
That's the beginning of the journey.

The meteorologists predicted 32 degrees Celsius
Which all of us put up summer dresses,
Gallivanting from enquiry to allusion of the city.
The disrespect of the climate teases our wishes.

There is a heavy downpour of snow plant
In the land that brings us an immaculate regret
To the land of taste. The feel of bitter language.
Choose one of the many flooded around.

Audience flock in numbers to hear their
Heart-breaking-funny narration that tell them
That old stone they rejected was their live smile.

Penetration

We thought the smiling-thought
Would not articulate
Solomon into the ears
Of the withered weather.

Joints on the wall can't
Challenge the foundation builders.
The harvests of the present life
So, we need to do surgery

On the wrongs. Nature speaks
The facts on his birthday.
The cloth on us, don't question nature.
The results are our answers.

Tell the spectators what they
Don't want to know.
More research,
More pain in the integrity.

We're not assuaged with
What the years are
Telling the jubilee.
They're not content with being on
The welkin, the motionlessness in trials.

Dissatisfied with the virid tor
In the forbidden woods.
The susurration hasn't attained
The goals in the race.
Is it bribed several times?
Let's walk in the fire.

The taste of our shortcomings.
The miles to fetch what we
Could not describe.
Other skins were & are still chasing
The living life of action.

With what the fresh air tells them.
Look into their faces,
The functions of a turpitude.
The canoe brings fishes which are
Allergic, we asked for them,
Tastelessness at the banquet.
To our health because we are
Notoriously stubborn,
Temporal sweats, little products.
We eat them, &
We're dancing to the music.

Cafe Time

In the ambush smells of him,
With also Lucifer on the throne.
The gaze travels far in the veins.
Constantly, closely & continuously.
The news of the day. The images of a
Half-yellow night. The friends of the
Malicious hours. The ugliness of
Fertility. The hands of stone-
Heartedness. The efforts cannot answer
The investigators now. The jubilee
House has an answer to the IMF.
Let's see. We see the ailment of fakeness
At the back of a palm. The great
Conversations have shown their
Underwear. Transparency weeps.
We're not glad about that.
The purpose is the heart
To come out. The fourteen February
Wants to be one. Flowers & roses
Have missed their targets.
The channels to the
Blueprints of cries & affliction.

Oversight Calculation

Before the prediction on the mountains
We've descended at the foot. We count

The left stars around the sphere.
The environment has already sent the

Awaited telegrams to the respective
Subscribers. The whispers of the snakes

Told us to cut nonsense & dismantled hearts.
The talks of flying birds tolled birthday songs,

That remind us how old are we & our
Achievements. The questions we prepare for

Five years plus months are eroded away
By a wicked shower. But the hidden answers,

Not ready for the baseness.
At the long last the truthfulness

Has come on the top of the water.

Reigning Silence

We set on a lioned journey &
A cloth of moisture
Ceases the arms. Our views,
Shroud - in - blanket.

We don't purchase
The siblings of nature.
Even now a thunderstorm
Cannot speak in his own land.

Do not understand this cantata.
We do not hear good things that
Are happening under the grass. If we
Have known we would have

Built mountains on the
Pyramid but we listen to the earth.
The materialistic hearsay; Show us.
It will not assist ears to have his siesta

In the house of vultures.
We trust him but nature has
Taught the real lesson.
Voices bury prematurely.
We prefer to listen to children's songs
In the kindergarten to lies of the president

Whose lies are more than
The hairs on his head.
Since he mounted the throne children
Have been cursing their destinies.

We can now feel bitterness &
Thorns flooding homes.
Pains reign over the sea, dry lands
& Sahara battle for purity.

Fingers Across

Fingers across toes in
The foreign pockets. Writs
Resting on the bridge. Across
The cross starts the mystery
Of arms weave through legs.
Billow crosses over the sun.

We touch the climate &
Everywhere is darkened.
The touch of the barrel,
Their pot is brimmed
Staring at us from
The horizontal kneels

Of his eyes. Our spirits
Stab through the cement
Walls of Nsawam prison
& we could only sell
The items on sale, quickly.
We could not fish out everything

On their fingertips.
All the truths are indefinite break
Under the serpent carpet,
The true friend of darkness
& destruction. We saw the doors
Of worries patrolling on the beach

Road. We waited for the last call &
We took to our heels, reading
The stem there. They involve
The storms of yesterday plus
The practices of today's illustrations.

Mr. & Mrs Rainbow

Yes, time to visit,
We've now come home.
We could not respond to
Their welcome, new seasons.
The greetings are floating to
Mr. & Mrs Rainbow

What is occurring in the fruitful
Land. Not yet touched. Some
New foodstuffs cannot explain
Themselves to the customers who
Are ready to enjoy new creations.
We need to explore. It is an inventory.

A scanner is needed. Mr. Filter is
At the workplace doing research
On the publications of x-ray
Machines. As we scanned the rainbow
In the mirror, we jumped into a poem, deep,
& pursued courses in poems. There're the keys.

Securities

The plant of glimpse of hope
& assurance have been
Kicked out from their legitimate

Houses because *Naada's* lips travel
Far beyond *his* territories.
We have noticed that outside amazon

Forests cry for a bailout.
Black soils complain to us severally.
Fear has been imported into the land.

Boldness has been bribed many times,
Wounded. The friend of sheep on the river.
Some days are numbered on

The lives of some folks. Herbs to cure
The sick wandering in the wrong wilderness,
Are impatiently on guard. Hearts

Cannot peacefully enjoy their sweet
Homes. Lions & tigers have illegally
Overthrown peace & a good

Standard of living. Day & night have
Become our enemies. He took the lives
He never created them. We hope the

Morning star has engineered to don
His baptismal clothes.

Black Sky Has Become Homeless

Every day knows what he's going to deliver
But he doesn't know himself, said his soul.
If every week knows himself then let's leave
Or let's not jump into the sky for answers

Rather let every month revisit history.
Let those have ears do not travel far,
For eyes have already answered them.
We receive letters from the earth,

Containing complaints.
The languages in the letters are
To be read to those
Who don't have ears to save information,

For we're not ready
To be a spokesperson for an
Empty-headed leaders *like him*.
Reading, understanding is for those

Who ready to deliver with the assistance
Of the shining sun. Not the children of
Nebuchadnezzar, we see today, who cannot
Stop stealing what they didn't sow. The

Same hands that cause crime, the same
Hands pray & receive the body of Christ.
Sayings & idioms always predict games high,
Pieces of information & advice look at them,

Trying to score goals that grab the attention
Of the rivals. Upon the unbearable propaganda
Flying here & there, we don't notice any
Actualisation on their floating minds. But

They are rather smart at cooking blatant lies.
The black air is ill, worried. The conceive of
These acts cannot fish edible ideas.
Things up in the ceiling & down in the gutter.

The rising is about to rise.

Ailment's Visit

Heads, tails cannot sail on the same boat.
We paddle mightily but the boat directs us into
A ditch. We feel emptiness in the sphere at the
Corner. There is no fuel to transport the hell out

Of the destination now, but the dream is to
Communicate now. Two shoulders dribble
Between legs on the field.
Meet at the table & there will be food to smile at you.

Eyes are soaked with brimmed oceans.
Black clothes dance around the stubborn festival.
Nadaa has dislocated our lives. If we're bathing
In enjoyment, arms don't reach the point.

Legs have numberless responsibilities to carry
At the marketplace. It has been years
We have slumped into a chair & read
Rich articles that are ready to kill a barrel desire.

This is because the golden light has vanished into
An unknown place. The system is dead. Presently
There are neither fertiliser to wake up the death nor
vehement prayers to divide the river Bosomtwe.

Trust, resurrection, look back. Both the old &
The young have combed within life & lifelessness for
The departed glory. The sorrowful sun has illegally
Taken the presidency. *He dives in the rich water*

& sinks with the land. We promised them reversible
Curses, taking us into lamentation & dropping
Gallons of acid in our mouths. The promise,
That, we will never lack heaven but now

We're swimming in the pool of disappointment.
We're Now married to backwardness & suffering.

Breaking News

To live like the gruesome elephant in the Jubilee
House which always comes out in the night,
To salute the lobbies & conflict & accelerates
At the nose of Judas. The smell, the allergic

Pen of harmony. Is it true? We shall reflect on how
Shark helps him to devour the meats reserve
For millions plus billion lives. We promised pyramid
Before the sacrament of baptism, that there are

Numberless promises. Beautiful ones, of course
Like knowing the features, black & white standing,
Apart from the seven diamonds that everyone
Wish to see, challenging the layers of the

Sacrifices at the daytime. We wished tribalism
Would tell the truth. What a pain that destroys
Harmony. Ashes cannot stop us from the good work
Of a good shepherd. The chronic wound is shaking

The souls up with that reason, *postures.* Let's gaze
Into each other's eyes & tears will never drip
From the eyes of angels.

Spiderman

All the news saunters on the surface
Of a holy lake. Neither with legs
Nor with feathers fly into the haze.
Up there are ears fighting for seats
To hear the gossip in the wind.
Even under the sea the fishes &
The sharks tune their radios on.
Spirits question ears whether they
Are safe in their own horizons. Fishes
Could not prepare the information
& sell it at costly prices. The news
Stabs twice at the back without a second
Thought. We can't do it because it is an
Inexplicable pain, bitter than reality.
But the rising sun will be proud of the muscles.

Weaving Through the Wilderness

This summer, the sugar creates
Nothing for the world to see.
Meanwhile desires track
Far & near to grab whatever
On their list. Innocent likeness
Is washed away. A new time is
Created for those who want to
Jump & somersault in the air.
As the true book stayed away from
The truth in time of need,
Stay away from duplicity.
We can no longer ask the sieve to overwork.
Admiration is locked
Down in the grave. We can't see
In the daylight because the sunglasses
Shield the attack of the enemies.
Devil & holiness are in the same boat
Feasting on the same plate.

Good Friday in Dilemma

i

There are so many dates in our lives.
On the calendar
We are different from wine & Fanta.
Ask your destiny
Laughter & sadness will narrate
Uniquely different stories.
So, let's hear

ii

Very essential to ash
We owe hello to breath & say *hi* to strength.
Well to ancestors who drive
In the same vehicle with us.
We can't forget the day we
Married our enemies on *Good Friday.*
The talk on *Good Friday*

iii

Reminds us of our baptismal joy.
The conversation on the floor
Does not match with the poems read to
Us on the graceful day, the institution
Ordains elements. There are also
Uncountable, unattractive clothes
In the wall drop, which we love to wear
On *Good Friday.* They don't

iv

Have any ideas to manage even
A stall but kissing an angel
At his rips. Now we are living with the
Hell in the fabricated paradise, we die
For them when they go to market &
Their asses are wide open.
We feel malevolence. The message is
That he wants to eliminate us.

v

His teachings blackmail the greedy.
His explanations sweeten
The banquet on the *holy Thursday.*
The treasure in the doctrine.
We need it badly. Whenever we wear
It we fly to a lonely place &
Invite trust & control to sing their
Victory songs so that we can

vi

Be born again. The scanner speaks
To us & even takes us
To the riverside to watch a spotless
Play of *Good Friday in dilemma*.

Funeral Services

We can't hold ourselves because
The red & the white cells
Have reduced their sizes.
We don't see the *Solomon of yesterday.*

They're smiling with the funeral
Service, not the moonlit.
Cement can no longer hold a
Sign bond with water now.

Drivers on the streets
Have diverted their channels
But our new saloon cars won't
Float on the same lane with them.

The children of elephants continue
To smuggle out lives through slim
Windows to the thespian. *Nadaa*
Is interested to turn our gain

Into pain & cloth our joy with stygian
Uniforms. The persistent
Tolling of voices above the earth,
The lungs cannot control throats

At work. The soak of voices.
The syrinx of the souls. The dance of
Souls. The melodies run businesses
Outside of homes. Life is precious

To the land of vision. We can't buy
It twice and it does not hold an egg.
There is no pure transparency. The pool
Cannot get dry when we say *alla Prossima.*

Over The Bank

We fear to welcome a new day
Which we want to experiment with.
Over the bank, on our lives.

As rich as the green grasses were,
They cannot conjure a new ideology
In summer, still today.

Now, it has become a satanic day.
Teeth of yesterday have lost his title
To a culture of silence.

Blunter than gossiped lips. Still in his shield.
No machine guns to resurrect intelligence.
Intelligence is under a spell when

He cannot excavate mountains,
Iron contoured lines, they're coiling rapidly.
The state of duplicity is hot cake.

There should be there
When there's not there to fight
The withered weather

The daylight has been consumed up
Because a day cannot shake hands
With a night likewise chiming &

Tolling cannot share *a Holy Communion*.
Eyes are still swimming in the dirty
Rivers. Truths are bleeding sorrow.

Agony & fear is sorrow's friend, here.
Souls here & beyond there.
We need independence

From an unseen object. Oppression,
Uncultured like *him*. Under the pretext
Of emptiness, no sanitation,

No voice on a shoulder.
Problems are stronger than solutions.
Because of that voices have passed on.

Still, freedom & Justice laments, Hearts.
Martyrs can no longer witness dictatorship.
Even civilisation is laughing at us.

A primitive act & barbarism in the same shoes
Of dirtiness & shamelessness. Why?

Gifts

Seeing the handwork in the labourers,
The day has spoken itself.
Counting the days, counting yourself,
Ask yourself, how're you?

We have now gotten to the stage
Where we hate our existence.
Much ado about nothing. Behind us,
Nothing has been growing on

The fruitful field. These questions on the
Tree of wisdom but our knowledge distances
Itself. We conjure what we need from
Nowhere, strolling among visions.

Falling, church & mosque
Celebrate their feasts. We race in the sand
But In the middle, deeper than the problems
Around deities. Knowledge & research

Applauses loudly. Nowhere in the chapters,
Cassock is better than music. On the
Foreheads is the start of the lesson.
We jog to add more credits to the little

Ingredients in the basket. Library never
Dies at the end but we do not see his
Name in the book of Who's Who
In the month of no importance, all the

Flowers close their eyes on their birthdays.
Despair & taint is wrestling over only a seat left.
There are uncountable seismic features
Smiling at us. Paths spread around demands,

Decorated with mourning clothes. A painful flog
Wandering anyhow saluting every tree it comes
Across. Melodious names are found struggling
With dead names. We look at the palms of rain,

Pieces of information clapping loudly in fire & in
Homelessness. We have no fruit &
Fruits & vegetables to serve you but respiration
For decay. They are not gifts from the womb.

Scattered Streets on The Waters

We wait & wait for the world to come.
It has already existed on a peaceful planet.

Days aren't happy within themselves.
Weeks still bang their chests to come out

Of the custody. The tension is hungry.
Months relax on the beach, counting

The sea breeze & creatures. It's unaffordable
But as cheap as lies & long arms.

Years have waived up. They wait that
Gossips will soup feed them. No vitamin

No protein, no gasoline to renew
Their stone-hearted hearts.

Heads are heavy for necks to reason up quickly.
The blossoms in the vessels are lamenting.

Spark agitation, every minute in tribulation
But still, we do not have life in the account.

Bloody hands constantly wave & we reject
Their offer. Because they have nothing to offer

But crooked tongues, long arms, hardened
Hearts. The metal doors around are

Heavier than heaven doors, electrified
To lean against the wing.

Notoriously stubborn he is.
We interpret his words. Roses turns into

Grasses in the white garment. The trust
In the food questions our life expands.

The deepest regret chases him. Failure
Is written all over him. He has turned our joy

Into death. We're without heads & feet
Because of him. Where did we go wrong?

Are they our faults to vote him into power?

Suffering In the Air Over Here

I like to read the sight mars irrespective
Of what the atmosphere we're being starved

Of. & to start a business, we need
Productive tools that can shove away

Mountains Everest & Kilimanjaro instantly
Not like criminals we're having today, litter at the

Wrong places at the wrong time munching
On feeds they do not toil for. On the left side

Is the motor of a life, red fish in the soup.
Rising above the level, we crawl over dry

Ambitions, pile up at the entrance of the trip.
No rosy life as he promised. No breath at

The tail. We swap & swim in the swamp.
To attain the rank of alumina, we picture the

Movement of the civil wars in the developing
Villages in individual lives. We push away

Nonsense. It was an allergy.
We want to touch the heart of passion

We want to din with them as it
Happened at the last supper but.....

Suffering in the air over here.
We do not hear the golden songs from

The green forests. Hungry in the air,
For good listeners.

The eyes of the sun undress the graves,
We salute nature for staying peacefully

With her family.
When are we going to lick honey again?

When are we going to live
Without fear & panic? How long? When?

Multiple One Plus Ten

It's a shock to hear the mix of
Melodies of frogs & cats manuf-
Acturing *multiple one plus ten.*

We cannot climb the hills around,
On the far away are the good
Words & sugar in the life of obedience.

Meal for the soul to eat. We're
Not satisfied, although we haven't
Eaten for years because we were

Disobedient to nature. We are now
Paying for the price which earlier on
Green, black & red warned about.

Our trust is now taking
Us to a mortuary. Now, the
Problems are copious

Singing a joyful melody in combat.
Our seedlings, they are offertory.

Hunting Season

Dreams. Hollow dreams have been
Having fun in our slumber.

Weakness & decay in the daily songs,
Short & ugly like him who

Is the wrong image in the soup.
The chocolate colour has not told

Us the truth of the Air hovering us.
We cannot dance to these rhythms

& listen to down-hearted recitations.
Dresses now are helpless.

Tears soak every walk of imagines,
Displaying the wretched photos of the

Season. Laboratory test could find where
Energy is operating on the seventh planet.

The drain of motivation & empty vision
Paces faster than a criminal.

We can't run like that because
Our legs do not know the oblique path.

We have rich ideas like geography.
We do not stare into the tabernacle.

Research is always the navigator of life.
No solution, fruits, laughter are on the skin.

We're eager to speak to our ancestors
In the comfort of law & order of music.

New ideas & visions laid untouched.
The computer still tests the abilities of man.

We don't want to be lazy like him who doesn't
Like him who doesn't read.

Chances are handcuffed & its lights
Are having holidays at the cemeteries.

Their morning stars are paving for invention.
Time isn't pleasant at home.

The blow is full of a mix of hope & trust.
Loss of homes to illegal men. We are impatiently

Waiting for a rainy season to plant new lives.
We are keen to see, smile on the confirmation day.

Where Is He Now?

We have come to see. We have
Come to walk alongside the globe.

We sense something from very far wandering
From an arm of the wings. We don't want to describe

It now because the doors to the description will be
Slammed behind us. Fathers on the hills have

Refused to open their eyes & describe the
Danger of the broken bridges. We can't cross

The streams in the front of us. because we
Have been forbidden to say the kind of

Sickness which is deteriorating us. They weren't
Born blind until the world opens their eyes to

Things which aren't theirs. Differentiate between
The falling off, of your life on the promised land

& seeing what isn't h*is Made rather than that*
Of babies with sharp teeth. They are there

Watching things visiting the land of pains
But they are cursed with their sights.

He isn't among us. His smell sickens us.
But the river Jordan

Is ready to house them.

Behind The Bridge on The Hill

If we see .... what we're seeing .... now then,
What .... are we seeing .... in the daylight?
Then .... the nightlight .... will suicide..... Itself.
..... Behind the bridge on the hill ......

We ...... shall cross ...... the bridge.
Inform them ...... that we're seeing ...... the hill.
The thick ...... forest is ahead of us, behind,
Crying of the rejected paradise.

Miscalculation, heads bend in mud.
Imaginary faces on the stems.
Go, walk on the bridge now. .....
Listen to the type ...... of songs played around.

Songs in the air respond to questions & answers.
We already.... knew the lifestyle.
They knew but .... under the pretext ......
Under the watch..... the air of ...... the

Venus has informed the earth.
Not existing ...., on the eyes of the fit,
Sweet action ...... vanishes in the system
Before the opposition ...... of the world.

History Has Repeated Itself

We were extremely hungry to the extent that
We had to revisit our history because
Genesis is ever ready to uncover, read to us.

They're ill of magnet, acid & fungi
Zero - idea & foul-play - intention
Deliberate - shameless - fools.

That the ingredients are on the way.
Do not wear the same shoes with him.
We don't want to see the ugly

Features of their symbol.
We're supposed to shield
Against the thunderstorms.

We see a long history, an untold story.
The storytellers have sharpened their lips
But ears do not fear to be deaf. The old

Testament is displaying the rooms in
The house but clauses & phrases have
Much more to narrate to the hungry, the inquisitive.

We can't invite these unclear ingredients
Into the kindergarten.
The immaculate lessons do not teach them at all.

The cost can put up hundred mansions
Because our parents do not like the scent.
Neither will we minus the days. The echo

Of the history has been a good friend of a war song.
We play them severally & the sounds laugh
At the audience. We refuse to do the homework.

The results have become hip-hop
Dancing ups & downs on our noses.

Where Are the Men?

The comb travels far & near. It
Doesn't fetch a single grey hair.
The mirror has finally confessed
& the artists cannot open their

Doors to these stories. The talk
Of the senseless barrels. The fruits
On the ground do not need to talk
About the qualities of foodstuff in the market.

We're still on the search for the *so-called - the men.*
There's something we know you don't know.
Better people make a better government
With their fruits we shall know them.

The earth is hungry for living men,
Much more than the living word.
We can only hear worthless
Noise drumming in the living ingredients.

Acidic bomb vomits from their mouths,
Anytime they release their guns against
Innocent earth.
We notice that the atmosphere is getting sick of

10+10=13. Speeches are longer
Than tongues & are more countless
Than sand in the grave.
When it comes to it, their hands

Harvest the fruits they have rejected.
Not their seeds on the bed. The bed
Faces disgrace & loses respect.
The imbeciles are the men sitting

At the false places. The songs of
Today are on different lanes.
Tomorrow defines another beat.
We know them from the creation

They know very well that 3 + 4 = 7
But their functions are not interesting.
Their dreams are their goals & their scores
Are deliberate drives in the desert.

The Listed Points

Stand up, stand up for the land,
The land is like a canoe in the ship,
Stranded on the high sea of sorrow
Rudderless & with broken navigational aids.

The land is crying for liberation.
The land demands your devotion
The land is on the crossroads,
& its future hangs precariously in a balance.

Your stools have divorced you now, completely.
They are tired of seeing you around them.
The streets are hungry for its taste & choice.
A match of red eyes across the land is needed now.

Let your red t-shirt fly over, beyond its territories.
Let your voice roar like a wild tiger which
Is fighting for his missing life. Hand to defend
Its title. For prestige is an honour & glory.

Apocalypse

We love languages & we want to dislocate
& live in the mere. because there is a Pentecostal
Home, tell them that you want to know more about

Half of the *Arctic Ocean*. The pregnancy of
Apocalypse has finally & revolutionarily burst out.
We can meet people who love languages

& articulate a multitude of tongues. We
Dive into expressions in the walk, left under
The mercy of scorching flame & shrills of

Talk thunderstorms louder & clearer. The
Contents of the body do not need services to
Resurrect the death. The foundations have now

Been recklessly disarmed. Cracks are being axed
On us & the teeth of the economy have been
Graded away. The present market confesses to

Camel, which transports beauty from Africa to
Australia. We need synonyms to explain
Antonyms. The floor of traders fades sharply.

The shout does not kill the noise.
Ghosts take over the challenge.
The marks commence the exams on the

Foundation. On their foreheads light
The cats & dogs, which keep watch of the
Movement under the breath. The land of

Gold has become the hell of poverty
& the discomfort of affliction. We impale
The heart of Cyril & sail through. As the net

Of fishes heard the angelic whisper of John,
Apocalypse, secrets & plots, the sun
Opened our eyes wider.

No More Smiles

We look at ourselves before
The graves in question.
The assignment is unfriendly & lifeless is to

Smile at but the hairs on our
Arms convey the messages.
Others have been breathing without

Air. Fingers massage air & shoulders
Kiss their foreheads multiple times.
Brains expect much more from us

Like they demand from the masters of old.
They throw a big light In their lives & only
Debris carpet. We unlock the first folio of

The vision. White sand blows. As the
Apparatuses were laid on the fingertips,
Proposals dribbled plans. Policies hang

In the throat of assignments. We comb
Thoroughly & cry like a sweet mum
Who wants to know what is dirtying the climate.

As we were washing out the excrement,
No more smiles. Legs could not believe
The situation. The world of ache.

Who invited this world now?
New paint brushes walk to walk.
Photos of smiles run for their lives. We did not

Know the devil until now. Where are we?
The agitated spirit wears His red shirt &
Starts to sing the melody, which takes us
To the land of sleeplessness.

Ghosts Speak ooooo….

Island refuses to flow at the time
Drought needs them dearly.

It's extremely hard to tell the truth.
It's medically healthy to confess

Your crime. It's recklessly stupid
To continuously lie. We can't sleep

Well because of the sermon.
Pillows refuse to enable us to have

Sweet dreams. A comfortable bed
But it belongs to the creation.

The tongue can no longer run
Away from the foul play.

The house commences to slap
The main gate. To tolerate each other,

We deliver a powerful speech.
Born-again words. This was the time,

This is the time. No word will land
Without a gunshot. There should be

Sentences that will earthquake
The society. Reading,

As hobbies, has dropped into dustbin because
There is not a waking sentence to digest.

We've come to see the dodging side
& the side of the hand palm.

The unmade places are the virgin truth.
Ghosts speak ooooo....

Vacant Old Man

Teeth find heaven & Dubai.
Lips have become jobless now.
Rivers are the best enemies
To natural resources.

Old age is the best enemy to flowing blood.
The strength for the ordinary is
Crawling in the mud. We find the illness
Of nose, is unclear now. The sand

Tints the sky. We hear dogs now
Growling loudly, losing their capacity.
They will rob Peter & pay Paul on the cross.
They will accept anything that will

Disgrace their tribes.
We slap the rips of the bells,
Then they dance to the tune.
The followers ensue the wind,

Float on the eyes, it stays behind
The waste, flushing out the dirt,
The end of the trek is the beginning
Of the readings.

Munching On the Matters

We can't continue to inhale the polluted scent
Sweeping away one-in-all on the assured soil.
We pump up from the triangles of the holes.
The mosquitoes have already disseminated
The information. Continuous cough & the slap
On face, on the notice board. Finally, nose has
Grabbed fever. The typhoid fever, the bosom friend
Of death. Even a wall could smell the danger
Stretching his arms to employ us into his barbaric
Palace. The blowing of nose has communicated
The message. Mothers on the seats have crossed
The comfort. Because of the cold rain dropping
At the back door, they could vomit the poison out
From their sick system. The rattling of leaves has
Been sealed by look-into-our lives. we don't see to
Communicate to Now, neither do we believe that
Wings will assist us in the white-moonlit night.
The seed of hypocrisy is planted in every walk
Of life because brown envelopes cease to slump
In its armchairs. But now a nose mask is aiding
Hypocrisy to keep functioning.

Lamp Without a Tail

Standing before our last hope
At the angle of the dilemma
We question the faculty hanging
On the dying tree. Confidence
Still remains where it is. No
Blow can cut off a tail. We've
Become sharp & fearless,
Wanted to remain undefeated.
We listen to murmurings in the wind
The north wind confuses coolness.
Tasks cannot answer a lamp why
She is without a tail but lamp
Continues to fight for her life.

Birds On the Tree

I see the weather uncovers the good ideas.
Birds aren't happy with aeroplanes for
Intentionally sneaking into their recreational
Centres. Masters in realm welcome the discontent
In the cold room. The third day is born. Muscles
Stand against ideas aggressively. Plans dance
Around problems. Swollen problems are
About to deliver its babies. We have become
Homeless in our own paradise. We cannot believe
That planes are greedy & allergic to peace.
The same feathers that convey food to the poor,
The same features steal state's money &
Resources in folds.
We're searching for palaces in an abode.

Greetings In the Morning

We knocked at the gate of nature
Innumerable times with the might
Of a lion. Then trees came forward

& chuckled at us freshly.
This morning, we don't see any
Good about this morning, we thought.

It was shocked to hear the thunderstorm
& rain was shouting at each
Other above the agony of little children.

We saw soil complaining that
There was no water to drink
& that very soon its neighbours

Will set off early in the morning
& will see stones at the table.
There will be neither oxygen nor blood.

The talk in the wind whispered & the chase
Of money. *Nadaa* came to destroy
& he is making nature sorrowful

& unsafe in its kingdom. The smoke in
The Southern Ocean tells the move
On the platform. We stared at him.

No help appeared on his skin. He
Sings praises whenever the earth
Opens her mouth. There is time.

Crucifixion

When night is about to commence its business
Homeless children begin to count the sand particles
They play with. Seeing the decorated crucifixion

To lose belief in the natural resources at the sight.
They drip curses on their destinies. They stab
Their sights into the hearts of the first soul of the

Village. Rhetorical questions have been
Reverberating frequently in the temples of the
Children. They wished night was not created &

That the daylight will persistently conquering
The wicked night. The crucifixion we carry on
The heads is heavier than what our mothers

Went through during labour, they thought.
Other activities that are struggling to pause
After twelve stations are tedious labour

But the wicked *man* has already planned to
Transport much more, frustrate us destructively
To the point of no recovery. He needs to sleep

On the bed of poems so that he can procure
The *Solomon* to bail the children from prison.
Although the sirens of the poems keep

Resounding him of his rightful responsibility
But he thinks of family & friends. How to
Empty the public purse is number one on

His scale of preference. The village has
Visited the land of no return but only the
Funeral should be organised. Rich

Village has become ghost land. Daily
Prayers travel far but destroy neither
Sodom & Gomorrah.

The cry of the children rings outside of
The prayer camps. The light of the poems
Is battling against the moon & clouds
For room to operate in.

Discover

The secret cameras are piloting far distances
& discovering new events that are breeding
Ill fruits & vegetables. Searchlight is still
Demonstrating its maturity at work. We believe
No polluted oxygen could deflate from the
Saver. The basket is brimmed, flowing over

Horizons. Liver & lungs could not help
The ingredients park in the homes to celebrate.
The items at the market could not propose
Love to customers. More than seventy-seven
Billion dollars went for fishing continuously &
There was -0–0=-1. Scandals upon scandals

Are floating their boundaries. The looting monies
Are more than the particles of sand on the coast,
Swollen in ugly shapes & sizes. Things are
Falling apart quickly to the land of lifeless situations.
The scanner reports the incompetence of the empty
Headed men whose barrels could contain a drip of

Water to save a dead candidate. Life rather chases
Death but the arrival of a new baby has a living smile.

Salvation

Does it exist at all?
The revelations speak
About uncountable
Incidents in nowhere

& but from somewhere.
We still wish we'll comprehend
The little babies' cry &
Their laughter on the

Roofing sheets. The songs
Are somersaulting over
Over problems & the tales
That are being hunted by

Tigers & lions are
Farms' products, which do not
Win the hearts of consumers.
But we only hear delicious tone

Outside on the resurrected
Day. with our fishing nets, we
Set the trek in the unmade place
& we never found salvation

Rather Lucifer welcomes
Confusion & we could not
Arm the presence of a fake
Pastor Mensah Otabil,

False piety. He’s a scammer
Your life shakes, auction sale,
Your little property, his target
He has nothing to offer in time

Of need. He offers hell, your
Suffering never ends at his
Presence. Salvation is neither
Seen in him nor in his sanctuaries.

Burning Minerals

What are we hearing now?
What are we seeing now?
What are we inhaling now?
What are we feeling now?

A new home is being created
From the seat of mercury.
Homeless hell has finally sneaked
Into the paradise of the living.

Satellite has seen fire on
The mountain, worse than
Hell at the nostrils like hell
Controlling activities in a church.

Like a new constitution in the
Parliament. The wall of the
Forest has heard the rustling
In the waves, the pollution

In the brain has banished
The beads but tongues in
Palaces & conferences
Like those we see in church

& institutions refuse to wage
A rebellious war against fraud
& pharisaism which is demanding
The kingdom blessed with

Natural resources, emulation
Of incoming aspirants who are
Very keen to replace the aged.
The waves are on strike.

They are kicking off cliffs on
The move to the mother sea,
The strong pillars of the food
& water. The guide of the trip.

The Game of Today

When things trail off the main lines
The church runs away for her life.
She sleeps on matters that concern
The broken house because she has
Not finished sleeping with an air conditioner.
Like *Naada* constance sleeps on
Issues lashing the state. The roots of
The stem has vanished from under the
Pillars. We sink our heads & the road
Traps are set on every junction. The
Weather is unfriendly to us. The con-
Flicting stories & audience feel bitter
Side of the meal is being served on the table.

Decomposition

Around is as empty as a hollow heart.
We always hear that there are
Elements in the offices executing in mud,
In sweats. The seats are full of ashes & trash.

We always hear statements
Aimlessly & lawlessly
Which set traps aspirants.
Basket of water in the offices.

Deadly goals killing the green juice.
We stare at Jupiter & the hills in him
Look at the earth scornfully &
The spicy meals direct

Its glance to somewhere else.
We weigh the elements
& compare them to gold & bauxite.
The laboratory results flog the

Elements as many as they could.
We turn back & we hear in the
feelings, spirits are showering
Insults & curses on them.

We could only feel empty
Knowledge is occupying the earthly Eden.

Not Our Biological Brother

A few minutes ago
We had calls from the
Above which stated
That the nightmare we
Had were because
Of the false boat we
Boarded & we did
Not dream about
That he doesn't
Belong to the earth
& that he is on
Lease to the ingratitude
To taste pepper soup
Being prepared by an
Importer whose
Features are totally
& completely scary
But we give a trail
& he has disgracefully
Disappointed creations
& white paint but this
Season is reading out
The offence & we shall
Show him the door.

Epidemic With Its Matchet on The Field

To say hello to the matchet,
The strength in the pocket
Will estimate the products on the market.
Day in the night; night at the
Corner of the pause. The purposes
Is greater than the target. Beyond the
Capacity of tiger like a camel tripping
Miles, carrying the problems &
Troubles on his tail at the end of the
Month. We reap any fruits from the
Field but we do not see our money in our
Account because of religion has deceived us,
Because rich substances have lost their credibility.
He hates beauty. The act we see within is
Contrasting from what we see on the skin
Of a wolf. The river *Niger, Sweet*
Mother of Africa wishes she will visit
Her children & baptise them in her
Name, them anew.

Jogging On the Endless Road

He starts the journey
Like a serpent swimming under grasses.
Before we got to know

Where he was driving us to,
The journey had started moving in
Us anyhow. The curve in

Question dribbles curves
Plenty of times. If our desire
Is always the scanner of

The heart, then there is no need
To think for the second time.
The chemistry which shows us

The way, the same biology has taken
Us into fire. We see problems
Solving problems at

The same table. There is no
Need to dig million feet into
The Indian Ocean. The mirror

Can smartly tell you the true
Love in the store. Nose could
Not tell the mouth the true taste.

The scent outside. The end of
The road is yet to start.

A Walking Stick as A Fashion in East

Some alien voices amplify in many vicinities
& stations will not allow us to communicate
With our guiding & guarding spirits. We wake up

From our struggle because we know that
The start will climb stairs & descend into a trash can.
The half-closed night is dawning near

& we hear a fake cough that is ordained by the
Withered edges, making irrelevant noise to the
Breath & the length. The confusion is chosen

Outside the circle. The loyal & royal people
Of the throne are out. The blind radio presenters
Support the walking sticks to be stronger

& more vivid to the listeners. They dance in a
Dilemma. They listen to the duplicitous voices
& answer the wrong questions.

Now, the people in the darkness have seen a
Great light shining broad, beyond measure. The
Gods of our longing have defeated the night so

Let us build the land of ours.

Itching Tongue

Things have happened behind the black curtain.
The centre can no longer hold itself again. Cry
Cannot entertain smiles & jubilation is far to fetch.

Unfold the hungry story on the dining table.
Itching tongue looks into the mirror.
We've to confess, says the itching tongue.

Things have happened in offices
When vegetables are still losing their pride.
Then religion is still practising prostitution.

Pray that fruits will resurrect to his feet.
Let everyone know the other side of the
Amazon. Things have happened at the shrine

Before the season.

When prayers travel miles beyond their capacity,
When rain is falling heavily in the harmattan,
When moist is carpeting your views at the harvest

Point, things are happening in the dark rooms.
More things will happen everywhere, that will
Open the chapters of this new collection of poems.

Who is hungry to devour more than
They've been served?
Who is thirsty to drink from the pool

Of rivers in the veins?
Too much for the reserved *Jubilee House.*
Crime in socks.
Its name has been published in the
Life of many faces.

The holy fire could no longer stomach them.
Time has finally shown its face.

New Leaves

Before the creation a place has been prepared
For us & for those who cross the river seven
Times & return fourteen times. This man is

A living testimony. The rest of the least. No present
Vitamin for him. The continents have no room to
Share with him. Now we cannot be

Measured by thermometer. Oven as the senior.
The meteorologists cannot understand aromatic
Products on the display. Arms between legs.

The entertainers totally forgot the stanzas of
The poems. We're the nature, the very good friend
Of sightseeing. We're not happy about what's

Going on in the kingdom. New leaves are speedily
Depreciating. The winners of poems say the truth.
They are concerned & they are crying for the

Restoration of truth in the blood. Microphones
Sneak out from its mansion. They now vow to
Expose them if they don't allow nature to maintain

Its position as the most hospital child of the earth.

Yellow Life on The Run

The melodies of the little babies
Are questioning the language.
Problems wear much more cloths
& the styles are holding the noses.

We have been moved from the line of heart
Struggling with the mourning songs.
For the middle, not the start of the songs.
We miss their morning worship.

The yellow life is talking everywhere.
The sign of the cross, nine times.
There is a place to visit now, the first born
Of tomorrow. We're floating & the waves

Have come to stay in the community of
The wicked. We are the people that disown
The acid. We know him now. His presence is
To kick out the heavenly earth from the golden

Taste. Images parade there, reminding us of
The life. Poison sits on the false seat. Medical
Prescription is still at the tail, 100 metres.
Where are we now? Where do we go after here?

New Times Hit Again

We listened to homeless discussions
We did not know where they came from.
The daily newspapers float
Around from the surface

Of the sphere. Inside the hills,
We thought about the pregnancy
Of the discussions. How many
Months can be the pregnancy?

Unknown months stole her way
Into years. After countless times
Evil babies show their teeth
To the sun. Things in the dreams

Remembered the first day they
Visited the first soil. The homeless.
Unwanted seedlings lick up
The reserved cake for another goal.

It could be twins or triplets, only
Gynaecologists can predict confidently
The contents of sugar in it. It could not
Corrupt the minds of the listeners.

The words on the sight could not stop
Joy from escaping the plot organised
By disappointment. The stainless
Angels fly far away for their lives. They

Can not dance to the clap sounding
Loudly in our bodies. The nature of
Capacity on the ground soak away
The last strength accumulated.

Reminder In the Hostile Village

We're not dead but we're living with death.
We cannot sleep in the planet because so many
Things are imported from the land that

Does not exist on the sight. Stanzas of
Poems will be glad that the phrases on
Tongues will pay an attention to the blaze

On the houses. We commence to inhale
The fake oxygen before it misses its streets.
It's a street within responsibilities. The composers

Sing winter songs in summer & harmattan songs
In Europe. The climate tastes different food
Serves on the festival. As we read the reports of

The renowned dentists, the sharp teeth are
Uselessly decayed because the owners
Concentrate on the wrong tips. They refused to

Wash down ills & death in the houses because
Of the existence of perfumes. The green light
Is always on for those who're ever ready to channel

The useful path. The sharp teeth refuse to din
On the flesh rather targets the dry bone. The lives
In the bones still breath till the sky opens widely.

Matter Vomits Problems

Matters plus inconsistency are equal
To the prices we're swimming in.
We don't want to hear the parrot.
My late father didn't want to see
The sixth eye when he was
Caressing my sweet mother.

My eyes could not stop driving
Through the lines of hardship.
Then signs direct our tongues
To stop on the way. The skin of
Envelopes saddens our hearts.
To know the content of the formal letter

We have to sharpen our knives in order
To look for a cure. Inside our boxes are
Hotter than 600 Celsius. Because
Stomachs are fed, mouths cannot
Preach the good news.

A Day B4 12 Noon

Because the barrel is full
My two arms cannot
Communicate as they
Promised to turn hell

Upside down. We knock
Loudly but they refuse
To attend to our calls.
We cannot appear like

The children used to smile
At their parents in the evening.
We move but the direction is
Floating over channels. It's

Dangerous to dive with
The right waves.

Imagining Here & There

We walk on the ocean to visit summer in his world,
As harmattan is to visit her world in realm

& we could not stay there & see
The gloom of the stars under the

Mercy of a malicious oven baking their complexion.
Cubes of ice melt, ice cream

Sledges on a tongue, throat grades positions,
We do not see ourselves in the race.

Why? Jogging marathon, ascending with our efforts
& descending sharply with

Wickedness in the snow, day & night,
The strength in the pocket looks

An action, unhappy with the lazy dogs.
The seven days await us, in them, full duties

& restless periods. We begin the trek on the
Deserted land, alongside the roads

Are poverty, more wicked than death.
The roofing is broadly wide open, physically blind.

Souls Travel kilometres per hour in the minds
Of planners, testing them.

Nevertheless, the wrong tests are organised at
The wrong time at the wrong place. The moisture

Rains, things pray their last prayers.
Shadow faces morning. Pictures in winter are

Shown on our skins, impregnated with both dark
& inexplicable drawings on the public

Walls, displaying talent in individuals,
Not rich enough to alter the destinies of

The suffering. Sleep not rather----- wake from
Your slumber, arise from your sleep now,

The new day is drawing near.

False Boat at The Station

We don't know where
We've found ourselves now.
We do not study the paddle
Which is controlling
The wind, which is ceasing
Our breath when the cool
Temperature wants to pay
Its unusual visit. We could not
Trust the ticket in our hands.
He promised us an amazing
Love which hasn't touched
Water & soil before. We have been
Looking for the rivers of
Pleasure in our lives. We wished
We could hide under the cliff of
Sea so that waves will swerve
Them from their sights. He has
Rather reduced our heavens
To hell. Grace to grass.

The Movement of The Curtains

I follow the moves of reality &
My good friend imagination will not
Allow the moon to beat me in

The ring. because his lights are
Innumerable. The same words in jeopardy,
Have their ways into sanctuary, celebrating.

The same tongues that baptise
The sinners in the desert,
Wear the cloth of wolf on his birthday.

The other side of the circle
Is broken down. It has gone round
& receives the body of his believer.

Cry In, Cry Out, Cry Loudly

I cry in & walls ignore me.
Lucifer sings in between.
The Bible says the Lord's prayer.

He dances around himself.
Koran says prayers four times a day
Mecca has another vision & mission.

Both travel on the different lane
But meet at the same point. No goal.
If the grey hair refuses to learn

How to say black is black
& white is white then cooking
Pot can also boldly say he is better

Than white cassocks of the bishops.
Because he has lied seven hundred
Million times a day. & he has

Strangled us to death three
Trillion times in an hour.
My wounds have

Become portraits to others
To see in the museum.
Folds are unfolded & are in numbers.

He thinks his students will continue
To blow dust into the eyes
Of innocence.

Hear My Story Now

We live in the world,
Where we don't know

Where we belong, now.
But our ancestors

Wrote me letters that
We belong to this land

& that they fought
Hard for us all to live

With sincere love &
Harmony. We know

The problems at hand,
Mystery to monster in act.

Their bellies are getting
Swollen more than before.

At the banquet, our mouths
Tell us the truth,

More bitter than illness,
More heartless than stone-hearted

Plea. Our daily rosary prayers
Will never let us down.

Nobody knows the second coming.

Crawling To Ashes

I have touched something that has subtracted
All the vitamins in the system. I now hang

Somewhere in the west. Out of the page. Already
In the ears of the inquisitive, gossip has scored

The marks to be crowned the king of kings.
True confirmation in the store.

The stems warn leaves to be more careful
Order than that, the sun will disgrace them.

We want to scan the bag. We cannot smell mango
& eat pawpaw. Where are we now? The landlord

Can send us a notice at any time but the crucifixion
Will not abet evil action. We aren't visitors today

But the prices of fuel pay us an unceremonious visit.
Hoping for hope in the sky, not the time of showers.

Hands have not rested at all. Period of goodbye.
Sweats of litters are measured. Night,

Strength fights nature in the rain, I remember the
Day I was baptised in the streaming weather.

I never waive up the decision, twist & bend,
Blend & weave, through the thorn

& tears, I still wait for the dialogue. The oily day.

Slow To Anger

The weather in me
In you up there or
Here in her, which
I cannot see at all,

But if I could have
The other eyes I'll
Perceive in my life.
I will jump over the
Pathway of a
Leaked gas in the
Refined centre.

The red lamp at the lips
Of the compound house
Consistently brightening
Whenever I'm there
With my working tools
On my timbered shoulder
Preparing to deliver
The best services

Those hundreds of thousands
Of millions already
Approached with the
Best know-how but ended
In the dust ..... hearing
The misunderstanding
In the waves of Akyem

The slap on the face
Of the Sharon cliffs
The flash & the splash
Kicks away the murderous
Israelites that have
Devoured thousands of lives.
So, I farm only healthy
Fruits & vegetables

Plus flowers & roses.
The big trees are sheltering
The fishing pool
That purges away the explosion.
The butterflies on my
Chest flutter around my feet

They bring the evil in
Them out & show them
The best in me.
The water in the glass
Is colourless, colourful
When it extinguishes
The fire under the hot debate.

The moment of ecstasy
Of happiness & joyous
Madness dies instantly
Because of him.
We are still in search of truth.

Hands In the Pocket

The temperature in the office
The matters on the desk in
The Jubilee House, what
The new site describes
News, floods, places of interest.
Newsletters haves inexplicable

& indescribable organs.
The cold temperature has no information
For us. No case has been reported.
I hardly open my letterbox. I could
Remember, I've rented it over to cobwebs
& spiders. They are extremely glad &

Accommodative that they have
No concern in the left pocket. Right back
Pocket will take care of itself at the appointed
Time. But the sun on my face wants
To undress the other side of the story
However, the time isn't at hand

At the curve, my hand forks out more
Problems in the questions, mean why
My cat isn't ready to pump out from the sack
Neither do I expect any mail from anybody
But it has been a long time since I called
To check on my salary.

Do I fit into the present world? Let me see
What inventors will tell me. I keep on
Watching through the windowless,
Uncomplicated images parade at my toes.
The blending of a road burst into a thundering cry,
Then a picture appeared.

In The Middle of The Drama

Brains comb everywhere for
The answers hiding within/themselves.
The immigration of the answers

Asks the jobless grey/hairs—
Who have forgotten/the dates of their birthdays.
In the middle/of the drama,

Tongues keep/awake for work.
Assignments/dancing in their throats,
Nowhere to be found on the kneel.

I encounter the light/of lights in the dark.
Hope runs in/my veins like 6 months
Pregnancy, telling his/parents that he's fit.

The barrier on the sea. The other side of life,
We have already/tasted it, bitterly.
The sight of the/drama enlarges its zone.

& I/challenge the big/challenge about to
Dig the last layer i fly. I float & I fight/against
The weight, the cliffs in the lake/with

Their sharp teeth. What I saw were the
Children/of another handmade
In the sand, were that/of calamities hanging

In/the air. In the virgin/forest has spread
The information/from the above,
From/the conflicting roots. Their interest

Of words is trade on boot-for-boot pages.
I'm now swimming/in the restless stream.
Tomorrow is predicting/swollen worries.

Both Sides of The Coin

Under the telescope,
Hundreds on his path.
Thousands don't buy the system.
They are working with their might.
Millions are tired of the rules
& regulations, walking ups
& downs above mountain level.
Billions have relaxed in their armchairs.

Sounds of words of messages of
Stories Of articles of books stood
Out from their best on the floor.
The sunshine in the sun.
The answers in the sack.
The eyes in the darkness.
The fingers in the black, hooting at
Heavy rain in the winter,

Planting a new life.
Showers of snow in the summer
Composing riddles in the war zone.
The muscles of fishermen stand alert.
Things rail off their lanes. I have taken
Plenty of notices. The boards are full
Of announcements. They are as sharp as
Made-in-Japan knives, as rich as on

The mountains, as aggressive as tornadoes
In Alaska. Life kicks off. Squatting & jumping
With the music, Google tells the truth in the saver.

It's Clear Now

Around the clock from the start, from
Where we are now in the muddy water,
Walking to the place in the daytime
Adding & subtracting the existing globe,

Things are falling apart under the watch
Of activities, the images in the churches
Continue to preach another news. Looking
Through the black suns, we saw Bawuincompetency

Receiving the award of incompetence. He's
A drop-out image among the lowest waste
At the sight of reflection. He could not handle
The difficulties of sun & sand in the river.

After the result of the day, he has failed to
Pour honey in the bitter river to change the
Taste & choice of a poisonous river. The
Fruitful fruits have stopped to produce

Their results in the reaping season.
Bawuincompetent is ineffectively &
Inefficiently incompetent to the extent
That darkness has run away with huge

Shame.

The Side Other

World, be on your ears before tornadoes
Paint unworthy pictures on your birthdays.

Ask the earth about Bawuunskilled. That
Days are older than their years, if we've

Perfectly added the figures to shame the
Bad odour, which championing the fresh

Winds sitting on their throne. He is married
To a undefeated ineptitude & has made his

Mind not to divorce. Even though, ineptness
Does not love him, he clings inability. He is

Unable to provide rainfall in the dry season
& destroys the existing rivers & lakes for irrigation.

Nights are still crawling
Behind the rejection. Goods.
Brains have done nothing to praise the disowned jobs.

Vacant Palace

Nights are still crawling
Behind the scenes. Full
Rejections scatter all over
The surface of records

& mirrors. Failure has
Nothing to disprove
Disagreement. Bawuempty
Could not calculate a

Simple arithmetic. Since
His birthday he started
Fishing, he has not even
Netted tilapia for supper.

He has no idea to transform
Desert from no place to
Some place in debate. He
Lacks IQ to solve simple problem.

Because he doesn't qualify to
Be a class prefect. I would
Recommend the book "Animal Farm".
He needs to conjure Solomon.

Hate For Sunlight

NPP have said countless times that they can change
The seasons we have. But they have forgotten that
Actions speaks louder than voice. And that scanning
Darkness has no hope to plant into hopelessness.
I know, I know, is from the mouth rather from the brain.
Under the sunshine, pride dances on their foreheads &
I saw a package of deliberate acts circulating in their
Blood veins. The white & the red cells have visited the
Lands of wickedness. NPP have sowed arrogance in the
Fertile Soil & harvested the chain of shame & backwardness.
The face of hopelessness & disbelief has sailed through a
Narrow paths. Now their song is, we came to steal, to kill &
To destroy. Their performance demonstrates what we are
Perceiving now.

The Full Labour

We were told the type of seeds planted in NPP
Before the announcement in the public. Studying
The weather smiling at us, we could emphatically

Say that they are expired seeds needed to be
Thrown away from the land of the living.
We did not check the invasion of the spoilt plant into

The spotless, fertile abode. The genetic lineage never
Diverted its way his ancestors navigated on. There is
No change between yesterday & today. Close look

Into the wide road, spreads around the nature, winter

Will not replace summer, whiles day has not made
Her mind to change into week. The threat of tornadoes,
The whisper roaring in the wind, there has been no a

Single earthquake to correct the behaviour of the nature.
They are still arrogant to a particular number that even
Disgrace has taken her dirty clothes & run for life.

Unattended Assignment

The white darkness is still unactive
In his own land. He travels far & near

To effectively discharge duties assigned
To black suns. He promised the virgin

Bushes & holy waters in shrines. He tried
To fly into another planet with the help of

Rain of waterfalls, the life of saints in
Sanctuaries. The hands of goodness.

The care of the rivers has been snubbed.
He claps for ruin to box on heartless does.

The cry of rich cultures & traditions smashes
Into atoms. No life is seen on the body of

Heritage. Everything is signalling red & black
Colour. All the jobs are left unattended.

Friend of recklessness in action, deliberate
Incompetency as the result. Wear your

Shame as your achievement.

The Myth of Being….

I can count well without missing
The missing stars among us. Several fouls
& failures. His crimes as plenty as sand

On the beach. It always rings in my tiny ears.
That's heart-breaking news, of course
The bell of the churches around could only

Dance around the request. We need to bring fishes
In the houses for the babies but all disappear
Into his pocket. Er ist *Mafia.* The fire at home

Builds an unbearable life, baking one another
To nothing. The appointed time will spring up
& we shall laugh together around one table.

No Way No More

The cry of the children now
Toll in my heart.

I'm in the same shoes as well.
The stanzas of poems

Study every feeling in the blood pressure.
I've to let immaterial out.

Their rooms convey the message of intimate
Care, the promise hunts me & hurts me,

Here & there,
Today's work cannot decide the strength.

The song of that day is the master
Counting on his head, yes!

Yes of course,
Falling a minute & standing up in two minutes.

The period is still dead at my goals.
There isn't much to exercise,

The fridge in the summer, freezer in the desert,
The motor in the body,

I can fly over mountains.
The ears are closed for spiders' stories.

The layers of work litter on his arms.
Excuses are in the pipeline.

Neither green blood nor milky mirror
In the cabinet running up & down

Ascending into the moon for assistance &
& descending into the kitchen to say hello

To the empty cooking pots is the drive at
The moment.

THE BIG BUT will salute him four times &
He'll return injured, memorable times.

Still in the constitution, voices cry saying,
NO WAY NO MORE.

Wake Up Uprightly

Wake up now. Awake before it's too late
Your bed doesn't want to see you anymore.

Wake up now. Awake before it's too late
Your pillow doesn't love you anymore.

Wake up now. Awake before it's too late
It will not help you to have sweet,

Powerful dreams. Wake up now.
Awake before it's too late

I can't breathe in with this polluted oxygen.
Wake up now. Awake before it's too late

A golden heart stops beating untimely.
Wake up now. Awake before it's too late

Things are slipping out of hands.
Wake up now. Awake before it's too late

The present clouds form unkempt blankets.
Wake up now. Awake before it's too late

I can't continuously weep beyond control.
Wake up now. Awake before it's too late

Now I have come out of darkness.
Wake up now. Awake before it's too late

Now I have seen the great light.

Arise

Arise from your sleep
How long will you keep
Quite over wrong things
Occurring in your own
Land. Your precious land
Is all that you know &
All that you have now.

Arise from your sleep.
The deception is too much
For the ears to hear,
For the nose to smell,
For the stomach to contain,
For the soul to entertain,
For the lips to uncover now.

Arise from your sleep.
The hell of duplicity is
Quickly expanding its
Horizons without fear & favour
& no mercy for the people.
Feelings have touched them &
We need to conquer the night

Ring The Bell

Ring your bell loudly
Ring it countless times
For the deaf to move
It's ass. For the death
To resurrect from the
Neglect. It's my time,
It's your time to ring the bell.

Ring your bell loudly,
Ring it so that less interested
Citizens will know that
Time has come. The vital
Ingredients need to be cooked.
They long to eat every delicious
Soup in every home.
It's your time to ring the bell.

Ring your bell loudly
Ring it beyond the size of God.
The intimidation is too much to bear.
Mouth can now eat as much as he
Wants but labour as he is being
Created for. I now live with full of
Warning because I speak the truth.

It's your time to ring the bell.

It's Your Life

Say truth to power
The promised land
Is still mourning bitterly.
Hard working hands at rest.

Our souls will never sleep.
So, they cannot dodge the fire
From the above.
Say truth to power

Now it has come to it.
Thunderstorm will persist to
Drum at their doors. Fire
Will never assist darkness

To accomplish its mission
Or escape its disgrace.
Say truth to power
It has broken our hearts

See the system has taken away
By the merciless flood.
It's enough for this nonsense
To win the league, oneness,

Boots for boots spirit is ever
Ready to say truth to power

Healing Gun

It's my turn now
To renovate the broken world
It's your turn now

To set fire at their stench asses
It's our turn now
To undress them to the village

It's our turn now to wash their
Dirty clothes outside
Yes, we're sons of the morning

Yes, we're the daughters of the day
For let our tears be turned into joyous dance

Red Oil

By now land should know
The type of rainbows.

Hungry & angry will box
On to open the eyes of

Blind. The unique land
Cannot allow serpent to

Bite her & lick her ears.
My wounds are still advising

My brains. Time has come
To say bye to a dark village.

Now I have seen what is
Eating the village up & I

Cannot wait anymore.
Fight the epidemic killing us

Rapidly. I have the great
Weapon & I don't want to see

Darkness anymore. Because
I'm the pillar of the village.

War In Wars

Don't be lazy. Be on your knees.
Laziness is your greatest enemy.
Don't be lazy at all. Be on your feet.
Your paradise has been turned into

The wound of discomfort. The black smoke
Is too much for us to inhale now.
We must run 100 metres to catch
Up the hidden golden lives.

The golden moment has been taken
Away from us. You don't need to marry
What's happening. The moment hates
Our existence. It's not a good friend of poems.

He came to change Mars to Jupiter.
Now we have woken up from our planet.
Now poems have turned darkness into
Awareness. Let our actions shine & expose them.

Actions

Action is jobless
By now we would have
known & taken *action.*
Morning doesn't want

To be in the same ship with sleep.
I have the requisite tools
To effectively carry out
An unattended work, says action

In the evening. Too sorrowful
To feelings. Gentle words
Are too soft to cook
A delicious meal for supper.

I must move now, says action.
Houses are empty. Our holy
Land now is allergic to friendship.
New births are needed to fill

The right places. Our holy land needs
Fresh air to breath. Go out now.

Boiling Loudly

Your immaculate voice
Does not want to miss
The arranged matches.

Ears want to be fed
The living message.
For some time now

Illusion has been changed
Into ruin. Fruits have been
Created into vegetables.

It's tasteless to eat your own
Flesh serves at the banquet.
Let our voices trek beyond its

Boundaries, now.

Chapters On the Screen

You have used me
You have abused me mercilessly
Switch on the beam of the street
Knife into the sea. The colours are out.

Shout above
Drum persistently
Too much for the soul. Mouth is always restless.
The talking drum. Nonstop with all the might.

Read out
Storm in
Waves against cliffs on the way
Spelling out the words in the box.

Your presence
The face
Fearlessness is the weapon on the field.
Your time is up. No more acid.

Wild beast
Eagerness
Ready to face them squarely
Screw the words in the ears. All die be die.

Uproot

The sea is severely hungry.
The fishmen have kept quite enough.
It's time to construct a sea defence.

Says the canoes parade on the shore.
The waves have changed their movements.
The bends are innumerable & paddles

Can't iron them out alone. Hammer can
Energise the paddles. The fire is consuming us.
Water must deliver more services. We need

Hammer to fix the broken structure.

Erosions

Dirt is reigning everywhere
Swallowing tons & people
& I pray to the god of rain
To fill my belly. Yes, come

Down & renew the face
Of the earth. I won't sit
Down looking on like that.
I must walk like a thunderstorm.

I must behave like an excavator.
I must eat them like a shark on duty.
I need to construct a new home to live in.

Wake up Ashantis
Wake up Akyems
Wake up the promised land

We are sinking in our own land
Arise Ghana now from the gutter
Against ***NPP. Vote NPP out of power.***

Speak Out

Let the tiger speak
A new day is dawning near for those who
Haven't seen the faces of the seven stars

Send the message across
Neither do I relate to polluted smoke nor half white.

Solomon doesn't sleep
I must speak to green, blue before despair
Plays its dirty games with me.

With the clean heart
Enough is enough for continuous intimidation
& threat, says the apocalypse.

It is my might
I support you & iron rods are being
Planted at the junctions.

I am a martyr
Till the assignment is accomplished the sound
Of toll is not allowed into the land.

Toxic Odour

We look into the driving mirror severally,
The children of elephant are not Solomon
But has liberty to enjoy the fresh oxygen from

Under the sea. Liberty cannot be bought
Rather must work for justice & peace which
Is longing to come back home & dwell with us.

We attend to our books & their names are
Not found in the rich history books. They are
Not fruitful to pull down honey on the peak

Of the mountain. They have smuggled out again
What they do not labour. They do not have
Anything to build the world on but wide

Mouth to swallow roses & drink blood for
Coffee. We can only hear them making
Noise around. Their smell has sickened
Us & we need the bailout now.

Famished Road

Let's waft on the dead land.
It's a oblique journey
To a short destination.
It takes a palace &
A paradise to reach there.

The song of awareness.
We run faster than before.
We spring like kangaroos.
We reach somewhere.

Here are the answers:
Things have completely
& totally fallen apart.
The road has opened

Its mouth, widely.
It affects the beautiful assets.
The pandemic is malicious
I need to fix it immediately.

The road has been famished.
Go to the field now.
Everything is sleeping on
The left arm.

Come from out of the shield.
Notice all the paths
Don't sit down, for, grace is
Losing the match to nothingness.

Not to look at the arms to suffer alone,
Says Mr. legs, the minister for
Employment. I've also visions
& missions to execute before

The earth swallows us up, says
Miss arms. Brain has helped
Your hands to write powerful notices.
Send out your notices to the false prophets,

Go away you devil
Go away you impostor
Go away you murder
Go away you looter

Go away you destroyer
Go away you liar.
The wind blows.
The roots have spoken.

The stem has been confirmed.
We don't need you anymore.

The Microphone

Amplify your voice above the mt. Everest.
We shall install an X Bass in the air.
Speak loudly, speak sense now.
Pump air into the ashes.
The youth blood is speaking to you.
A "youthless" land is a useless land.

Green colour stands against retrogression.
We can't hold ourselves together
To the *Holy Communion.*
Neither can negative plus positive
Dance on the same platform.
The situation on the heel is on flame.

We can't wave to the air.
Heat isn't our mate in summer.
Drum loudly & let your shoulders
Stand out for right.
Let the microphone bob on the sea.
Finally, the microphone

Has found a productive job.
He has plenty of homework to carry out.
The smell needs to be fumigated.
Go to the remote, the grassroots need
To start the engine. Their souls have been
Starved of the healing food for so long.

Welcome songs. Tune of the broken roads
Even the animals are ready to listen to
The messages. Proclaim to the city.
Let us build the city of ours anew
Our light is our goal. Our love has turned
The night into a day.

Intentional

Nadaa is the pain &
The misery at the sight truth
The brightness can't sleep
Under the blanket of darkness.
Worries don't have peace
To devour summer, to display
The natural attraction of the heart.

Look at us & we will never salute
The wrath of the black serpent.
The greetings of today can't
Record everyday music in the waves.
Read the steps of a baby in the sand.
The heat in the winter read
The lives of the sea water in the
Sun in the bright day & we can't
Say no to sanity in the harvest.
We feel acidic pepper in the rain.
We are now running away from our *Yes.*

Uselessness's Uselessness

Now sun & darkness pretend they are combating
In the realm of toothlessness. They always make
Noise around the ears of the winds in the dreams.

But sun is overall, write the song of
The nightmare, what you would invite a simple discussion.
Of course, I'm not sparing the rivers or lakes in the lagoon.

And such the direction of the cries,
The usual darkness about the land,
Is much less declined to play the clown

& far from displaying too much pride is frequently undignified.
Nadaa is very notoriously stubborn the allergy of Eden
in heart
Just chuck him underneath the wasted time or flog the hatred

Or tornadoes from generation to generation.
He'll run away meanwhile nobody is running after his life.
He's such an idiot. He'll answer any hell or the fall apart.

Again, we must remind our souls & we shall curse
Our first birthday celebration.
A liar's a liar - a thief's a thief

A murder's a murder - a strangler's a strangler
An oppressor's an oppression - a tyrant - tyrant
A hypocrisy's a hypocrisy - a scammer's - a scammer.

Biography

Live your life well
So, we don't lie
At your funeral
No subtraction
No addition
No multiplication
No division
The record is there

www.ingramcontent.com/pod-product-compliance
Ingram Content Group UK Ltd.
Pitfield, Milton Keynes, MK11 3LW, UK
UKHW040402200225
455254UK00001B/69

9 781977 267917